Bitter Harvest

MÉXICO
State Boundaries
Railways 1910

0 100 200 300 Miles
0 100 200 300 Kilometers

UNITED STATES

El Paso
Ciudad Juárez
Cananea
San Antonio

SONORA
CHIHUAHUA
Hermosillo
Chihuahua
Ciudad Guerrero
Parral

Ciudad Profirio Diaz

COAHUILA
Laredo

BAJA CALIFORNIA

GULF OF CALIFORNIA

Guaymas

SINALOA
Culiacán
DURANGO
Durango
Torreón
Saltillo
Monterey
NUEVO LEÓN
TAMAULIPAS

GULF OF MÉXICO

Mazatlán
ZACATECAS
SAN LUIS POTOSÍ
San Luis Potosí
Tampico

PACIFIC OCEAN

AQUAS CALIENTES
Tepic
JALISCO
Guadalajara
Chapala
GUANA JUATO
Celaya
HIDALGO
VERACRUZ
Tuxpan
Jalapa
Veracruz

YUCATÁN
Merida
Valladolid
QUINTANA ROO
Campeche
Chetumal
CAMPECHE

Ayutla
Colima
COLIMA
MICHOACÁN
Morelia
Cuernavaca
D.F.
MORELOS
Tlaxcala
Puebla
PUEBLA
Rio Blanco
TABASCO
Villahermosa

GUERRERO
Chilpancingo
Acapulco
OAXACA
Oaxaca
Salina Cruz
CHIAPAS
Tuxtla Gutiérrez

GUATEMALA

Bitter Harvest

The Social Transformation
of Morelos, Mexico,
and the Origins of the
Zapatista Revolution, 1840–1910

PAUL HART

University of New Mexico Press
Albuquerque

First paperbound printing, 2006

Paperbound ISBN-13: 978-0-8263-3664-4
        ISBN-10: 0-8263-3664-7

YEAR	PRINTING
10 09 08 07 06	1 2 3 4 5

Library of Congress Cataloging-in-Publication Data

Hart, Paul, 1964–
  Bitter harvest : the social transformation of Morelos, Mexico, and the
origins of the Zapatista revolution, 1840–1910 / Paul Hart.
      p. cm.
  Includes bibliographical references and index.
  ISBN 0-8263-3663-9 (cloth : alk. paper)
1. Morelos (Mexico : State)—Social conditions—19th century.
2. Mexico—History—Revolution, 1910–1920—Causes. 3. Morelos
(Mexico : State)—History. 4. Morelos (Mexico : State)—Economic conditions—19th century. 5. Morelos (Mexico : State)—Rural conditions.
6. Peasantry—Mexico—Morelos (State) 7. Peasant uprisings—
Mexico—Morelos (State)—History. I. Title.
  HN120.M58H37 2005
  306'.0972'4909034—dc22
                    2005019250

Book design and composition by Damien Shay
Body type is Utopia 9.5/13.
Display is Poetica Chancery and Utopia Bold.

Contents

Illustrations

Preface

This book is about the origins of the Zapatista revolution in Morelos, Mexico, from 1910–19. I began the study because I wanted to know what started the revolution there and how a defeated rebellion in one of the smallest states in Mexico helped initiate a nationwide land-reform program that lasted for most of the twentieth century. Originally, I thought the study would concentrate on the hardships imposed during the dictatorship of Porfirio Díaz, from 1876–1910, but I soon found that understanding the origins of the revolution in Morelos required examining a much longer history of agrarian unrest there. That meant exploring the seemingly lost decades of Mexican social history from the 1840s to 1870s. I then concluded that, instead of simply being a localized peasant rebellion born out of circumstances unique to the area, the forces at work in Morelos on the eve of the revolution represented an intense version of similar processes taking place across large parts of Mexico, especially in the North. I was driven to that conclusion by the discovery that many of the people who fought in the Morelos revolution were not only, or even mainly, peasant villagers, but were sugar workers. That fact tied their experiences to the working-class revolutionaries of Chihuahua and Durango and created a different picture than the one portrayed in most of the books I had read in graduate school.

What was unique in Morelos, though, was that instead of having to migrate to mining and urban industrial centers where they became subjected to the industrial regimen of company towns or the anonymity of urban living, displaced peasants became part of a local agrarian working class, serving the needs of the expanding sugar industry. During the late nineteenth century, Morelos sugar producers began to dramatically increase production and to monopolize natural resources, especially land and water, at the expense of neighboring villages. The proximity and seasonal nature of sugar work, though, meant that while some people were forced to become dependent peons on the estates, others were able to get jobs on the plantations while continuing to live in their pueblos. That allowed the old structure of their communal villages to survive. While workers in other settings tried to resist the conditions of the early industrial era by creating new organizations like mutual aid societies or labor unions, people in Morelos turned to established social structures such as local self-government and the communal use of resources offered by their pueblos as a source of mutual defense. The example of the free landholding village, or *municipio libre*, provided an important alternative to the process of land enclosure and the harsh working conditions that characterized early industrialization in Mexico. It also offered a basis on which to build other ideas about how to divide resources, structure work, and live life that differed radically from the demands being imposed by sugar manufacturers in Morelos and by other industrialists in other parts of the country.

Contrary to romanticized images of peasant villagers attempting to stop time and fighting for a world already lost, peasants and workers were trying to realize their own vision for the future. From the middle of the nineteenth century, rural people in Morelos adopted modern ideas and demanded equal rights and the personal freedoms advanced by Liberalism, but they adapted those ideas and extended them to their communities, which they saw as the starting point for reorganizing society. When the revolution broke out in 1910, the Zapatistas soon moved away from elite rebels like Francisco Madero and, although they joined the calls for democratic reforms at the federal level through the guarantees of effective suffrage and no reelection of the president, they believed that "municipal freedom is the first and most important of the democratic institutions."

The Zapatistas offered two main revolutionary changes. They demanded a major redistribution of land and wealth through a grassroots land-reform program that would take property from the largest owners and redistribute it to peasants and workers. They also challenged both the national dictatorship and local boss rule that plagued political life by seeking democratic reforms from the base, including the direct election of town and city governments, officers who would serve one-year terms, and an end to corruption by having all civic business conducted in public. During the course of the revolution their ideas regarding land reform and municipal autonomy attracted many rural Mexicans, but proved alien to the primary concerns of most urban and industrial workers who could not aspire to communal land ownership or local self-rule. In the end, the Zapatista's inability to translate their goals into an urban context helped prevent a broader working-class alliance from taking shape during the revolution.

This study is intended to provide a social history of nineteenth-century Morelos and to explain the causes for the Morelos rebellion. It is hoped that it also suggests parallels with other parts of the country, shows how what happened in Morelos fits in the larger story of the revolution, and contributes to the comparative study of rural rebellion in general. The book is not primarily about the military phase of the revolution nor its results. However, when considering the successes and failures of the Zapatista struggle, it is important to remember the almost feudal social relations that existed before the conflict and to recognize that although the Zapatistas helped overthrow the Díaz regime and won major concessions from ensuing governments, they lost the war. It is, therefore, a mistake to judge their motivations for fighting the revolution by the deeds of future generations that "institutionalized" it.

The revolution accomplished some Zapatista goals, but not others. As the appendix of this book indicates, a significant redistribution of land ownership took place, especially in Morelos where the old landowning class was destroyed and the communal pueblos regained their lands and earned the right to increase their holdings in order to accommodate population growth. Local control was never realized though. Instead, popular pressure from below pushed national leaders toward land reform, but those reforms did not last.

The writing of this book was made possible by the financial support of several institutions. The History Department at the University of California, San Diego, (UCSD), UCMexus, the Center for Iberian and Latin American Studies, and the UC system President's Office all provided grants that funded the initial work. Later, the Center for U.S.-Mexican Studies at UCSD provided a visiting fellowship that allowed me to put aside teaching responsibilities and write. The Pennsylvania State System of Higher Education and Texas State University, San Marcos, both funded further research in Mexico.

Beyond the necessary financial assistance I have received, it is with real gratitude that I acknowledge some of the people who have helped me along the way. My dissertation advisor, Professor Ramon Eduardo Ruiz, provided much needed guidance when I was a young graduate student at UCSD, and he has remained a continuing source of encouragement ever since. Professor Eric VanYoung introduced me to works that broadened my theoretical approach, and Professor Michael Monteon provided valuable criticism of my dissertation that helped when writing the book.

I would never have been able to gather the material necessary for this project without the help of many people in Mexico, and I would like to thank a few in particular. Antonio Saborit, of the Instituto Nacional de Antropologia y Historia, lent his assistance on all my trips and helped me gain entry into some hard-to-access archives. He also introduced me to some of the leading experts on Morelos, including Salvador Rueda Smithers and Laura Espejel. Both were very supportive and generous with their time and knowledge. I particularly want to thank Laura Espejel for her help and hospitality; her kindness cannot be exaggerated. During my stays in Morelos, Valentín López González allowed me access to his personal archive in Cuernavaca and shared personal stories of the area's history. I also wish to thank the archivists and librarians in Mexico for their help and expertise, including those at the Archivo General de la Nación, the Archivo Porfirio Díaz, the Hemeroteca at the Universidad Nacional Autonoma de Mexico, the Secretariat of Agrarian Reform, the Archivo Judicial del Tribunal Superior, and those at INAH. I also thank the staff of the Benson Latin American Collection in Austin, Texas.

I am fortunate to work with many fine colleagues in the History Department at Texas State University. I am glad to be able to express my appreciation to Jesús Frank de la Teja for all that he has done for me and to also thank the two people who have served as chairs of the department, Kenneth Margerison and Eugene Bourgeois, for their consistent support. I am especially grateful to Gregg Andrews, who read the entire manuscript and who has been a true mentor and friend. I thank John Mason Hart of the University of Houston, who also read the whole piece and shared his knowledge of Mexico on a regular basis. David Holtby, editor of the University of New

Mexico Press, has been a pleasure to work with; I thank him for his early and sustained interest in this project. Of course, any remaining errors are mine alone. Finally, my deepest thanks go to both of my parents who have always been there for me with moral and material support, and to Michelle for her friendship and patience.

DISTRITO FEDERAL

MÉXICO

HIDALGO

MÉXICO
D.F.
TLAXCALA

MORELOS
PUEBLA
VERACRUZ

GUERRERO
OAXACA

Gulf
of
Mexico

Pacific
Ocean

MÉXICO

Tepoztlán

Santa María
Amanalco

Apanquezalco

Cuernavaca

Oacalco
Pantitlán

Atlacomulco

Yautepec
Borromeo
Cocoyoc

Temixco
San Gaspar
Atlihuayan
Calderón

San Vicente
Casasano

Puente
Dolores
Hospital
Sta. Inés

Sayula
Buenavista
Cuautla

Chiconcuac
Xochimancas
Cuahuixtla

Cocoyotla
Miacatlán
Barreto
Anenecuilco

Actopan
Mazatepec
Villa de Ayala

Tetecala
Acamilpa
Tenextepango

Las Estacas
Jonacatepec
Santa Clara
Montefalco

Cuauchichinola
San José
Vistahermosa
Treinta
Temilpa
Atotonilco

Tlaltizapan

Puente
de Ixtla
Zacatepec
Tenango

San Gabriel
Tlaquiltenango
Chinameca

GUERRERO
Lake
Tequesquitengo
Jojutla

PUEBLA

MORELOS

▲ Haciendas and Mills
■ Towns
⌇⌇ Railroads

Introduction

The state of Morelos, immediately south of Mexico City, became the crucible of Mexico's agrarian revolution. Between 1910 and 1919, it turned into a bleeding ground. Government troops burned villages, cities were abandoned, and two out of five people who lived there either fled the fighting or died in it. The roots of the conflict went back to the middle of the nineteenth century when the region began an intense economic transformation that turned its peasant economy into a network of plantations and mills that became the heart of the Mexican sugar industry. The transformation of industry and agriculture in Morelos coincided with developments in much of Mexico that created the conditions that led to the outbreak of the revolution of 1910 that reshaped the nation's history.

This book suggests that developments in Morelos, instead of being isolated or local in nature, reflected a broader pattern occurring in other parts of the country that also erupted in revolution. From the 1840s on, Mexico pursued a national policy of economic growth and modernization that included the promotion of commercial agriculture at the general expense of village communities. Yet, it is not inconceivable that the social tensions and conflicts caused by those policies could have been overcome by continued economic growth. That did not happen though. Instead, contractions in the Morelos sugar industry, as well as in the silver and cattle industries of the North, exacerbated the social problems created by an exclusionary political regime after 1907. Displaced peasants, small-scale farmers, disgruntled ranch hands, and unemployed miners in northern Mexico joined Francisco (Pancho) Villa, while in Morelos, displaced peasants, small-scale farmers, and disgruntled sugar workers made up the bulk of the insurgents who rode with Emiliano Zapata. First the dictatorship of President Porfirio Díaz, and then reformist, but hesitant, revolutionary leaders resisted the call for deep social change. As a result, violence and turmoil engulfed much of the nation for the next decade. In the end, the popular forces of Zapata and Villa were militarily defeated, yet they were still able to force major concessions out of the national government, the most obvious being the adoption of a widespread plan for agrarian reform.

The Broader Appeal of Zapatismo

Born in the pre-Columbian pueblo of Anenecuilco, Morelos, Emiliano Zapata emerged at the head of an agrarian movement made up, in part, of villagers whose communal land inheritances were disappearing into hacienda sugarcane fields, and hacienda workers whose lives were spent working long hours in the fields and mills and living in miserable conditions in thatched huts on the plantations. Those two groups formed the backbone of the Zapatista insurrection. Displaced by the loss of communal land holdings, subjected to harsh working conditions on the estates, met with government neglect, and lacking other options, they took up arms to demand a reversal of the sweeping process of enclosure that had been taking place for the last sixty years. When they did that they challenged some of the most powerful economic interests in Mexico and faced fierce repression.

The significance of the Zapatista rebellion extended beyond Morelos. Three main reasons for that stand out. First, although their concerns were initially local, the revolutionaries questioned the human costs of a national program that sought economic growth through the promotion of an economy based on cash-crop agriculture, mineral extraction, and the exploitation of other natural resources. During the late nineteenth century and first years of the twentieth, that approach had sparked impressive economic growth and fantastic profits for a few. However, it undercut the subsistence basis of people living in the areas where it was being carried out, and, importantly, the approach proved unsustainable. Second, the government's pursuit of export-led growth benefited large-scale landholders at the expense of smaller producers. That alienated peasant pueblos in the center and south of the country, as well as independent small-scale farmers across much of the North. Third, the Zapatistas gained national stature because they helped overthrow the dictatorial government of General Porfirio Díaz, who ruled Mexico from 1876–1910, and, more importantly, because they fought any new "revolutionary" government that failed to address the needs of Mexico's impoverished and politically excluded rural population, which represented the majority of the country's people.

On the eve of the revolution, Mexican citizens of all classes had begun to protest the antidemocratic nature of their government and the lopsided benefits of its economic policies. Workers in various parts of the country resented the fact that large foreign-owned enterprises paid Mexicans lower wages than their foreign counterparts for the same work and excluded them from management positions. The government, meanwhile, repressed labor organizations and allowed foreign concerns to treat Mexicans like second-class citizens in their own country.[1]

The regime faced problems at the upper end of the social spectrum as well. Some domestic capitalists felt that by offering foreigners preferential tax incentives, relinquishing subsoil rights, and granting massive land giveaways totaling more than twenty-five percent of the surface of the country, that the Díaz regime had placed the interests of foreign capital above their own. As a result, some, like Francisco Madero, whose family owned substantial mining and agricultural interests in the state of Coahuila, began to call for the president's removal. Foreign investors, by contrast, who profited from the low wages of Mexican workers, low taxes, and the dictatorship's commitment to control the labor movement and maintain social order, applauded Porfirian Mexico as a model for other modernizing nations to emulate.[2]

During most of the Porfiriato (the reign of Porfirio Díaz from 1876–1910), foreigners and a small domestic elite, including the Morelos sugar hacendados, benefited from the government's policies. Meanwhile, higher wages that trickled down to workers in the fields of Morelos, or the mines and forests of Chihuahua, helped mitigate the hostility that many of them felt toward their government and employers. Mexico's dependency on foreign capital and markets, however, meant that the limited benefits reaching the working classes evaporated when the economic recession of 1907 hit the United States and other industrial nations. The downturn diminished foreign demand for Mexican goods and restricted foreign investment in Mexico. That helped drive the country into a recession, and it soon exploded in seemingly disassociated regional uprisings that actually formed part of a broader, more coherent, picture.

With its economy reliant on a cash crop vulnerable to the vagaries of domestic and global markets, Morelos fit a larger pattern found in the states of Durango, Chihuahua, and Sonora where surveying companies, the railroads, timber and cattle interests, and mining enterprises led a significant land transfer from common to private hands. That altered the social structure, displaced people from the land, and turned them into wage laborers dependent on market forces beyond their control. Dissatisfaction with those conditions made it possible for the agrarian ideology driving the insurrection in Morelos to spill over its borders, gain broader appeal, and profoundly impact the course of the Mexican Revolution, ultimately resulting in the adoption of a national agrarian reform program and helping to shape the polices of what would have otherwise been a more conservative postrevolutionary state.

Roots of Rebellion

Beginning in the 1840s, well-financed investors responded to the increased market opportunities created by Mexico's growing urban centers and began to expand sugar production in Morelos. As the haciendas grew, they overwhelmed small property holders and suffocated the traditionally communal and subsistence-oriented campesino villages. Facing limited options, many villagers abandoned their pueblos and moved onto the estates as dependent wage earners, share croppers, and tenant farmers.[3]

Modernizing ideologies such as Liberalism accompanied the political and economic changes taking place and, initially, represented a challenge by the emerging bourgeoisie to the remnants of aristocratic privilege left from the colonial period. Following Mexico's independence from Spain in 1821, an aspiring middle sector of lawyers, journalists, and middle-level merchants, who felt frustrated by impediments to their advancement, attacked established practices such as tax exemptions for the Catholic Church, legal exemptions for the church and army, and state concessions for things like the tobacco monopoly. The Liberals advocated broader political participation for the educated middle class and greater social mobility through more open markets, especially in real estate, which the church dominated. Their social program also called for a commitment to equality before the law, which attracted many rural Mexicans familiar with the discriminatory and castelike nature of the prevailing system.[4]

Conservatives, most from the old landed families, large merchant houses, and church and military hierarchies, sought to defend the prerogatives of those institutions, such as the benefits for the state monopolies that provided key products to Mexico City, as well as exclusive import-export contracts for foreign trade. The Conservatives also considered most Mexicans, especially Indians and mestizos in the countryside, unprepared for full participation in civil society. As a result, they viewed the Liberal program as a recipe for chaos. Seeking to maintain social stability and their own privileged positions, they hoped to perpetuate legal inequality and maintain special privileges inherited from the colonial era.

Probably the most important consequence of the battle between Liberal and Conservative leaders was that it inadvertently opened the door for the Mexican peasantry and rural working class to interject their voices into the national debate. During the nineteenth century, an often illiterate, but not inarticulate, rural populace entered the fight over what principles the country would be based on. They effectively adapted elite-inspired ideas and language to meet their own needs and defend their interests, and they changed the debate in ways that neither the Conservative nor Liberal leadership anticipated. Mexico, however, was not left to settle its internal disputes on its own. The U.S. invasion of 1846–48 and the French intervention from 1862–67 brought widespread devastation. They also threw the Mexican elite into disarray, creating the social and political space necessary for the expression of repressed grassroots aspirations.[5]

By the 1870s, the issues dividing the national elite had been decided on the battlefield in favor of the Liberals. Many people in rural Mexico hoped the Liberals would deliver on a combination of promises that included greater autonomy for the pueblos from a less intrusive federal government, legal equality for all, and an end to feudal-like labor conditions on the estates, where workers were bound to the haciendas through debt. Instead, the Liberal victory resulted in a legal assault on the pueblo's communal land ownership, and then, ironically, instead of decentralized power, rural Mexicans got increased centralization under Díaz.

During the Porfiriato, a wealthy Mexico City-based planter elite consolidated their rule in Morelos. They maintained their position thanks to a stable national government that exerted control over pueblos and workers through a strong police presence. The sugar planters and government functionaries combined to push forward rapid socioeconomic changes in the state, while managing to impose greater order on a region notorious for unrest. Underneath the glossy veneer of perceived Porfirian peace, however, dissatisfaction simmered.

Questions of Causation

The privatization of common lands and the transition to commercial agriculture proved traumatic and disruptive in Morelos and was resented and resisted by many who lived through it. The process, however, is a common one in world history, and although it often generates social tensions, it does not necessarily result in revolution.[6] The standard interpretations of the revolution in Morelos maintain that pueblo villagers rebelled in response to the dramatic expansion of the sugar haciendas and their expropriation of communal landholdings and water rights during the Porfiriato. That is true as far as it goes, but the expansion of the sugar industry was not sufficient in and of itself to cause the revolution. Current explanations actually lead us to an apparent paradox. If the revolution in Morelos was mainly a response to pueblos losing land, water, and other resources to the great estates, why did open resistance by pueblo citizens decline during the Porfiriato when haciendas continued to acquire land and water at pueblo expense and when sugar production shot up dramatically, more than doubling between 1898–1908? The contradiction calls for a fresh look at the revolution in Morelos and requires moving beyond vague generalizations about the capitalist transformation of the countryside. That transformation is an almost universal occurrence in any society attempting to "modernize" and is, therefore, inadequate as an explanation for something as remarkable as a revolution. Examining what happened in Morelos, then, may offer comparative insight into explaining how agrarian unrest turns revolutionary.[7]

Although pueblos and workers protested the changes taking place during most of the Porfiriato, three main factors discouraged open resistance. The first, and most obvious, was the sheer repressive capability of the state. Repression alone, though, does not guarantee compliance. The critical element to hacendado hegemony in Morelos was that while they were destroying the old way of life, the planters were replacing it with a seemingly viable alternative. That alternative was well-paying wage labor, which mollified pueblo resistance to the changes being imposed. So, the second, and probably most important, factor that explains a lack of open resistance at exactly the time one would expect it the most was that the sugar hacendados employed the peasants that they displaced from their communal lands, provided them access to rented land, and offered the material security that came with being a dependent peon on an estate.[8] As a result, even though people resented the loss of their autonomy and other changing conditions—and this study provides ample evidence that they did—there was little motivation for villagers and workers to resist in a way that might put them in jail, or an early grave. The absence of rebellion, however, did not mean that they accepted the conditions wholesale, or felt they lived in a just society. Due to the balance of power, people resisted in other less confrontational ways, often choosing litigation first, then turning to other options when that approach failed.[9]

The third main factor limiting open or violent resistance was that not everyone rejected the changes taking place. Rifts within communities between local elites, wealthier peasants, and poorer villagers often contradicted idealized visions of a communalist utopia under siege. While many pueblo citizens defended a lifestyle and identity that prized economic independence, communal land ownership, mutual aid, and an important degree of local political autonomy, others wanted to pursue different options. Some dreamed of owning their own independent small farms; others wanted to escape the sometimes stultifying confines of their pueblos. Some tried to realize those goals by taking advantage of the Liberal land laws of the 1850s that were designed to privatize agriculture and break up communal holdings in order to create a class of small-scale property holders. Reality, however, proved much harsher. Instead of moving from peasant to independent yeoman farmer, as the Liberals had advertised, most villagers found themselves making the move from peasant to hacienda worker. The transition involved a change in life from communal based, self-sufficiency to wage dependency. It was a historic step and, like the initial stages of enclosure and industrialization elsewhere in the world, it did not come easily.[10]

While employment opportunities temporarily mitigated the hostility of displaced peasants, the overproduction of sugar soon created a glut because of Mexico's inadequate domestic demand. The Morelos sugar hacendados began to overproduce at the same time that outside problems surfaced and limited export possibilities. U.S. and European tariffs against Mexican sugar coincided with surging Cuban sugar output following the Spanish-American War of 1898. The combination drove the Morelos producers out of the global market. As a result, hacendados were forced to curtail production, and by 1909–10, many displaced peasants found themselves both landless and unemployed.

When the national movement to oust President Díaz broke out, angry pueblo villagers and hacienda workers in Morelos joined in, demanding their land back and rejecting the social costs and instability of an economy based on sugar. The revolution that followed ripped apart the society the sugar hacendados had created. It represented an exceptional episode marked by extreme violence, but it also was part of a longer process of adaptation and resistance to the commercialization of agriculture and the transition from self-sufficient peasants into dependent workers. The Zapatista revolution gained symbolic power beyond its borders because it merged with other rebellions across the country, and because it represented both a rejection of the wider failure of the Porfirian path to development and a clear, culturally appealing alternative.

The Unique and the Universal

Morelos was unique both culturally and ethnically, but it shared some common experiences with other parts of Mexico that underwent accelerated bursts of commercialization, which helps explain why the values articulated in Morelos gained more widespread appeal. Ethnicity played an important role in the Morelos countryside. When the Spanish conquerors first introduced sugarcane there in the early sixteenth century, they brought Africans and forced them to work as slaves in the fields and mills. Many slave descendants became workers living in the hamlets that sprang up on the fringes of the sugar estates. The mixing of Africans, Americans, and Europeans led to a social milieu of Indians, mulattos, and mestizos at various stages in the turbulent transition from peasants into workers. The one constant, though, was that Spaniards and their cultural descendants sat atop an evolving and highly exploitative social hierarchy. The situation bred deep animosities.[11]

One of the most important aspects of rural society in Morelos, from colonial times to the revolution, was that many mestizo and mulatto hacienda settlements adopted the inherited values of Mexico's rural indigenous culture and its emphasis on independent village government and shared community landholding.[12] The Spanish Crown granted many indigenous communities legal rights to village communes and a degree of local self-government. Most hacienda settlements were made up of non-Indians, though, so they generally lacked the legal rights that Native Americans held to land and local autonomy. During the mid-nineteenth century, predominantly mestizo and mulatto hacienda towns began to challenge their ambiguous position in the prevailing system by fighting for recognition as legally incorporated pueblos with all the civic and land rights that status entailed. Their identification with the values and organization of the communal village, in lieu of the blanket acceptance of individualism, capitalism, and wage-labor alternatives, was probably the most significant social development in Morelos from the 1840s through the revolution. During those intervening years various Mexican government's attempted to dissolve communal landholding and instill the love of private property in its place. Hoping to defend their special status and way of life, Indian villages normally sought to safeguard their old colonial land grants. Mixed-race hacienda settlements, though, began to push beyond those traditional efforts and demanded that the right to land and self-governance be extended to all rural communities. When they did that, they radicalized an agrarian ideology that gained broad appeal throughout Mexico. Their wider vision had a profound impact on the revolutionary goals of the Zapatistas, and because it resonated with desires elsewhere, it heavily influenced the eventual reforms brought by the revolution.

Method and Organization

This book follows a basic chronological order. Chapter 1 presents the human and physical geography that help define Morelos as a region. Chapter 2 discusses the late-colonial period and independence movement, when localized agrarian rebellions began to assume wider significance. The main purpose of this first section is to trace the historical development of grassroots political consciousness in Morelos and the culture that informed it.

Chapters 3 through 6 treat Mexico's unbelievably turbulent mid-nineteenth century.[13] The intent is to connect regional social history with the nation's more well-known, but largely superficial, political history in order to explore how different groups experienced and shaped the larger narrative. Chapter 3 discusses the U.S. occupation of Mexico, the usually neglected popular efforts at national defense that surfaced after the collapse of the Mexican army, and the local meanings of that episode. Chapter 4 presents the major ideological and military conflicts between the Liberals and Conservatives, the different ideas Mexicans had about issues of race, equality, federalism, and centralism, and how those struggles opened the door for wider public participation in deciding the major questions of the day. Chapter 5 deals with the French intervention, rising nationalism, and the meaning of social banditry in the notoriously dangerous Morelos countryside. Chapter 6 is a case study of a bitter legal dispute between the community of Apatlaco, Morelos, and a powerful hacendado, which exemplifies the wider pattern. It demonstrates how the structural changes at the macrolevel affected localities and considers how what happened there reflected similar battles being waged at local levels across much of the nation.

Chapters 7 through 10 cover the Porfiriato and the revolution itself. Chapter 7 documents the rise of the Morelos sugar industry, the expansion of the sugar estates, the intricacies of the sugar-making process, the jobs and wages associated with it, and the impact the industry had on people's lives. Chapter 8 links events in Morelos to conditions outside of Mexican control, especially the international economy. It presents the thesis that it was not just the expansion of the great estates that led to the revolution, but rather their economic instability. The chapter explores how the rise and fall of global and domestic sugar markets affected Morelos and offers a picture of the associated social costs during the Porfiriato. Chapter 9 integrates elite and popular perspectives on the Morelos revolution, based on hacendado responses to surveys sponsored by the government of Francisco Madero and on interviews of former Zapatistas.

Although the efforts of the Morelos insurgents had a deep impact on twentieth-century Mexico, the society they imagined did not take shape. Today, the Mexican government pursues many economic policies reminiscent of the Porfirian era, including the pursuit of modernity by recruiting foreign investment and industry through low-wage labor and low taxes, promoting export-led growth vulnerable to changing global conditions, and privatizing communal landholdings. Those policies hold important social implications. If past experiences offer any lessons to learn from, they suggest that the benefits of those choices must outweigh the costs, and they must prove sustainable. Otherwise, the government that imposes them will be rejected, perhaps not peacefully.[14]

Chapter One

THE LAND AND
THE PEOPLE

The modern-day state of Morelos lies only fifty miles south of the Valley of Mexico, which has stood at the center of Mexican civilization, politics, and commerce for at least the last millennium. Morelos became socially, politically, and economically integrated with the central valley and its continuous movement of people and goods in pre-Columbian times. The rugged and heavily forested Sierra de Ajusco forms Morelos's northern boundary and presents a natural border that separates the state from the central basin and Mexico City. The mountains range from six thousand to seventeen thousand feet and stretch from the peaks around Tres Marías in the northwest to the massive snow-capped volcano Popocatépetl towering at the northeast. As one travels into Morelos the land drops off sharply through pine forests and steep hillsides. Moving down from the mountain town of Milpa Alta into the Yautepec Valley, for example, the altitude drops almost seven thousand feet in only seventeen miles. Passable throughout the year, the northern mountains have never posed an absolute obstacle to the movement of people, but have presented a natural border that helped define the region and set it apart from its neighbors. Close enough to the central valley to share a common cultural experience and heritage, Morelos is also removed enough to have developed its own distinct characteristics.[1]

When the steep slopes level out into a gradual piedmont, one finds a denser population supported by a temperate climate and varied agricultural activities. The semitropical valleys below run north to south and are separated by low-lying hills with scruffy vegetation and deep ravines. The rich volcanic earth, seasonal rainfall, and year-around warmth in the valleys provide excellent conditions for raising sugarcane. The northern reaches of the principal valleys of Cuernavaca in the west and Cuautla Amilpas in the east lie in the *tierra templada*, or temperate zone, and their southern parts lie in what is called the *tierra caliente*, or the hot lands. In general though, Morelos's major valleys are referred to as tierra caliente, to convey their warm climate, fertile soil, and semitropical agricultural products.[2] Despite their differences, the social and economic interaction between Morelos's ecological zones developed in a complimentary way over time to form an integrated and recognized region.[3]

Accessed by the relatively low mountain pass at Amecameca, and the route from Mexico City-Tenochtitlán to Cuernavaca, Morelos was a thoroughfare between central Mexico and peoples to the south before the Spanish arrived. Following the military defeat of the Aztecs, the conquistador Hernán Cortés recognized the wealth of the region, and in 1528, King Charles V of Spain awarded him twenty-two Mexican towns populated by twenty-three thousand Indians, and named him the Marqués del Valle de Oaxaca. Cortés's domain covered much of the present-day state of Morelos. He and other Spaniards began to funnel labor from the central plateau to the lowlands and mines, or wherever they needed workers to exploit the natural wealth of their "discovery." The forced internal labor migrations led to frequent contact and mixing among the indigenous peoples of the highlands and lowlands and the various newcomers who soon arrived from across the ocean.[4]

Cortés and others immediately embarked on a variety of business enterprises and agricultural experiments. The most important for the future social history of Morelos was the cultivation and processing of sugarcane. Cortés had prior experience with sugar production in Cuba and brought the plant to Mexico, where it flourished in the warm climate and rich soil of the Morelos lowlands. Soon Cortés's mill, called Tlaltenango, was producing 125,000 pounds of sugar a year. Mule trains hauled the sugar to Mexico City's urban population, who consumed most of it, and the rest went to the port of Veracruz for export to Spain.[5]

Indians and the Land

European diseases decimated the indigenous population of Mexico and benefited the Spanish in their conquest by weakening resistance. The ravages of smallpox and influenza afflicted all ethnic groups, but struck the native inhabitants particularly hard, spreading with "inconceivable rapidity" and killing millions. As a result, the population of central Mexico fell from as many as twenty-five million people in 1519 to only seven million by 1548. The people of Morelos shared this unfortunate fate. The number living in the region declined from an estimated 725,000 prior to the conquest to about 600,000 three years later. Then, after one generation of further contact, the population plummeted drastically, with only 150,000 indigenous Mexicans left alive by midcentury.[6]

With their population depleted, Indians had no reason to hoard the land since they had as much as they could use, at least for the time being. That held true partly because they focused on subsistence agriculture rather than cattle ranching or raising and selling cash crops. Indian land sales and rentals to Spaniards due to the widespread native death of the early colonial period would come back to haunt them when their numbers recovered and their needs increased. That event was compounded by the Spanish policy of *congregación*, which was an official program of relocation and concentration of Indians from smaller communities to larger towns for easier control.[7]

Local native rulers often found themselves in the contradictory position of procuring what the Spaniards demanded in tribute, while trying to serve as guardians of their people at the same time. Under Spanish rule, Indian villagers in Morelos adopted an Iberian style of governance, electing town councils. Despite the outward form, they managed to maintain the function of their traditional ruling elite as late as the twentieth century. That included unelected but prominent members of their communities, usually made up of elders.[8] Yet, at the same time, the adoption of Spanish surnames, language, and dress by some Morelos *caciques* (local native rulers) indicated their rapid Hispanization. The voluntary contributions of lands, laborers, and monies donated to construct and maintain convents, hospitals, and haciendas for Catholic religious orders pointed to the willingness of some indigenous leaders to accommodate nearby Spaniards and assimilate into colonial society. As a result, no universal solidarity or culture of resistance materialized in Morelos, and villages often fractured internally.

The conflict between individualism and communalism within the native pueblos manifested itself early and could be seen in the towns of Anenecuilco and Cuautla. Postconquest *principales* (local indigenous leaders) claimed community lands as their own and sold them or subdivided them among selected individuals despite the fact that they belonged to village communal patrimonies. Spanish authority and practice, including the changes they brought in pueblo governance and administration, increased the opportunity for individual aggrandizement and the Indians' sense of acquisitiveness. Internal rifts emerged, usually between relatively rich villagers and others in the community, especially during periods of stress. Competition between pueblos trying to protect their royal grants and communal holdings surfaced too, like the one in 1685 between "los naturales del pueblo de Atlacholoaya" over possession of communal lands against rival claims from nearby Xochitepec. These early land struggles between pueblos took an important turn in the nineteenth century when, instead of squabbling amongst themselves, these same two towns put aside their differences and joined forces with other pueblos to challenge the claims of neighboring hacendados. That demonstrated their increasing awareness of a shared condition in their struggle against hacendados "*españoles*."[9]

The native population disaster led to new patterns of settlement and land tenure. The effects of death and the congregaciónes combined to eliminate many towns. As people died, the land fell vacant, and private Spanish interests assumed a rather morbid inheritance. For example, as disease and death ravaged central Mexico, a special commission was formed to investigate lands "vacated by the deaths of Indians in the Villa de Toluca."[10] As the number of indigenous people dropped, concern grew among the Spaniards about feeding the swelling urban population in Mexico City, since Spanish conquerors and colonists relied on Indian tribute and labor for both their food and wealth. With a growing Spanish and mestizo population in the city, and a dwindling indigenous one in the countryside, expanding Spanish commercial agriculture became a necessity. Naturally, the sizeable preconquest Indian population had occupied most of the best agricultural areas. But as it plunged, Spaniards acquired the vacated properties and began to organize their holdings into what would become the haciendas. They moved to consolidate their estates through a combination of leases, purchases, and grants. The resulting land turnover during this brutal period laid the foundation for much of Morelos's future social strife.

A primary vehicle behind land transfer in Morelos was the *censo perpetuo*, which was a permanent land grant bestowed on an individual by Cortés and the heirs of the Marquesado del Valle. For example, in 1632 the *naturales* (natives) of the pueblo of San Juan Huitzilac asked for two pieces of land granted to a Spaniard named Francisco Prieto de Espinosa in a censo perpetuo from the Marquesado. The people of Huitzilac owed tribute to Francisco Prieto, but could not meet their obligations because death had decimated their community while their tribute obligations remained the same. So, while they were at their weakest, "when this pueblo had very few Indians," they sold the land to Señor Prieto to make up for shortfalls in tribute. The same thing was happening across Morelos. The naturales in Atlacholoaya suffered a similar experience and contested the takeover by purchase of a censo perpetuo of four *caballerías* (one caballería equaled 250 acres, or 42.79 hectares) of land in Cuernavaca and *una estancia* (a pasture) by the Spaniard Don Lesmes de Astudillo in 1629.[11]

Meanwhile, the Crown, often facing bankruptcy, also provided avenues for transferring land and water rights to private individuals through *composiciones*. The composiciones bestowed state authenticity and legal recognition to lands acquired by Spaniards, either legally or extralegally, in return for a cash payment. The process encouraged usurpations and fraud.[12] Paying between eight hundred and four thousand pesos each, Spaniards renting cane fields and operating mills paid the Crown to gain title to the land and legitimize their claims. Later, those old titles would give the hacendados important legal footing in conflicts that arose when Indian communities recuperated and asserted that their lands had been unfairly taken from them in the past.

At the same time, however, an important viceregal decree of 1597 created the pueblos' *fundo legal*, the social ramifications of which reached well into the twentieth century. The fundo legal was an allotment of communal land granted to every Indian community holding pueblo status and was deemed the inalienable property of the community. The size and parameters of the fundo legal evolved over time, but by 1695 came to measure six hundred *varas* (about six hundred yards) in all directions emanating from the village church at its center. It is partly for this reason that the church as both a physical structure and spiritual sanctuary has held such an important place for rural Mexicans.[13]

Despite various efforts at limiting the abuses suffered by Indians, the Crown was primarily interested in gaining a profit from its colony and, therefore, actively supported the development of export-oriented activities that would provide goods desired in Spain or that would enrich it. That mainly meant silver production that could be subjected to the royal treasury's *quinto*, or one-fifth tax, but also included cash crops like sugar. Even in the midst of these economic interests, some general protective legislation for the Indians emerged, most importantly, the fundo legal and the official recognition of their right to communal land. That provided the pueblos with some defense in their disputes with expansionist hacendados during the ensuing centuries.

The importance of the fundo legal extended beyond providing the Indians their material needs and allowed for much of the local politics and economics of village life to be run by the pueblo itself. It formed the foundation on which Morelos's villagers built a large corpus of legal cases and moral appeals. The fundo protected pueblo integrity and allowed pueblos to retain political rights and organizations, to control religious events and celebrations, and to build and maintain schools and civic buildings. Morelos's pueblo citizenry jealously defended the fundo legal as a way to maintain a degree of local political, economic, and cultural independence from both hacendados and the state.[14]

The fundo legal also formalized another basis for cultural competition. It gave legal sanction to Indian preferences for communal land ownership and accepted the *vecinos'* (citizens) rights to divide and dispense the land as they saw fit. The establishment of the fundo, however, did not recognize individual rights to the land. Rather, pueblo vecinos considered their fundo the collective property of the community, not just as a group of living individuals, but as something more durable and venerated stretching back for generations. Even in the twentieth century, villagers in Morelos still viewed the land as an inheritance from their ancestors and believed it was the duty of the living to safeguard it for future generations to use and share, as those that came before had done for them.[15] So, royal decrees tempered the rate of land turnover and provided some basis for villagers to fight back through the courts on the merits of generally vague pronouncements. Government edicts, however, did not stop the aggrandizement of the hacendados and the process of land alienation in Morelos. Larger socioeconomic forces exerted a profound effect.

Africans, Labor, and a Changing Ethnicity

Sugar production demanded heavy and intense labor. The phenomenon of dying Indians not only facilitated the expansion of commercial and industrial export agriculture but also led to the importation of African slaves. Spanish landowners bought slaves in growing numbers during the seventeenth century in order to satisfy their increasing need for labor. By 1650, they had brought an estimated one hundred thousand Africans to Mexico, bound for the mines, coastal plantations, and the sugar-producing zones of Morelos. Slaves worked in the boiler rooms of the mills, as cart drivers, cane carriers, and field hands. Their arrival brought the third major element in the ethnic transformation of rural Morelos as it became a new mix of peoples and cultures.[16]

Cortés contracted to have five hundred African slaves work on his estates in 1542, and in 1549 he had eighty slaves at the family mill at Atlacomulco, while twenty-one house slaves served his residence in Cuernavaca. Another major *encomendero* (holder of a grant providing labor and tribute from the native population) and sugar planter in Morelos at the time owned twenty slaves. The institution of slavery spread, and by 1630, the hacienda of Guajoyuca employed eighty slaves, and the nearby hacienda Atlihuayan had the same number in 1632. There were 230 slaves of all ages living and working on the hacienda Xochimancas in 1653. Slaves represented a substantial investment to the hacendado and made up a relatively sophisticated group of skilled workers whose descendants worked on Morelos's sugar haciendas for the next three and a half centuries.[17]

Despite regulatory laws, in practice few restraints controlled the behavior of slave owners. Hacendados in Morelos housed their slaves in special quarters called the *real de esclavos*. Slaves were routinely disciplined, subjected to corporal punishment, had their bodies branded with searing-hot branding irons, and sometimes hacendados had their overseers brand slaves on the face for easy recognition in case of flight. Estate owners kept whips, handcuffs, neck irons, and chains for their administrators to use to restrain and punish rebellious or disobedient slaves.[18]

Slaves represented an economic asset to the Morelos hacendado, but they were also considered potentially dangerous. Escaped slaves were a cause of fear. Morelos planters maintained a repressive police presence in order to discourage outbreaks of organized resistance. Even so, some slaves in Morelos plotted a revolt as early as 1536 to achieve their freedom. They elected a "king" and attempted to induce Indians to assist them. The instigators, though, were identified, captured, taken to Mexico City, and executed in a public display. Despite the outcome, the episode pointed to the potential for blacks and Indians to identify with each other based on their mutual oppression. Spaniards dreaded the possibility, and the authorities passed laws to keep the exploited groups separate from each other, and therefore more easily controlled. But, over time blacks, Indians, and mestizos ended up living together and belonging to the same extended families and communities.

Spaniards felt surrounded by the other *castas* living among them. Reflecting Spanish attitudes at the time, Gómez de Cervantes complained to the Crown in 1605: "We are surrounded by enemies who outnumber us; the danger is great because Indians, Negroes, Mulattos, and Mestizos are present in much greater numbers than us who have to serve your majesty and defend the realm." Openly referring to other ethnic groups as "enemies," Cervantes revealed an attitude that would die hard in Morelos.[19] Just because Spaniards feared the castas in Mexico did not mean that the darker-skinned lower castes were able to ally themselves effectively. Alert to the possibility, though, King Philip II ordered Africans segregated from Indians because "besides treating them badly, they teach them bad habits and vice, lead them astray, and thus are able to prevent the achievement of our goal of their salvation, prosperity and tranquility." Philip worried that African slaves infected the Indian mentality with ideas of resistance. Despite the efforts of the state and slave owners, the daily realities of work and leisure time overcame the official efforts to limit contact between Africans, Europeans, and the indigenous, as the larger process of *mestizaje* prevailed.[20] Spanish overseers in sixteenth-century Morelos supervised a mix of enslaved Africans and nominally free Indians and mulattos. With a Spanish ruling class, a subjugated, but still somewhat functionally independent Indian community, and a supply of imported African labor, the dye was cast for the future social history of Morelos.

Because they created, maintained, and sat atop an unequal caste system, the Spaniards feared retribution. Their concerns were well founded. One late sixteenth-century traveler in Mexico noted that "the Indians and Negroes hate and abhor the Spaniards whole heartedly."[21]

Trying to escape lives of captivity, runaway slaves formed cimarron societies that attempted to re-create African village life in Mexico. Pitched battles between cimarron groups and Spaniards broke out in several places during the latter sixteenth century, including both Río Blanco in present-day Veracruz, and Cuernavaca, Morelos. Later, violent episodes driven by anti-Spanish attitudes exploded in Morelos during the nineteenth and early twentieth centuries that reflected the perpetuation of bad feelings originally generated in the colonial era and re-created over time. Violence was only part of a wider popular response to the elite's persistent effort to maintain an unequal, ethnically divided, caste-ridden rural society.[22]

Despite Spanish efforts to segregate blacks from Indians and other members of colonial society, the rising number of mestizo and mulatto residents in Morelos served to transform the ethnic makeup of rural villages over time. Some descendants of African slaves remained hacienda dependents until continued mixing eventually rendered them ethnically and culturally indistinguishable and they became absorbed by mestizaje. Today, however, some haciendas in the sugar valleys of Morelos, where the slave population was the most dense, still have churches decorated with black and mulatto saints and religious figures, pointing to the ancestry of their parishioners and, probably, to the efforts of priests to provide symbols to which those parishioners could relate. The best known of these figures is the Cristo Negro de San Gaspar, which hung from the church wall of one of the major sugar haciendas south of Cuernavaca. Legend surrounds the figure, but artisans probably crafted the image during the mid-seventeenth century. It was later moved for safe-keeping during the campesino uprisings that accompanied the Wars of the Reform in Morelos. Today it can be found in the old church of Jiutepec.[23]

Reflecting the legacy of slavery, the population of the Valley of Cuautla Amilpas was "perhaps mostly Negroid" during the mid-eighteenth century, while Zacualpan was also largely black and mestizo. The jurisdiction of Cuernavaca recorded the marriages of black male slaves to Indian women, which resulted in a large number of so-called *zambos*. Those relationships were common throughout the tierra caliente. By 1743, for example, there were 4,954 Indian tributaries in Morelos and a total of 2,690 non-Indian families of Negroes, mulattos, and zambos.[24] The native population eventually merged with black and mulatto field hands and sugar workers to create their own localized version of the mestizo, and the cultural practices and histories of the contributing subgroups were evidenced in their places of worship and work. Ethnic diffusion in Morelos led to a fluid and varied cultural setting, with peoples from around the globe being brought into contact, broadening and changing the emerging society.

While some people with African lineage moved to the larger provincial towns and disappeared into ethnically diverse places like Cuautla, Cuernavaca, and Yautepec, others stayed close to the estates. One important example was the large, still identifiable mulatto population of Villa de Ayala in the 1740s. Ayala is the place for which Emiliano Zapata's famous Plan de Ayala was named. Many rural settlements in the Morelos lowlands began as mainly mulatto and ethnically mixed hacienda *rancherías*. Some then eventually became pueblos, or even villas. In the mid-eighteenth century, for example, Ayala was known as the *congregación de Mapastlán*, comprised of six mestizo families and fifteen families of free mulattos. Generations later the old hacienda settlement became Villa de Ayala, and although it had fought with the once indigenous pueblo of Anenecuilco over land, both communities played prominent roles in challenging hacendado rule during the revolution. That convergence symbolized a larger pattern that indicated the rejection of imposed caste distinctions by the rural working population and a self-perception that recognized a shared condition in the evolving social order.[25]

Most hacienda towns began to identify with the spirit and ideals of the "Indian" pueblos. Identities in the pueblos and hacienda settlements were shaped by who the inhabitants were, but also by who they were not. Eventually, a broader campesino identity emerged, partly in opposition to ethnically distinct, wealthy, landholding Spaniards and their cultural descendants. The Morelos peasantry and rural workers in the hacienda towns shared inherited cultures and traditions of resistance born from experiences in slavery, conquest, and exploitation. Over time they formed a rural mestizo culture that embraced enduring indigenous beliefs and practices regarding land, community, local autonomy, and mutual aid.

Meanwhile, the world demand for sugar rose after 1580, and Mexican producers responded. The first dramatic growth of the sugar estates came in the latter half of the sixteenth and early seventeenth centuries and encouraged the expansion of the sugar haciendas, which grew piecemeal.[26] Once the process was underway, Spaniards began to buy and lease small parcels from local caciques, other Indian individuals, and pueblo governments. They then bought, sold, and traded them for neighboring plots and consolidated their holdings into contiguous tracts. The rural landscape went from communalist native villages and small ranches operating alongside scattered sugar-cane fields with mule-driven cane-crushers, to large Spanish-owned haciendas looming over neighboring villages and giving rise to hacien-da hamlets of Indian laborers and African slaves. The long and painful process of land transfer from Indians to Spaniards, and from commu-nity property to private capital had begun.[27]

Chapter Two

CULTURAL COMPETITION
AND THE STRUGGLE
FOR INDEPENDENCE

The struggle for independence from Spain unleashed social forces that foreshadowed Mexico's turbulent history during the nineteenth century. The independence movement brought forward violently conflicting ideas about citizens' rights and the nature of civil society, while changing material circumstances exerted new pressures on the rural population. The expansion of hacienda agriculture and the collapse of the mediating role of the colonial state made the relationship between hacendados and campesinos even more contentious than before.

The economic growth the colony experienced during the Bourbon reforms of the late eighteenth century brought uneven benefits to Mexicans. Mexican sugar producers benefited from the relaxation of colonial trade restrictions and from the great slave revolution in Haiti, which brought down the world's largest sugar producer and overthrew one of the harshest and most exploitative colonial regimes in the world. The new conditions offered the Mexican sugar industry increased opportunities on the world market. Meanwhile, and more importantly for producers in Morelos, Mexico City's urban population continued to grow, demanding not only sugar, but more corn, beans, and other foods. Traditionally, peasant villagers and small farmers had actively participated in supplying those goods. But as the sugar hacendados responded to the new opportunities, expanded their operations, and provided more foodstuffs to local and regional markets, including Mexico City, they entered into more direct conflict with pueblo agriculture. The old, always uneven but somewhat symbiotic, relationship between haciendas and pueblos became even more unbalanced.[1]

One of the primary goals of the Spanish colonial project in Mexico was the transformation of the Indians into acceptable and productive vassals of the Crown. Spaniards and Creoles (people of Spanish descent born in the New World) agreed on the need for the social and cultural transformation of the Indian. The process had been underway for centuries, but it could not always be controlled by social engineering from above. As economic circumstances changed, traditional indigenous resistance in defense of land and community also changed because of changing ethnicity and increased experiences with wage labor. The result was a rural mestizo working culture that retained important indigenous elements, but adapted to new circumstances.

Cultural Resistance

Following the conquest, official religious ceremonies transformed from Aztec priests practicing their religion on the temples of Tenochtitlán, to a Spanish and mestizo clergy preaching Catholicism in the countryside. Observed from today's historically removed vantage point the overall effort at conversion proved quite successful. However, localized resistance during the colonial period provided a constant countercurrent to the larger pattern, both in Morelos and across Mexico. For example, in 1761, Antonio Pérez, a poor and wandering mestizo shepherd, drew the attention of authorities in Morelos. He gained short-lived notoriety by preaching a syncretic religion that featured the worship of wooden idols, and he managed to generate a cult of followers who gathered in a remote cave in the volcano Popocatépetl. Pérez blended Catholicism with indigenous religious lore for his listeners in the grotto, creating a hybrid form that became a focal point of local cultural resistance to both the clergy and Spanish landowners. Morelos's social climate proved fertile for that sort of activity, and Pérez attracted five hundred followers across central and northern Morelos.[2]

By that time, Spaniards, including both private individuals and members of religious orders such as the Dominicans and Jesuits, had expanded their sugar estates and displaced increasing numbers of Indian peasants who raised staple foods such as corn, beans, and chilies on their small plots. Emerging from that context, Antonio Pérez told his followers:

> Christ's soul was corn. When they buried him a shoot
> was born from the heart of Christ . . . crows stole the
> ear and hid it in a field. An angel heard them shouting
> and found the ear where they were. He took it to Saint
> Isidore and Saint Luke with instructions to prepare
> the earth and sow the kernels of the ear. . . .
> The saint cut open the furrow and sowed the corn,
> which grew abundantly, and they continued to sow
> it so the Soul of Christ was spread throughout the
> whole world.[3]

In the contest of cultures taking place in the Morelos countryside, corn became the body of Christ and the food of the people, especially the poor. That cultural, religious representation brought corn, and those who grew and ate it, closer to Christ and differentiated them from Spaniards who preferred wheat and sugar. The struggle reflected the emphasis of pueblo citizens on subsistence agriculture versus the Spaniards' desires for commercial production and the greater profits from raising and marketing wheat and sugarcane.[4]

Pérez's resistance to the colonial order reinforced what many undoubtedly already believed when he preached, "Tribute must not be paid to the king, for it serves only to fatten the Spanish, and that is why the world is coming to an end. . . . Everything should go to the naturales (natives, indigenous). . . . They alone should remain, while the Spanish and the *gente de razón* (well-born and educated) should be burned. . . . All the riches should stay in the hands of the naturales."[5] Pérez was a mestizo, but he identified with the naturales. Pérez's conversation hints at a wider experience as new cultural determinants of ethnicity emanating from below began to transcend older racial ones imposed from above, and they helped shape political and social attitudes. Despite the presence of men like Pérez, however, most people probably accepted the church as brought to them by the clergy, and they definitely took employment on the haciendas, sometimes becoming debt peons or accepting other conditions of limited freedom. Even when considered within that larger more general acquiescence, the Pérez movement still revealed some of the stresses and strains in rural society and offered at least one expression of the way that material conditions, beliefs, and identities of both self and others interrelated.

Pérez, as a mestizo, was caught between two worlds. He belonged to a growing group. The non-Spanish population of Cuernavaca, for example, grew by 89 percent between 1743 and 1809. Some people in smaller communities in the countryside worked their village plots and remained basically peasants, occasionally working part-time on rural estates. Others lost their land or were born on the estates and lived in the growing hacienda settlements that people from the southern part of the region called rancherías, and those in the north called *cuadrillas*. Others migrated to larger towns in Morelos, or to Mexico City. Pérez was just one of many caught in the middle of this transitional society. But the message he preached as he traveled the Mexican countryside by foot, calling for the elimination of so-called Spaniards in Mexico more than two hundred years after the conquest, challenged the prevailing social order on several levels.[6]

His views apparently resonated with other poor Indian and mestizo peasants who joined him. When the authorities discovered a gathering of 160 people worshiping two idols, they quickly moved to repress the Pérez-led movement. The priest of Yautepec reported the incident and, based on confessions of some of those apprehended, the officials implicated five hundred idolaters from a dozen Morelos pueblos. The effort to apprehend Pérez and his followers led to a melee that left one Spaniard dead before the rest of the cult members escaped to the cave or dispersed across the countryside.

The priest who first acted against the movement reflected the rapidly changing nature of local society. He was an Indian cacique whose two brothers were also priests who had been indigenous leaders. Their roles underscored the lack of a homogenous non-Spanish group in Morelos, as indigenous elites often associated with the dominant culture. Some indigenous leaders, like these two, joined the Spaniards and criollos in opposing popular expressions of resistance and tried to marginalize dissident members of the community, be they Indian, mestizo, or mulatto.

Although the authorities repressed the Pérez movement for its religious deviance, that was only the most obvious component. Antonio

Pérez gained followers the year after an agricultural crisis eroded the demand for labor on haciendas and left a hungry rural population scrambling for a way to pay for corn, the price of which had become prohibitive due to shortage. That material hardship exacerbated other tensions. Despite the brutality of the conquest, pre-Hispanic practices, beliefs, and ideals mutated and survived into the mid-eighteenth century, sometimes blending with the religious practices of slaves and providing a platform from which rural people pursued varied strategies for cultural survival.

Occasionally, an incident or accusation of some kind of deviant behavior resulted in the submission of an unfortunate soul to the Inquisition. Two cases bracketing the Pérez episode offer telling glimpses into how economic change, religious conversion, and an evolving ethnicity interacted. They revolved around hacienda sugar workers in an area where religious imagery featuring black saints is still on display in an old hacienda chapel near Cuautla that hints at its ethnic past, and the larger process of conversion, mestizaje, and cultural adaptation that took place there. One case involved Pedro Nolasco, a mulatto laborer on the hacienda Cuahuixtla who faced the charge of "evilness" leveled at him by a woman who accused him of poisoning her when he concocted a brew that made her temporarily blind in 1787. The other case was an accusation by the priest of San Jeronimo Aculco against a blind, one-armed black slave named José Manuel for "fortune telling." It revealed that underground counter-hegemonic religious practices were taking place on the haciendas among the African-descent population. Such cases disturbed those charged with their religious instruction and echoed patterns evident in Haiti, Jamaica, or wherever tropical plantation slavery took hold and a repressed population sought escape, solace, or revenge through voodoo or some other imagined alternative to the unbearable reality they were condemned to endure. The degree to which these kinds of activities represented conscious resistance, and what meaning workers and peasants imparted to their actions is open to debate, but the fact that they engaged in a variety of behavior that contradicted elite efforts at social, cultural, and economic domination, and that the authorities moved to repress it, is indisputable.

For people born or settled on the haciendas, cultural resistance might take the form of witchcraft or some alternative religion, but for those in the pueblos with a realistic chance of retaining some local autonomy, one of the most important elements underlying their cultural resiliency was the evolving ideal of the municipio libre, or autonomous, communal, pueblo-based way of life. At that historical moment the municipio libre included a lifestyle with a corn-based diet inherited from the pre-Columbian past, a syncretic religion combining African, pre-Colombian, and European imagery, and a sense of being ethnically distinct from, and exploited by, the great landowners, local representatives of the state and, sometimes, the church. Taken together, those three groups represented the imposed power of the dominant culture, backed up of course, by the police and military. The concept of the municipio libre evolved over time, but in a basic political sense it included participatory local rule, based on local representation and leadership. Materially, the municipio libre implied collective labor, shared natural resources, and shared expenses at the municipal level. Those communal values persisted throughout the twentieth century.[7]

Antonio Pérez's movement surfaced during an economic crisis in 1761, as did Zapata's movement in 1910, when, in the midst of another corn shortage and economic recession, pueblo citizens and landless sugar workers pursued a vision of greater social justice that included another indictment of the oligarchy and a new call for a redistribution of resources. Both movements were also tinged with folk Catholicism, with Zapatista troops fighting under the banner of the Virgen de Guadalupe. Although Zapatismo matured during the revolution, part of the fight was rooted in the past and called for the restitution of inherited rights. The other part was forward-looking and offered an imagined alternative future. The combination allowed for Zapatismo's continual political evolution as the struggle wore on. Although much transpired between the days when Pérez preached in the grotto and those when Zapata rode the countryside, some continuity remained. The alternative views campesinos expressed expanded, reflecting the changes in Mexican society and demanding new meanings of citizen and nation.[8]

Legal Defenses of Communalism

A key enabling element for the survival of a campesino-based worldview in the face of the capitalist transformation of the countryside was the continued access to communal land. Even though the percentage of people able to support themselves by tilling their village plots dropped precipitously over the centuries, communal landholding provided the foundation on which a self-sufficient agricultural lifestyle stood until the middle of the nineteenth century. The only real official guarantee to communal landholding, though, was the fundo legal. The fundos legales were intended to provide common access to land, water, woods, and pastures that would guarantee the maintenance and growth of the community. Population growth and expanded commercialization reduced available land over time, so although it survived for centuries, the fundo legal was not sufficient to sustain pueblo independence, and outsiders did not always respect it.[9]

The leaders of Zapata's hometown of Anenecuilco de las Amilpas, for example, complained in court in 1798 that neighboring haciendas were hemming them in. They claimed their remaining land was insufficient for their needs and comprised less than one-half of what they deserved as part of their fundo. By that time the population in Morelos had recovered from the demographic disaster and had changed considerably. The land was more crowded, and the haciendas had spread a great deal.[10]

José Nicolás Abad, the owner of a hacienda known as San Francisco Mapastlán during the 1790s, challenged Anenecuilco's assertions that he was usurping their lands. He claimed that Mapastlán had held the disputed lands for more than two hundred years. According to him, Anenecuilco sold the lands to the hacienda in 1597, tried to recover them in 1608 and again in 1685, but the courts denied their claims both times and recognized the land transfer as a legal sale. Regardless of whether he held legal title, the hacendado's recitation of events established the sheer duration of the conflict, which was already almost two hundred years old in 1790, and it illustrated the deep roots of the land problem in the sugar-producing regions of Morelos.

Using terminology frequently employed by Morelos's hacendados, he labeled the Anenecuilcan's claims "repugnant" and insisted that the "barrio" of Anenecuilco was "not and never has been a pueblo." Pueblo status was crucial; without it a hamlet stood almost no chance of defending, recovering, or acquiring land. With it, everyone, including hacendados, recognized that *pueblo vecinos* (a word that meant residents, but increasingly implied citizens) were legally entitled to at least some land in order to support civic culture. Not until the middle of the nineteenth century, and the advent of the Liberal reforms, did the validity of even pueblo claims become openly rejected.[11]

Abad's statements also brought forward the cultural divide developing between pueblo communities and the planters when he argued that the land in question belonged to the hacienda Mapastlán and that Anenecuilco had no use for it because it was planted in sugarcane.[12] People in Anenecuilco planted their lands in corn. Apparently, most village communities did not grow sugarcane for sale to local mills and, instead, devoted most of their energies to raising crops for consumption. That pattern held through the revolution.

The vecinos of Anenecuilco pressed their claims through the testimony of several old men, including Cristóbal Mora, José Cuellar, Martín Carlos Flores, and Ignacio Baez. Flores was a seventy-two-year-old mulatto *labrador* (campesino, or peasant farmer); Cuellar and Baez were seventy-two-year-old mestizos; and Cristóbal Mora was an eighty-year-old mestizo and resident worker at the hacienda. Mora swore before God and the "Santa Cruz en forma de oro" that "the pueblo of San Miguel Anenecuilco is a pueblo, and a very old one." As a youth he had heard his *antepasados* (his elders) say they had known various old Indians who were *gobernadores* and recalled that the church " that existed then was already ancient: and that they had seen people buried in the same church, and one witness remembered one of those old men saying it was the pride of the town."[13] The citizens of Anenecuilco also produced a sixteenth-century map showing trees, hills, and rivers, and in the center a drawing of a pueblo that was labeled "San Miguel Anenecuilco" in Nahuatl (the preconquest indigenous language of the area). One of the other old men supported Mora, saying it was common knowledge that the church of Anenecuilco was in its original state and one of the oldest around.[14]

Beyond the particular issues involved in the case, the oral history these men related demonstrated the ongoing land conflict, how it was debated, and how rural, usually illiterate, people transferred knowledge through time. Although not its original intent, the dispute's records showed what they thought, what they considered valid, how they remembered their past, and how they kept the past alive. The people of Anenecuilco relied on the personal memories of what they considered four living oracles. The fact that the eighty-year-old Mora said that his parents had heard "some old Indians" say the church had existed for a very long time also points to a number of things. First, Mora was a mestizo who identified "old Indians" in a way that made them sound like relics of the past. Yet Indians in the area still comprised an essential element of the populace. A census of Anenecuilco that accompanied the lawsuit listed thirty-two people, all of whom were classified as Indians, at least for the purposes of the case. Because of the colonial decrees recognizing the land rights of Indians, these ethnic classifications are not entirely reliable, because it made more sense for a community claiming pueblo status and pre-Columbian roots to label as many of its inhabitants as possible as

Indian instead of mestizo or something else. For example, of the ten witnesses brought forth to offer sworn testimony on behalf of Anenecuilco, four were Spaniards, two mulatto, two mestizo, one *castizo*, and one Indian. The distribution revealed the changing ethnic composition of the Morelos lowlands, on the one hand, and the weakness of Indian testimony in colonial courts, on the other.

The demographics also suggest that by the late eighteenth century, pueblos of the Morelos lowlands were not closed communities, although they retained a keen sense of their past even as some members migrated in or out of the population. Rural communities in Morelos probably did look inward for protection and resist some aspects of integration into the larger society. That behavior was only logical though, since much of their contact with outsiders would have carried negative connotations and subjected them to things like exactions of tributes or taxes, impressment into the military, or some other imposition of central authority and deprivation of local autonomy.[15]

Anenecuilco's experience was not unique. Cuautla Amilpas, Anenecuilco's neighbor and the most important town in the region, also became embroiled in multiple legal disputes from 1796 to 1804. The vecinos of Cuautla found themselves in direct conflict with many powerful neighbors, including the owner of the hacienda Cuahuixtla, which was impinging on the town's fundo legal. The hacienda, one of the major sugar estates in the area, eventually grew to surround Cuautla on the south and east, and it surfaced repeatedly over the centuries in disputes with its pueblo neighbors. Other haciendas caused problems for Cuautla too. The hacienda Buenavista built an aqueduct on lands claimed by the townspeople, and Cuautla also lodged a major complaint against the hacienda Santa Inés for another land invasion. All these cases must have cost the people there a substantial amount to litigate, but community leaders felt that it was worth the expense to defend their lands and the relative independence and self-reliance they ensured.[16]

People in other sugar-producing areas of Morelos shared many of the same experiences as those in the Cuautla Valley. The pueblo of Jiutepec, in the valley that descends gradually to the south of Cuernavaca, and now totally absorbed by the larger city, filed a complaint against the hacienda San Vicente in 1807 over the invasion of lands the town had held under a viceregal grant since 1661. Meanwhile, vecinos of Jantetelco, in the southeast portion of the state, protested that Don Nicolás Icazbalceta, owner of the hacienda Santa Anna Tenango that dominated that region, "despoiled" them of their lands.

Jantetelco had purchased the land from the Duque de Terranova, heir to the Marquesado, in 1694, and almost one hundred years later Icazbalceta claimed it and attempted to charge the pueblo rent to cultivate it. The case resembled many before it and others to follow. The villagers claimed that the hacendado had taken land that belonged to their fundo legal. Disputes like these intensified over the years. The experiences of these towns indicated the scope of land conflict throughout rural Morelos, while the emergence of Antonio Pérez laid bare the social and ethnic antagonisms seething underneath a supposedly protective colonialism. These episodes were local manifestations of a regional process in the tierra caliente, where commercial agriculture spread, bringing with it both increased opportunities and increased conflict.[17]

On the eve of independence, ethnically mixed townships and independent Indian villages existed side by side with sugar haciendas and their still substantially mulatto hamlets. When colonial rule ended, 25 percent of the rural population in southwestern Morelos already lived on the haciendas. More than 60 percent of hacienda residents were mulattos, 25 percent Indians, and the rest castizos, mestizos, and Spaniards.[18] Considerable ethnic diversity existed within the free pueblos also, as well as variations between them. Some, like Tepoztlán in the northern highlands, were Indian pueblos with few members from other ethnic groups. Towns below the mountains, like Yautepec, were mixed; those further to the south, like Jonacatepec and Xochitepec in the tierra caliente, had more non-Indians than Indians. Xochitepec, which had pre-Colombian origins, had undergone the transition to mestizaje during the rise of the sugar estates during the colonial era. Although removed from one another, these latter towns all lay in the sugar-producing zones of Morelos and figured prominently in future episodes of social strife.

The Estates

The larger sugar estates of Morelos generally extended over several thousand hectares, with lush irrigated cane fields, open pasture lands, scattered unirrigated corn fields, and nearby hills and forests supplying the firewood that fed the furnaces of the sugar mill. With their smokestacks towering above them, billowing the pungent smoke of burning cane into the air during the *zafra* (sugar harvest), these imposing estates could be seen for miles around. They derived their major income from sugar sales to Mexico City, and had blacksmiths, carpenters, slaves, and *peónes* (resident landless estate workers) toiling in workshops, working in the fields, and sweating over boiling cauldrons in the mills. They raised grain and alcohol for local consumption and sale and maintained hundreds of animals, including horses, mules, and oxen. The oxen they rented out to workers and neighboring pueblo residents for cash, or a share of their crop. The hacienda administrator and the overseer lived in smaller houses near the big house. Permanent tenant farmers usually clustered their straw huts and wooden shacks, called *chozas*, into small hamlets and walked to their subsistence plots out on the fringes of the estate (see Figure 1). Day laborers from neighboring villages arrived in the morning and left in the evening.[19]

The main house of a Morelos hacienda was a large, thick-walled two-story stone structure with patios, archways, and high-beamed ceilings. The main house stood near the chapel, which all the large haciendas in Morelos had, and some even claimed a resident priest. Hacendados equipped their feudal-looking estates with parapets, ledges, and tunnels. The massive walls provided both durability and defense. The architecture of the buildings revealed the defensive posture of their owners and an understanding of the hostility some native communities, and even some of their own employees, felt for them. With social unrest a constant threat because of conflicts over land, infringements on local autonomy, and attitudes of racial superiority, estate owners and administrators knew who the likely targets of violent social upheaval would be.

Independence

When Napolean Bonaparte's armies crossed the Pyrenees and deposed the Spanish king in 1808, long-standing social grievances in Mexico found a new outlet as the country entered a period of instability and turmoil. Events across the Atlantic shook the political authority of the colonial state, eroded its repressive capacity, and allowed both popular and reactionary forces to burst to the surface unbridled.[20]

The Mexican Independence Wars exploded on the scene and involved both a protest against the abuses of the Spanish metropolis and violent popular uprisings against the prevailing social order in the colony. The social movement, led by Padre Miguel Hidalgo and later José María Morelos, the insurgent mestizo priest for whom the state of Morelos is now named, demanded equality before the law for all castes, the abolition of slavery, the abolition of tributes, and the surrender of lands usurped from the villages. Among other things their followers called for "Death to bad government!" and "Death to the

Gachupínes!" They struck fear into many Spaniards and other defenders of the old regime who tried to rally criollos and middle-class professionals to the side of law and order with predictions of blind retribution and a genocidal caste war.[21]

Most sugar hacendados in Morelos felt threatened by calls for social reform and violently opposed the cause of the popular classes. Foremost amongst them was Gabriel de Yermo, a prominent Morelos hacendado who held the meat monopoly in Mexico City and led a coup by royalist Spaniards against the Mexican viceroy and his autonomist leanings during the French occupation of Spain. Following Mexican independence, Morelos hacendados displayed a consistent lack of patriotism during the nineteenth century; in fact, this same class of land owners would later seek the assistance of the invading U.S. army to repress lower-class militancy in rural Morelos during the late 1840s, and they would also seek a foreign monarch for a Mexican throne, settling for Maximilian von Hapsburg during the 1860s.

Other people in rural Morelos, while they did not join the insurrection in huge numbers and still had a basically "localocentric" worldview, did take advantage of the chaotic environment of war to right what they thought were old wrongs, a pattern that repeated itself several times during the nineteenth century. They attacked Gabriel de Yermo's rural estates and those of Juan José Irazabal, another wealthy Spaniard who had built a new sugar mill on lands rented from the

Figure 1.
Sugar hacienda and
the Morelos countryside,
nineteenth century. The
refinery and storehouses
are to the left where the
smokestacks are.

Indians of Nexpa and Tetecala. A significant number of local vecinos opposed that transaction, which the town council authorized over their protests. Given the chance, villagers sacked Irazabal's hacienda and took back the land. Large landholders responded to the threat by banding together for mutual defense, as they would again during the crises of the nineteenth century and in the revolution of 1910. Hacendados paid their dependent laborers to fight for them in support of the royalist cause, the perpetuation of the colony and, above all, the protection of their estates.[22]

Mexicans finally gained their independence in 1821, but the popular forces behind the cause were defeated. The political separation from the metropolis was brought about by surviving elites in order to defend their interests and blunt more radical aspirations for a new social order. The unfinished struggles of independence foreshadowed future agrarian unrest.[23]

Postindependence: Continuity and Change

Mexican independence did not bring fundamental social change to Morelos. Many haciendas remained in the possession and under the administration of Spaniards, while rich outsiders purchased estates and invested their money in the sugar industry, accelerating the change in land tenure. Much of the Indian, mulatto, and mestizo population referred to the owners of the great estates as

"Gachupínes," a derogatory expression that conveyed the popularly held image of the exploitative Spaniard. For their part, many "Spaniards" looked down on the darker-skinned laboring castes and, even though many Spaniards were actually creoles, with long ties to Mexico, much of the rural populace still loathed them. Increasing absentee landownership by metropolitan elites from Mexico City exacerbated existing social tensions in the years after independence and lasted into the twentieth century.[24]

The new hacendados gradually replaced the old guard who lacked the liquid capital required to create the larger, more modern mills that provided the economies of scale necessary for greater profits. Even though political turmoil continued after independence, a growing urban population stimulated sugar production for an internal market that was limited but stable.[25]

The rich new merchant landowners of Morelos, led by men like Pío Bermejillo, Manuel Escandón, Juan Goribar, Isidoro de la Torre, and the brothers Miguel and Leandro Mosso, could afford to upgrade and expand their sugar-manufacturing capabilities and experiment with new markets. When the domestic market suffered due to civil war and social unrest, export opportunities took on greater significance. Although never a major percentage of the total product, export potential played an important role in the sugar industry, especially when production outpaced demand.[26]

The new landowners moving into Morelos coupled their growing economic power with a move to consolidate their political influence as well. They transformed the political establishment as their relatives and friends assumed government positions previously held by local elites from the area's older landed families. Juan Goribar, for example, acquired the haciendas Cocoyoc and Casasano, and his son, Jesús, became the subprefect (comparable to a justice of the peace) of the district of Yautepec. Likewise, Ignacio de la Peña y Barragan, who came from a well-known, wealthy merchant family operating out of Mexico City, acquired the hacienda Hospital and became the subprefect of Cuautla. Miguel Mosso joined them, becoming subprefect in the district of Tetecala, where he and his brother had purchased the valuable and beautiful haciendas San José Vista Hermosa and San Gabriel. With a network of family and friends in powerful political and military positions, the new hacendados enjoyed local power and national influence. Despite the uncertainties and disruptions caused by turmoil in the nation's highest political levels and social rumblings from below, increasing consumer demand in the cities made up for a gradual decline in sugar prices after 1840 and provided the motive for growers to expand their enterprises.[27]

Life and Work on the Estates

The influential Spanish landholder, Nicolás Icazbalceta, owned the largest estate in Morelos, the hacienda Santa Anna Tenango, and operated it like most other hacendados at the time.[28] Tenango produced 35,666 loaves of sugar or, "*panes labrados*," in 1846, and, like other hacendados, Icazbalceta exported most of the sugar out of state, sending about thirty thousand panes to Mexico City and Puebla. Production on that scale required a lot of workers, and the hacienda offered the main source of employment to people living throughout the area. Icazbalceta's payroll reached almost five thousand pesos a week at certain times of the year, as it did during the last week of December 1846. Those payments exceeded the norm though, because they included the hacienda administrator's monthly salary of one hundred sixty-six pesos, his assistant's thirty-three pesos, the sugar master's twenty-seven pesos, and the overseer's twenty-eight-peso-a-month income. Along with those high-ranking administrative and specialized resident employees, an unspecified number of "*guarda tierras*" watched over the fields and made sure no one stole, burned, or otherwise damaged the valuable crop.[29]

These permanent and trusted employees earning monthly salaries presented a sharp contrast to the day laborers recruited from the nearby villages who lived hand-to-mouth scraping by on one or two *reales* a piece for their day's work. The major discrepancies in pay, security, and treatment between the permanent salaried workforce and the temporary, seasonal, or day laborers created a social gulf between the groups and the attitudes they held toward their employers.[30] The permanent, often Spanish, employees generally sympathized with the estate owners and, as the equivalent to modern-day upper management, many hacienda administrators hoped to emulate their bosses and aspired to be like them and acquire haciendas of their own. A new protoindustrial regimen with a labor hierarchy marked by income and outlook was beginning to emerge, and it altered life and work. For example, Icazbalceta's largest single expenditure during most of the off-season was for "*gañanes*," or day laborers, from villages near Tenango who, despite their low pay, could cost the hacienda up to 1,452 pesos a week. During the zafra of 1846, the hacienda employed an average of four hundred daily workers, reaching a peak of five hundred thirty during the busiest months.

Work was seasonal though, and the hacienda only paid about one hundred men from August to November, and sometimes as few as twenty-six. The sugar harvest always brought an increase in the number of temporary day workers cutting the cane, hauling it to the mills, and processing it inside. The entire social setting was in flux. More people were becoming workers earning wages, and that trend continued until the revolution. Many people, perhaps most, found themselves in some sort of in-between position, making their living from both subsistence farming and wage-labor.[31]

The In-Between

Most who lived and worked in the Morelos countryside during the nineteenth century were neither "peasants" nor "workers." Some villagers had petite-bourgeois aspirations for private property and small farms, hence part of their attraction to nineteenth-century Liberal Reforms and the promise of individual land ownership. Others, those on the bottom perhaps, traded the confines of their pueblos for the greater material security of the hacienda, while still others lived in a pueblo but lacked access to land and worked for wages in the hacendados' fields or mills. Most importantly, though, many people in rural Morelos, whether in pueblos or hacienda settlements, held onto, and expanded on, the traditions and ideals of the communal pueblo.

It was a time of transition, with the beginnings of a rural working class, still amorphous and lacking any real "consciousness" that set them apart, but coming about in a situation that mixed their new labor experiences with more traditional ones, including the defense of inherited values and community life. The implicit question is when does a peasant cease being a peasant and become a worker in this apparently inevitable move toward modernity? Was it when they lost their land, and with it their independence and self-sufficiency, and had nothing left but their labor power and became wage earners? A purely economic response would affirm that, but, as Antonio Gramsci has noted, the issue runs deeper. Gramsci's observations about this transitional moment in Italy lend useful insight into the Mexican experience and the transformation of peasant into worker during the nineteenth century when "mentally some landless laborers held onto more traditional values like ideas of community autonomy and communal landholding and, over time began to develop further expectations blending them with more proletarian concerns over wages and injecting their views into the changing political ideologies being circulated, debated, and fought for at the time."[32]

The process, of course, affected different communities both across Mexico and in Morelos at different times and in varying degrees. But, because of the industrial aspect of sugar production, it happened earlier in Morelos than most of Mexico and in a special way that allowed the heavy retention of agrarian values even in the face of rapid industrialization. Displaced agrarians in Morelos were not directly forced into cities or urban landscapes looking for work, but instead could find it in the sugarcane fields and mills of the haciendas. The agricultural aspects of the industry help explain the retention of agrarian values, while the industrial aspects brought new and more "modern" concerns about working conditions, hours, treatment, and pay. However, the work was seasonal, and while a basically free-labor ethic had replaced slavery, tribute, and peonage and some people were paid with money, large numbers also received compensation through sharecropping arrangements. Those non-wage agreements made people dependent on the estates. At the same time, vecinos in viable independent communities survived alongside the dependents on the hacienda real, offering a constant counterexample and keeping alive the kinds of communitarian values Gramsci discussed. Meanwhile, hacendados tried to expand their holdings and, when successful, accelerated the transition from peasant into worker.[33]

The process of peasants gradually becoming workers led to a polarized society because no significant rural middle class of prosperous, independent, small-holding rancheros developed. The main reasons for the absence of such a group was that there was very little unclaimed land in Morelos, and prices were extremely high. This combination mitigated against the creation of a class that could fill a niche in the transition to capitalist agriculture and whose personal interests could be further served by the alienation of pueblo commons that was being sought by the larger producers. Without a viable ranchero community, the result was a two-tiered society separated by a yawning void, both materially and culturally.

Meanwhile, hacendados tried to expand their operations even though the average sugar hacienda devoted only a small fraction of its total lands to actually raising sugarcane. But all hacendados still strove to secure access to a variety of resources including pasture lands for cattle and work animals, forested areas for wood and fuel, and some seasonal lands that could be rented out to workers. The irrigated sugar-growing areas comprised less than 10 percent of the surface area of most sugar haciendas.[34]

The growth of Santa Anna Tenango represented the overall pattern taking place across Morelos. Tenango only had 3,750 acres (15 caballerías of a total of 167) of land planted in sugarcane in 1824, but after the owners acquired the hacienda Actopan during the middle of the century, planting greatly increased until, at the turn of the century in 1900, more than 16,000 acres (65 caballerías) of fully irrigated land were in production.[35] Icazbalceta also acquired more pasture and forest lands, as well as greater access to water in that time. His gains came at the expense of neighboring villages and upset established practices. Hills, forests, and pastures had been considered public lands available for common use intended to satisfy the needs of all people in a given area since colonial times. Those uses included shared access by haciendas, ranchos, and villages alike. But the process of enclosure restricted the area available for villager's crops, as well as common lands from which to gather wood, graze cattle, or collect water. Once they took possession of it, large landowners charged villagers fees for gathering wood and grazing livestock. By privatizing the land and limiting access, the hacendados upset customary practice and outraged their neighbors. The pattern seen at Tenango was being played out across Morelos's sugar valleys, reinforced by innovations in technology, commerce, and the law.[36]

Some campesinos resisted changes that they felt offered little or no benefit, or even disadvantaged them. But with the mediating role of the colonial regime and its sometimes protective legislation gone, legal channels that had previously provided rural communities at least some avenue of redress seemed blocked. Feeling mistreated, and unable to express their voices through the political process, or to seek justice through the legal system, villagers grew increasingly resentful over the denial of customary rights. By the middle of the nineteenth century a deepening animosity was festering in the Morelos lowlands.

Chapter Three

THE U.S. INVASION,
NATIONAL DEFENSE,
AND LOCAL MEANING,
1846–1856

When the U.S. army invaded Mexico in 1846, it exacerbated the political crisis at the national level and impacted events in Morelos. Mexico's loss of its northern frontier to the United States after the Treaty of Guadalupe Hidalgo in 1848, highlighted the central government's inability to control peripheral areas and contributed to growing political fragmentation, *caciquismo*, and banditry throughout the country. Stepping into the void left by the defeated government, hacendados and campesinos in Morelos attempted to assert themselves.

With the power of the state eroded, the hacendados quickly moved to assume more official authority in the region and to increase their political and economic influence. But other segments of the rural population also responded to the invasion. Peasant and ranchero guerrillas from San Luis Potosi, Veracruz, Hidalgo, Puebla, and eastern Morelos staged attacks against American supply lines stretching from Veracruz to Mexico City. The communications exchanged between Nicholas Trist, the U.S. commissioner to Mexico who was responsible for trying to negotiate a truce, and General Winfield Scott, general in chief of the U.S. army in Mexico, offer important insights into the situation from the perspective of high-ranking North American personnel on the scene. When Trist asked Scott to provide him with a military escort to Mexico City in order to negotiate a truce, Scott responded:

> If able, I shall have advanced near to the capital, (and)
> I may, at your instance, lend an escort to your flag of
> truce; and it may require a large fighting detachment to
> protect even a flag of truce against the rancheros and
> bandits who now infest the national road all the way
> up to the capital.... Here, in the heart of a hostile coun-
> try, from which, after a few weeks, it would be impossi-
> ble to withdraw this army, without a loss,
> probably, of half its members...—which army, from
> necessity, must soon become a *self-sustaining*
> *machine*—cut off from all supplies and reinforcements
> from home, until, perhaps, late in November; —not to
> speak of the bad faith of this government and *people of*
> *Mexico*,—I say, in reference to these circumstances, this
> army must take *military* security for its own safety.[1]

Whatever stability the old colonial order had once offered was shattered, and independent Mexico, unable to effectively replace it, ran the risk of being devoured by its hungry neighbor to the north. Under those conditions, local ambitions, abuses, and grievances grew. As the national government reeled from crisis to crisis, social confrontations escalated in various parts of Mexico. The Yucatán, the Costa Chica of Guerrerro, the Huasteca, the Puebla Sierra, and Morelos witnessed peasant unrest in response to the negative effects of the growing penetrations of commercial agriculture into communal land tenure. Changing patterns of taxation led to challenges from communities attempting to levy their own local transportation and commercial fees to support both municipal services and an independent local clergy, and complicated the nature of some of these disputes.[2]

When the U.S. army occupied Mexico City in 1847 and flew the stars and stripes above Chapultepec Castle, it was a humiliating symbol of the Mexican government's total defeat. Demoralizing as that fiasco was, serious internal problems lurked underneath it. Villagers from the pueblo of Xochitepec, south of Cuernavaca, attacked the nearby hacienda Chiconcuac to rob it, repossess lands, and, according to those accustomed to demonizing Indians, to kill "toda la gente decente." Anger over previous land disputes prompted the attack, and the collapse of state authority due to the American invasion allowed people to act on their emotions. With the Mexican army routed and with peasants and rural workers in revolt, the hacendados of Morelos looked elsewhere for protection. Frightened of their pueblo neighbors and their own workers, hacendados turned to the commander of the occupational forces of the U.S. army stationed at Cuernavaca to send help in order to "liberate" the mill at Chiconcuac and impose order on the countryside.[3]

U.S. troops arrived, drove away the local insurgents, and remained encamped at the hacienda. Lucas Alamán, conservative statesman and historian, writing in March 1848, pondered the imminent North American departure, saying, "I fear greatly that revolutions of this character will be repeated, leaving us in a state of great uncertainty." Alamán worried about an outbreak of a caste war in central Mexico "between the various peoples that make up the population, among which the whites are the least numerous and stand to lose because of that, all of the properties that pertain to them."[4] Alamán was not alone; many hacendados in Morelos shared his concern. Their view of the social situation caused landowners to put their class interests above national integrity and to repress Mexican citizens with the invading troops of a foreign army in order to defend their own property and social position. As it turned out, that same army was being used at that exact moment to take half of Mexico's national territory. It was a sorry irony that Alamán and the Morelos hacendados wrung their hands and fretted over the departure of the American military. Meanwhile, some peasants and agricultural workers in Morelos joined national guard units raised to resist the North American invasion. While they were doing that, at least some hacendados there balked at national defense and saw armed campesinos as a greater threat than collaboration with the Americans. Rural society in Morelos at midcentury was extremely polarized politically, culturally, and economically. The propertied class, with its heavy metropolitan and foreign orientation, remained fiercely determined to maintain its privileged position by any means necessary, including behavior that was anything but patriotic. Thus, when looking for the origins of Mexican nationalism it is necessary to look not only at, but beyond the creole elite. Their posture in Morelos, though, differed from some local and provincial elites in San Luis Potosí and other outlying states, who did attempt to organize a defense against the invasion.[5]

Following the withdrawal of American forces, Mexico's political elites, stung by military defeat and harboring a fresh sense of national inferiority, pondered various options they hoped would spur development and head the country down the same path traveled by the more economically advanced nations of Western Europe and the United States. It was either that, or remain vulnerable and face more aggression. But Mexico's Liberals and Conservatives were unable to agree and engaged in a violent debate about the best course to pursue to promote the healthy economic and political development of the nation. The strategies implemented to achieve growth in the following years exacerbated the level of social conflict, and ideological differences precluded a spirit of cooperation even in situations as desperate as those posed by massive foreign invasions.

Elite Discourse: Liberals Versus Conservatives

Mexican Liberals envied the United States for its material success and political stability. One of the more outspoken early Liberal proponents was Lorenzo de Zavala, who, in his admiration for the United States, somehow overlooked American slavery and thought "the school for politics presented by the United States is a perfect system, a classic work, unique.... It is a living example of social utopia."[6] Hoping to imitate that model, Mexican Liberals sought the freedom of the individual, equality before the law, and protection against irresponsible government through the guarantees of free speech, a free press, and representative political institutions. They believed that laissez-faire economic principles and the privatization of property, including church estates and agrarian commons, would bring the economic growth needed to insure freedom. For the first thirty years following independence, they felt those goals required limits on centralized state power and its inherent potential for authoritarian abuse.

Hoping to achieve their ends, the Liberals turned their backs on Spain and its legacy of monarchy, colonialism, caste hierarchy, and religious intolerance, and looked toward the model presented by their northern neighbor.[7] But the historical roots of North American Republicanism differed greatly from Mexican realities. The emphasis on individual empowerment, commercial farming, and greater political liberties in the United States emerged from the combination of a mixed rural society of independent large and small free holders, and a strong native bourgeoisie of merchants, financiers, and manufacturers. Complementing these forces was a petite bourgeoisie of shopkeepers that provided a full array of goods, services, and technology to workers and farmers who represented a viable internal market and provided labor and foodstuffs.[8]

Looking at their own society with a critical eye, Mexican Liberals believed that the primary hindrance to their nation becoming modern and progressive was the communal ownership of the land and the retarding influence that they believed peasant agriculture had on the development of commerce and industry. Liberal intellectual José María Luis Mora's perspectives on the idea of property reflected Liberal thinking at the time:

> The right to acquire [property] enjoyed by an individual is natural, prior to society and corresponds to him as a man, so that society does no more than assure his possession. By contrast, the right of a *community* to acquire is purely civil, subsequent to society, created by the latter and hence subject to all the limitations which society wishes to impose.[9]

Liberals like Mora sought to forge a modern secular state and believed accomplishing that required reducing the cultural and political power of rural communities, along with the church and army. Some Liberal leaders sought European and American immigration in order to alter the genetic makeup of Mexico and what they perceived to be the overtly anticommercial attitude of the rural populace.

Mexican Conservatives, epitomized by influential and respected Lucas Alamán, argued that Mexico should pursue a path of national development rooted in its Hispanic heritage. They, like the Liberals, sought to marginalize what they saw as backward rural folk. The Conservatives supported a strong central state, Catholicism as the national religion, the preeminence of private property, and the industriousness of the creoles and Spaniards. They resisted political pluralism. Conservatives defended the existing division of wealth in Mexico and represented the interests of the old landed-aristocracy, including the church, while supporting a return to autocratic rule. Conservatives, despite their reactionary social agenda, recognized the weaknesses in the laissez-faire economic program espoused by most Liberals. Early on, Lucas Alamán called for the establishment of a national development bank, the Banco de Avío, to overcome the shortage of investment capital needed to encourage new domestic industry. Alamán also wanted a sufficient degree of tariff protection to stimulate native manufactures.[10]

Despite their differences, both Conservatives and Liberals shared a negative view of the Mexican campesino. For them, the transformation of the *indígenas* remained incomplete. Both based their views on presumptions of racial superiority. Many Conservatives approved of the perpetuation of the caste system and hoped to get rid of the dogma of equality. They argued that Indians should once again be treated juridically like children, disingenuously arguing it was for their own protection and welfare. In their view, Indians lacked civilization and possessed only a limited capacity for education and reason. As a result, all vitality resided with the whites who, naturally then, should constitute the leadership of society.

The Liberals opposed the continuation of a caste system because it restricted mobility and free choice, but they too found the bulk of the Indian population lacking. Their concerns did not revolve around the Indian's basic intellect, but with their ignorance of the enlightened vision that urbane Mexicans possessed. Mora, for example, writing in 1836, said, "One of the things that prevents, and will continue to prevent the forward progress of the indigenous, in all respects, is the tenacity with which they learn things and the absolute impossibility of making them change their opinions: this stubbornness is a result of their lack of culture on the one hand, and the cause of their slowness and an inexhaustible fountain of errors [on the other hand]." Although he himself did not make his living from manual labor, Mora's general impressions of the indígenas' physical weaknesses were widely shared by other members of his class. "When it comes to their physical strength, no one can doubt that they are weak, especially in all field-related labors, which is what they generally dedicate themselves to." As a result of their assessment of the native population's generally substandard quality, Liberals lamented that, in their present condition, the country could not be built around them. Mora believed, "The white population is dominant today, due to their large numbers, their education and wealth, their exclusive influence in public relations and negotiations, and the advantages of their position with respect to all other races: [as a result] it is in the white population that the Mexican character should be sought, and they are the ones that must set the example from which the rest of the world will form its opinions of the Republic." That sentiment persisted throughout the century.

Lorenzo de Zavala had expressed his apprehension about the ability of most of his fellow Mexicans to participate in a democracy because he found it "very harmful to a society when its working class citizens do not even have the capacity to discern between the people they are to select, much less understand the great tasks their elected officials are entrusted with." Later, the Porfirian regime sought to recruit European immigrants because they believed that would improve Mexico's genetic stock.

For many Liberals, the continued attachment to communalism confirmed the backwardness of the indigenous peoples. The cornerstone of an enlightened Liberal Mexico was to be the individual small-property-owning citizen. So, the mutual rejection of native culture, polity, and economy by Conservatives and Liberals alike left rural communities vulnerable to the imposition of state and local laws that restricted corporate rights in the 1840s.[11]

The Liberal rise to power in the 1850s and the ensuing legislative attacks on the traditional rights of peasant communities provoked escalating conflicts in the countryside. Yet, there is no reason to assume that the bulk of Mexico's communalist villagers would have fared any better under the Conservatives. Lucas Alamán himself served as agent for the Sicilian Duke of Terranova y Monteleóne, the heir to Cortés's vast rural estate. The sugar haciendas in Morelos, representing large tracts of productive private property owned by Spaniards and creoles, received the Conservative's favorable consideration over village communalism as well. Liberalism often receives the blame, or credit, for providing the ideological support for the encroachments of the rural estates on communal property during the second half of the nineteenth and early twentieth centuries, but that process would have happened regardless of which party ruled. The bulk of the leadership for both parties supported privatization of pueblo lands, and the process swept across other Latin American republics at the same time regardless of which party held power. What makes Morelos an interesting and important case for analysis is the popular resistance to elite imposed modernizing projects and the grassroots alternatives that emerged because of it.[12]

One of the most salient examples of the ideological differences dividing the political elite that eventually brought the rural masses into the fray was the conflict between Liberal general and politician Juan Álvarez of Acapulco, and Conservative general and many times president Antonio López de Santa Anna. Álvarez was one of the primary leaders of the Mexican resistance to the U.S. invasion, but his service was not always appreciated. Large landowners in Morelos and other political rivals accused him of inciting their hacienda workers to rebel, including various episodes at the haciendas Chiconcuac and San Vicente, near Cuernavaca, where workers attacked administrators and set fire to the sugarcane fields. The accusations against Álvarez followed his earlier support of peasant revolts along the Pacific coast near Acapulco.[13] Elite differences, though, were only one aspect of a multilayered struggle to define the nation.

Invasion and Instability

With the U.S. army still occupying Mexico in 1848, José Manuel Arellano, a lieutenant-colonel serving in a local national guard unit in Morelos, led combined forces of armed peasants and local national guardsmen in attacks on haciendas in the Cañada de Cuernavaca. Arellano came from Tetecala and was operating, at least nominally, under the authority of General Juan Álvarez. He and those with him took advantage of the chaotic atmosphere created by the U.S. occupation to readjust long-disputed boundaries between haciendas and pueblos in favor of community claims.

They started at Chiconcuac, where old boundary conflicts and antagonisms simmered. They took the hacienda's boundary marker and symbolically stuck it in the patio of the owner's house, which let him know exactly how much land they thought he deserved. Tetecala and Miacatlán were in the western part of the state, not far from the Guerrero border, and although Arellano officially served under Álvarez, he and the others operated largely beyond Álvarez's immediate control. Besides relocating boundary markers at Chiconcuac, the campesinos and soldiers with Arellano removed the markers at the hacienda Miacatlán, threatened to destroy dams and water works, and demanded that lands be returned to the pueblos. Álvarez reproached Arellano for his actions but, whether he authorized them, campesinos were acting on their own grievances, and the larger situation made that possible. Mexico's foreign minister at the time, Lucas Alamán observed the pueblo and worker militancy and complained, "Indian communities in this country are the implacable enemies of haciendas, and they will try any means, including force, to despoil haciendas of the lands they claim."[14]

Alamán's position was echoed, but also amplified in important ways, by Alejandro Villaseñor, the prefect of Cuernavaca, whose jurisdiction was analogous to the present-day state of Morelos. Villaseñor compiled a survey of the conditions in his district in 1850 that made clear some of the issues driving local protests. Although unsympathetic to them, Villaseñor concluded that rural communities in Morelos prized what was left of their independent local self-government, commerce, and landholdings and were struggling to protect them. He painted this picture of his district after the American withdrawal:

> Tlaltizapan, divided and in a state of continual alarm
> as a result of the suspension of its alcaldes: Tlayacapan
> and Tepostlán in the same state: Jojutla, upset and in
> conflict with the new hacienda established by Don
> Joaquín Fandino: Puente de Ixtla in open conflict with
> the hacienda San Gabriel over the open-air market the
> municipality decided to establish, removing that which
> had been on the hacienda; in sum, all the pueblos
> discontented and alarmed as a consequence of the
> last revolution of Arellano, which tried to destroy
> the haciendas.[15]

A combination of factors created those conditions. For years, going back to the 1820s, representatives in the legislature of the state of Mexico, of which the district of Morelos was then a part, debated enacting legislation to divide community-held pueblo lands among individual residents as part of an effort to form a class of small yeoman farmers producing for regional markets. In the fall of 1849, after more than twenty years of contemplating the issue off and on, and in the middle of a rising tide of agrarian conflicts, they passed a law abolishing community property rights in the state.

The new law came in the midst of general unrest including that attributed to Arellano, and a different disturbance in the district of Morelos. Despite the conservative nature of the church as an institution, Mexico had a tradition of independent-minded local priests who sometimes assisted villagers in obtaining legal representation and supplemented their sense of history and belonging from a local perspective. Individual clergy since Bartolomé de Las Casas and Vasco de Quiroga played important roles as protectors of the rural populace and as leaders of social movements, exemplified most obviously by Miguel Hidalgo and José María Morelos.[16]

During the summer of 1849, in the wake of the American invasion, a local activist priest known by the name "Rojo" led a short-lived alliance of pueblos against the haciendas in the Cañada de Cuernavaca. People from those pueblos demanded the restitution of lands occupied by the haciendas, and hacienda workers joined them, complaining about the bad treatment they received working on the estates. Frustrated by a lack of official support, the villagers and workers resorted to violence, damaging several haciendas. Alarmed, the archbishop of Mexico sent an order to the ecclesiastic authorities in Cuernavaca demanding the apprehension of the rebellious priest. The Mexican church, as a wealthy, landed, and conservative institution, moved quickly to suppress the inflammatory influence of the local curate.[17] But probably the most disturbing aspect for the authorities was the coordinated pueblo action, which demanded an immediate response.

Elites in Morelos knew their problems ran deeper than the agitations of one priest. Unrest spread throughout the lowlands. At the hacienda Santa Inés, indígenas from several communities bordering the hacienda began to organize. They demolished the stone wall the hacendado had erected around part of the hacienda and tried to reclaim lands that had been fenced off. The hacendado called on the military authorities to contain the campesinos. The national guard arrived, but commanding officers wrote to their superiors and reported that it was impossible to carry out their orders because their troops refused to obey them and, instead, supported the pueblo actions. The troops said they saw no threat to public tranquility. They sympathized with campesino exasperation because

> the haciendas usurped the lands of the fundos a long
> time ago, complaints were directed to the supreme
> government a year ago, and it's a long shot that their
> complaint was heard. They were forgotten, and the
> prefect apprehended numerous people who had signed
> the petition. Today, as a result of the disdain shown
> them, and lacking sufficient funds to present their case
> before the courts in order to have them return their
> lands, they have resorted to the only road left, in the
> belief that all the pueblos have the right to rebel and
> that it is justified when the laws are inefficient and
> their superiors and the supreme government ignores
> and humiliates them.[18]

The minister of war, General Mariano Arista, lamented, "Unfortunately, there is an immense restlessness among the towns according to the messages I have received, and it is incredible the advance that socialist ideas have made among the lower classes." Meanwhile, four hundred men gathered for a public demonstration in the town of Tlayacaque, near Cuautla, and demanded access to land and better working conditions on the haciendas. A demonstration of that size with participants coming from a variety of pueblos indicated advance planning and coordination. The proliferation of these organized efforts disturbed the authorities because it represented a shift from more traditional "peasant" type protests over land and water usurpations and included demands for better labor conditions and a wider recognition of rights that revealed a broadening consciousness.[19] The belief in the right to land was age-old, but suddenly demands for land were being voiced simultaneously with ones about low wages, inhumane treatment, and poor working conditions. A growing population, a nascent rural working class, and an emerging national consciousness sparked by the American invasion began to coalesce, and as it did, it clashed with the needs of the hacendados.

Managing Discord

Mariano Arizcorreta, the governor of the state of Mexico, grew increasingly concerned about the unrest in the Morelos countryside, so he addressed a circular to the hacendados there. He attributed the unruliness of the indígenas and the ease with which they were spurred to insurrection, especially in the sugar-producing area of the tierra caliente, to their resentment over the loss of their "*repartamientos*," the corruption of local officials by hacendados, and the poor treatment campesinos received on the haciendas. Arizcorreta noted that in the district of Cuernavaca in particular, various haciendas expanded their irrigated and seasonal fields onto lands rented from neighboring pueblos and then claimed the land as their own. The governor suggested the hacendados could diffuse the situation by either returning usurped lands, or by increasing the rent they paid for using pueblo land. He considered it a judicious move, and hinted at local corruption when he said that "the poor cannot improve their conditions, even more so if one considers that the greater part of these rental contracts have been concluded without the required legal protocols, at token prices, or with terms in fine print without provisions for the proceeds to go towards investments for the public benefit, but rather into the pockets of low-level local officials who made the contracts without informing others."[20]

Governor Arizcorreta expressed deep concern about the rebellious attitude of campesinos in Morelos because it blended with rural instability busting out in bloody insurrections in the Yucatán, in the Sierra Gorda, and in the area inland and south of Acapulco all the way to Oaxaca. Worried about the rising tide of unrest in the Mexican countryside and what it might mean for his jurisdiction if something was not done to discourage it, the governor attempted to persuade the landowners and sugar-mill operators in Morelos to act in a more conciliatory manner toward neighboring villagers and to offer better treatment of workers at the mills. He hoped those measures would avoid a much dreaded "*guerra de castes,*" like the one in Yucatán, from exploding in the Morelos lowlands.[21]

Morelos's hacendados responded to the governor's circular with outrage. They claimed that pueblo residents were the ones illegally invading private properties while disingenuously claiming that the hacendados had usurped the land. The landowners complained that pueblo villagers commonly laid claim to hacienda lands, even those with the most legitimate and ancient legal titles of ownership. Considered in the context of the social crises elsewhere in Mexico, Morelos's hacendados were appealing to one level of national consciousness when they insisted that the indígenas could not be allowed to foist their will on the rest of the Mexican population. They argued that pueblo claims constituted a threat not only to private property, but to Mexican society and, indeed, the greater cause of civilization itself. They accused Arizcorreta of supporting barbarism and pointed to the specter of Yucatán and the Sierra Gorda as examples of what might happen in the heart of the country if the indígenas of Morelos were not dealt with decisively. They warned the governor and others who may have been persuaded by him that "the sad example of Yucatán is not alone, nor is that which is presently occurring in the states of San Luis and Querétaro, under the pretext that the hacendados have usurped the lands of the pueblos, a plethora of rabid gangs rob, devastate and burn the fields and buildings. It is an even greater scandal to find the governor of our own state adding fuel to the fire with his alarming and impolitic announcement."[22]

Although mainly concerned that the legal codes and state power protect them, the hacendados voiced some legitimate fears. Their assessment that some rural Mexicans were not simply fighting against local injustices was partly true. Campesinos were indeed displaying an increasingly negative view of the changes toward privatization taking place nationwide, and their association with men of national prominence like Álvarez brought them into part of a larger whole. At the local level they attempted to forestall, or at least alter, certain elements of change, but because of the circumstances of the moment, local actions took on national significance. In that sense, rural rebels in Morelos did constitute a threat not only against large landed property there, but implicitly against the larger society that was defending what many peasants and rural workers considered a hellish status quo.[23]

Campesinos were developing an alternative vision of what a "civilized" Mexico should be like. The view coming out of the Morelos countryside combined two main experiences. The first derived from long-standing agrarian tenure, and the economic, cultural, and political patterns developed during three centuries of Spanish rule and clerical influence. The second involved more modern ideas circulating at the time about government, citizenship, justice, and law.[24]

Although influenced by many factors, campesino politics did not come into being solely because of outsiders like Masons, lawyers, clergymen, or local elites bringing ideas to the masses. It originated to an important degree from within the marginalized groups themselves. But, because they were a largely illiterate population leaving little written record in the form of letters, diaries, political speeches, or formalized programs, we must interpret their thoughts and feelings, in large part, through their actions. Viewed from this distance, campesino alternatives could appear as simply reactive and sporadic episodes of alarming but disconnected violence; people at the time, though, did not see it that way.

Elite sources, whether letters to presidents or governors, published political debates, newspaper articles, or arguments in court cases, reveal an awareness of a larger challenge to their rule. Yet, while that recognition was there, so was a consistent effort to portray the rural populace in a manner that made them seem as mindless and violent as possible. Since elites generated most of the documentation, one has to look at popular action itself and see what they were doing to make reasoned judgments about what they were thinking. Looking at the region's history with a broad lens reveals that the alternatives coming out of the Morelos countryside, while homegrown, were also part of a larger process that eventually coalesced and became more clearly articulated in the early twentieth century.[25]

Contested Visions

Legal, political, and economic developments in the Morelos lowlands aggravated existing social tensions that burst to the surface in the rebellions of 1849. The uprisings formed part of a larger wave of violent unrest sweeping the Mexican southwest, which made events in Morelos seem even more ominous to the hacendados. Feeling under attack, the large landowners tried to organize some kind of effective repression. The communiqués coming from the Comisión Central of the newly created Hacendado Defense League offer a good picture of events:

> Bands of wrongdoers have been pillaging the
> haciendas in the districts of Morelos and Cuernavaca
> for two months. *The wrongdoers come from some of*
> *these same haciendas,* those of Tenango, Atlihuayan,
> San Miguel Treinta, and, Miacatlan, Acatzingo and
> Vistahermosa. These episodes have taken on a charac-
> ter so alarming that one cannot see a quick or effective
> remedy. They threaten the ruin of all the mentioned
> rich and beautiful haciendas of the tierra caliente.
> The bands that commit the majority of these robberies
> are growing everyday, and some include more than
> two hundred wrongdoers.[26]

Similar stories appeared contemporaneously in the newspaper *El Monitor Republicano,* suggesting that this was more than hacendado hysteria. *El Monitor* reported "revolutionary" activity in the Cuernavaca area associated with demands for land restitution and improved working conditions. Noting the combination of pueblo villagers and hacienda workers, the paper commented that almost no pueblo in the district retained its fundo legal and that many of the "*operarios*" on the haciendas were tired of being paid in scrip redeemable only at company stores. As resistance spread, it became clear that these were not isolated local outbursts, but a more generalized rejection of hacendado land incursions, wage arrangements, and labor conditions.

The sustained nature of resistance revealed the inability of the national government to militarily enforce socioeconomic changes being pursued by a powerful few but violently rejected by a large part of the rural populace. That was clear when the national guard troops had refused to repress the campesino effort to regain land at Santa Inés, and their commanders reported that the guardsmen felt that the campesinos had not committed "any crime, and that they could not bring themselves to take up arms against their brothers and against their own rights, since everyone belonged to the popular class."[27] At the same time, local authorities uncovered a well-developed plot to attack large rural property in the tierra caliente. They captured and held responsible a lawyer and freemason named Perdigón Garay. The Masonic clubs in nineteenth-century Mexico, especially the "Yorkinos," wanted to dilute the power of the church and to expand civil liberties. The plan asserted the rights of the pueblo citizenry to land, called for dividing up the properties of the haciendas, and proclaimed that the lands and waters of the nation belonged to everyone and should be open to all the "children of the country."[28] The document, though, went beyond the persistent issue of land and recommended the establishment of a national bank, factory employment for women, and an army subsidized by the confiscated wealth of the church.

The effort to graft that plan onto local conditions reflected the fact that broader national concerns were filtering down to the rural masses where they were being attached to local actions and contributing to a growing agrarian consciousness from below. These developments brought home to mid-nineteenth-century Morelos elites and the readers of *El Monitor Republicano* that larger political ideals and objectives were merging with campesino activity. This was made patently obvious when the new governor of the state of Mexico, Maríano Riva Palacio asked that the circulation of some of Liberal spokesman Ignacio Ramírez's writings pointing out the abuses suffered by "*los indios*" and calling for a more fair distribution of land be suspended because Riva Palacio felt they were incendiary.[29]

The strategy of issuing plans was not new. The circumstances in which this particular plan was discovered, however, were of special interest. Prior to the independence wars, revolts in the colonial period had generally been local events, isolated in nature, usually not directly related to issues of land, and included no outsiders playing a prominent role in any of the known uprisings. But the rise of industrial production in the nineteenth century created new tensions that affected displaced artisans in urban areas and smaller towns. As a result, the growing agrarian unrest in Morelos mixed with the protoindustrial nature of work on the sugar estates and became part of that larger picture. After independence, outsiders who were generally nonpeasants, participated in twenty-one out of fifty-five recorded rural revolts in Mexico from independence to 1884, which illustrated that local issues were blending with wider events. Local authorities, interested in portraying the workers and peasants in their areas as happy citizens, usually blamed revolts, whether grassroots or not, on outside agitators like the priest Rojo or the lawyer Perdigón Garay. While the influence of urban and formally educated people and their ideas was indeed growing, the local participants in these episodes in Morelos were pueblo vecinos and hacienda workers.[30]

Governor Arizcorreta's futile efforts illustrated the inability of the state government to influence hacendados into ameliorating pueblo and worker hardships or to exercise a modicum of restraint. At the same time, the attacks on haciendas demonstrated the central government's alarming incapacity to defend the private property and interests of some of the country's most prominent citizens.[31] The government's weakness allowed the space for campesinos to express themselves, but it also made it easier for political parties and regional strongmen to manipulate the rural masses into supporting their particular agendas, resisting projects of the central government, or simply strengthening their regional influence.

With social conflict brewing, the hacendados moved to impose order on the countryside. Fully aware of events in other parts of the country, and feeling that they alone possessed the willpower to protect private property and insure social peace in the area, they decided to take matters into their own hands. They formed an armed mutual defense league and initiated a private rural police force to quell the threat of insurrection and pacify the region. Their actions came in response to the government's failure to bring stability, and also from their view that an ambivalent position toward the growing tide of rebellion, like that advocated by Arizcorreta, would only encourage it. Due to the negative images that hacendados presented of campesinos, and the fact that they portrayed them as retarding national development, it is important to note that the hacendados held ideas that were quite backward themselves. Their private police forces and jails, for example, contradicted more modern concepts about the monopoly of the legitimate use of force and the dispensation of punishment, which the more modern societies of the time reserved for the state. Morelos's hacendados rejected those notions though, because the state was not fulfilling its function in Mexico. After the Americans withdrew in 1848, hacendados in Morelos felt forced to behave as de facto rulers, interpreting the law and punishing the disobedient themselves.[32]

Lost beneath the more obvious events of the time period, such as foreign invasions, civil wars, and Santa Anna's ubiquity, was the fact that the rural population became increasingly incorporated into the broader national polity through exposure to the major ideas and issues of the day, and through their participation in the struggles around them. Some campesinos adopted aspects of the circulating political ideologies because they supported their own beliefs and provided new ways to articulate them. They were thus able to use Liberal language and the promise of individual liberty, full citizenship, and equality before the law to their own advantage.[33] During the course of the nineteenth century, different ideologies, not just Liberalism, appeared in connection with agrarian movements, like that led by Julio Chávez López, who grafted elements of anarchist theory onto local realities in Chalco in the late 1860s. The adherence to Liberal principles assisted Manuel Arellano in Morelos and others in the Puebla Sierra. As a result, working people in the countryside began to inject their own demands and ideals into the national dialogue, reshaping it. Their actions prompted at least some elites to consider and include them in plans, policies, and programs, and caused others to repress them. Although pueblo and worker militancy was not very successful in restraining hacendados during the nineteenth century, the great estate owners continually faced rural instability and had to weigh their actions for fear of losing their investments by instigating a "revolution be it general or local."[34]

It became increasingly apparent during the 1840s that the rural population constituted a largely unorganized but potentially powerful political force. To counter that potential and to foster their own idea of growth and development, elites in Morelos, with much of their power and wealth derived from the commerce and politics of Mexico City, opted to eliminate the long-standing property rights of rural communities. Those rights constituted the ultimate basis of peasant autonomy. The financially insolvent Mexican government, though, was too weak to carry out the program. Both the national government and that of the state of Mexico lacked the resources to enforce such a radical, sweeping, and unpopular change on the rural masses. Frustrated, the hacendados of Morelos grew increasingly intolerant of Governor Arizcorreta's conciliatory attitude toward rural communities and, ironically, accused him of exciting social discord. After a summer of discontent, Arizcorreta resigned from his post under pressure on August 16, 1849, making way for Governor Maríano Riva Palacio.

While they disapproved of Arizcorreta, the sugar hacendados found the new prefect of the Morelos District, Alejandro Villaseñor, more to their liking. Hacendados knew that if the general rebellion they feared ever materialized "the first victims would be the owners and administrators of the haciendas adjacent to the pueblos, and their estates would be the first to be reduced to ruins and left desolated by the uprising." Given those circumstances, they liked Villaseñor because he advocated "an agrarian law that would morally uplift the hacienda workers, giving the owners and administrators correctional powers over their subjects, but reserving severe punishment for those who exceeded their powers."[35] The proposal sought to legally validate the manorial social relations on the haciendas. Its implementation would have recognized the haciendas as juridically independent social units and granted hacendados powers similar to those of Southern plantation owners in the United States, who enforced their own codes of conduct on the people living or working on the estates. That would have included, of course, the hacendados' and administrators' rights to punish people who violated their rules. The key to Villaseñor's proposition was that it would have created the world the hacendados wanted, granting them immediate civil authority on their lands and allowing them to create their own social guidelines and enforce them with their private police squads outside of normal civil jurisdictions.

The idea came from deeply rooted attitudes of racial supremacy left over from the ideology behind institutions like slavery, the *encomienda*, and the repartimiento, where those of European descent ruled over blacks and Indians, often arguing it was for the benefit of the latter two groups. Villaseñor's proposal was interesting for what it reflected about the times. Its implementation would have legitimated what was already the norm in many cases. But, it would have also made the mainly Indian, mulatto, and mestizo citizens working on the haciendas in Morelos employees first, and Mexican citizens second.

Citizenship was an increasingly important issue and in the process of being defined. The political discourse in Mexico included debates about the nature and extent of individual, communal, civil, and property rights. Villaseñor's vision called for landowners to exercise authority over their subordinates in a paternalistic and degrading way reminiscent of the colonial past. Another, more subtle, way of achieving that end was to argue against the secular education of campesinos in Morelos. Hacendados claimed that the individual "*indio*" did not want education. They contended that the "dogma of equality" in the pueblos meant that as a people the indígenas were opposed to education in general because it disrupted their ideas of equality by elevating some individuals over others. The hacendados believed Indian ideas of equality reinforced general backwardness and lethargy.[36]

Villaseñor's proposition simply reflected the hegemony hacendados sought. It drew attention because it gave expression to the struggle taking place on the ground. Large landowners also had complaints with the way privatization was being carried out. They found litigation with pueblos inconvenient and bristled at suggestions that they placate peasants and laborers. Many hacendados regarded state mediation in their disputes with neighboring pueblos, and especially their own workers, as untoward interference in their prerogatives. They resented the idea that the government could tell them how to treat their employees living on their property. Hacendados expressed outrage that people they considered their social inferiors were continually allowed to contradict their social vision on almost every conceivable level, ranging from land and water usage, to wages, treatment, and the very definition of civil and political rights.[37]

Despite the hacendado's heavy-handed efforts at realizing their imagined world, turmoil continued through the early 1850s. During the summer of 1851 some estate laborers at the hacienda known as Treinta Pesos, south of Cuernavaca, complained about harsh treatment at the hands of the Spanish administrators there. Less than a year later, the residents and municipal authorities of the pueblo of Xochitepec, who had rebelled during the widespread uprisings of the late 1840s, again complained that Spanish estate administrators mistreated and insulted them. The events revived old animosities that had surfaced unambiguously during the North American invasion. Fear of a larger rebellion continued.[38]

The Conservative Dictatorship and Ayutla Rebellion

With Mexico's foreign debt rising, the government in shambles, and the propertied class feeling insecure, the Conservatives called for a limited dictatorship to restore order. They swept into office in 1852 with the "revolution" of Jalisco that came in the wake of the Liberal government's general inability to provide security. The many-times president and old general, Santa Anna, became the titular head of the government.

As is well known, the new Conservative government became totally personalistic and lethargic in its pursuit of national programs. Santa Anna took the title of "his most serene highness," and his final turn at the presidency was characterized by corruption, ostentation, and political one-sidedness. With the nation mired in debt, and social unrest brewing in the countryside, the ineffective army was decked out in lavish uniforms and military parades were held in Mexico City in an effort to lend prestige and authority to the dictatorship. Despite the trappings, the reality in Morelos was that hacendados continued to feel obliged to maintain security themselves as best they could.

Santa Anna's government, though, did provide important legislative support that came down firmly on the side of private property versus communal land tenure in Mexico. Santa Anna decreed a national law in 1853 that prohibited the public use of private pastures or woodlands. The new ordinance superseded any state laws, which, however unlikely, may have been inimical to private property. Another of his decrees went to the heart of much of the social conflict in Morelos. It forbade groups of families living on privately owned lands to incorporate themselves as villages and included the laughable requirement that to request incorporation they first had to secure the consent of the proprietor of the lands on which they resided. These laws represented the Conservative government's efforts, in conjunction with private action by the hacendados, to guarantee the transition from communal to private ownership of the countryside.[39]

Conservative legislation defending private property and openly attacking communal-land ownership and public access demonstrated quite plainly that on that score they behaved similarly to the Liberals. Their laws favored private lands over common lands and defined communities that emerged on the fringes of estates as company towns with no rights of incorporation and no civic autonomy. The Conservatives had hoped a limited dictatorship would bring political stability and secure the interests of private property, both of which they deemed essential for progress. Their efforts proved ephemeral. The central government failed to achieve widespread public acceptance and was financially unable to put enough armies into the field to maintain order. During the summer of 1853, General Benito Quijano wrote president Santa Anna:

> The indigenous towns do not give up on their petitions
> to acquire land and water at the expense of the sugar
> haciendas, which is their favorite activity, excited by
> certain mischievous individuals, enemies of all political
> order that play on the indígenas natural propensity
> against the white race. I have not found transgressions
> strong enough to justify teaching them a lesson that
> will scare them, because the Indians are profoundly
> reserved people and move with the greatest caution
> until they see a chance to achieve their goals when it
> looks most opportune.

The regime became more dictatorial, campesinos bided their time, unrest continued, and when Juan Álvarez rose in revolt in 1854 against the centralist government and its efforts to extend state control into the periphery, events in Morelos became part of the larger national struggle.[40]

Álvarez, an old federalist and Liberal and a veteran of both the Independence Wars and the U.S. invasion, launched the revolution of Ayutla. He found his main following among a cross-section of the country population of the tierra caliente, including the rugged mountains and tropical lowlands bordering Morelos, where he was known for defending peasants against the more egregious actions of hacendados, even though he was one himself. Álvarez's record of support for the rights of free villages in the region, however Machiavellian it may have been at times, was well established.[41]

Santa Anna, in contrast, represented the intrusion of the central government on local autonomy, and his decrees enabling private acquisition of common lands while denying communities the same rights alienated the rural folk of Morelos and gave them no reason to support his regime against the insurrection. As the rebel army of the south moved northward and entered Morelos, the town of Cuautla was fined three thousand pesos for offering no resistance to the insurgents. When government troops retook the town, they harshly punished citizens who had remained neutral during the rebel attack.

The revolution of Ayutla was not really an agrarian movement, but many rural people joined the struggle hoping to reform perceived injustices in their locales, which became possible when Álvarez offered them arms. In Morelos, pueblo vecinos and hacienda workers quickly moved to alter the existing property arrangements, and, as they had in the war with the United States, many, including those at San Pablo Tlayacopan and San Gaspar, took advantage of the opportunity to act out their own agendas. They carried out local land redistribution, revenge against landowners, and engaged in banditry and plunder. Conservatives and other property holders were understandably unhappy with the government's inability to defend them despite the taxes they paid to support the army. Álvarez soon held a wide swath of territory in the southwest and forced Santa Anna to abdicate in 1855.[42]

The triumph of Ayutla, although short-lived, was significant. It initiated a new Liberal government, paved the way for the Constitution of 1857, resulted in the abolition of military and clerical privileges, led to a new assault on church properties, and the nationwide disentailment of incorporated rural communities. Those principles formed the cornerstones of Mexico's Liberal modernizing effort, which lasted until the revolution of 1910 violently interrupted it.

The Liberal writers of the 1857 Constitution hoped to transform Mexican society by reducing the social, racial, and cultural cleavages inherited from the colonial past. They believed they could accomplish that by instituting the reign of individual liberties and laissez-faire capitalism. They worked to establish a state apparatus that could wield enough power and authority to ensure the creation and reproduction of the new society they envisioned. Their program, though, faced major obstacles. Conservatives, both lay and clerical, disliked General Álvarez because of his federalist leanings. Propertied people, Liberals and Conservatives alike, feared him because of his populist politics and the poverty of his supporters who, they worried, might influence him to redistribute rural properties. Meanwhile, increased social disturbances alarmed the landowning class. Hacendados in Morelos remembered Álvarez's role in the violent episodes directed against them during the U.S. invasion, and many hated him for his well-known advocacy of agrarian reform in favor of the pueblos.[43]

The Liberals faced the difficult challenge of winning the support of the rural populace. Santa Anna weakened his own position when he passed laws abrogating public use of private lands and stifled campesino petitions for the recognition of new rights as communities. The Liberals, despite their populist rhetoric, did the same thing. As a result, villagers and would-be pueblo citizens living in the hacienda rancherías found themselves caught in the middle. Earlier laws passed by the state of Mexico attacking community land entitlements became national legislation in June 1856, under the rubric of the Ley Lerdo. That event constituted a major betrayal of the rural armies that served in the revolution under Álvarez, who resigned from the government and returned home to Guerrero.

Implementing the Ley Lerdo

The Ley Lerdo, named for Finance Minister Miguel Lerdo de Tejada, called for a radical change in the way land was used and thought of in Mexico and soon contributed to intensified social unrest in Morelos. The Lerdo law mandated that the communal properties of pueblos, including all their farmland, were to be broken up and divided into individual private holdings. Other "corporate" properties belonging to the church were to be sold and put into private hands as well. The "corporate" property of pueblos was their communal land. Under the Ley Lerdo, that land could now be claimed or "denounced" by the local vecinos living on it, who could subdivide it among themselves by making individual down payments before established deadlines. If they failed to do that, the land could be "denounced" by people from outside the community who could then acquire it at the pueblo's loss.

One major problem was that most pueblo citizens in Morelos simply could not afford the down payments, or they missed the deadlines. That not only opened the door to wealthy outsiders but also allowed the more prosperous residents of the pueblos to acquire individual title to their own land, and to buy up the property of their neighbors who failed to make the down payments. Most communities, though, did not want to have their communal property divided up into small individual pieces, even if it meant people would gain individual ownership and legal title to their own plot. At the same time, some Liberal leaders, most notably Ponciano Arriaga, anticipated that those with the most financial resources would end up with the most land, so they denounced the Ley Lerdo as a land grab by the rich, designed to rob the pueblos of their communal inheritance.[44]

Some naive Liberal leaders hoped that the Ley Lerdo would precipitate the conversion of communal land into numerous independently owned small plots. The change was intended to increase agricultural productivity while creating a class of small-scale farmers. These Liberal leaders anticipated that the private ownership of land would instill in rural Mexicans the individual initiative deemed necessary for effective national citizenship, while at the same time contributing more directly to the economic development of the country. They hoped that personal ownership would redirect production away from the self-sufficiency traditionally emphasized by the Mexican peasantry, and toward greater market orientation. The reformers of the era wanted to emulate processes underway in the more modern industrializing nations of western Europe and the United States, and they hoped the political and cultural effects would be equally profound.[45]

Other idealistic, Liberal leaders sought to incorporate an ethnically distinct and often culturally reclusive rural population into the emerging modern nation and called for an agrarian reform program that would redistribute land in a more equitable way. Arriaga delivered a speech June 28, 1856, outlining his view of the situation and explaining his "*voto particular*" against the Ley Lerdo. Arriaga believed that the implementation of the Lerdo law would aggravate, rather than solve the agrarian problem and protested that

> meanwhile, a few individuals have possession of
> immense uncultivated lands that could provide

subsistence to millions of men, while a large population, mainly city dwellers, remains mired in the most
horrendous poverty, without property, without homes,
without industry or work. These people cannot be free,
or form a Republic, much less prosper, even with one
hundred constitutions and thousands of laws pro-
claiming abstract rights and pretty theories, but
impractical because of the absurd economic
system of society.[46]

The passing of the Ley Lerdo, and the incorporation of it as Article
27 of the Constitution of 1857, came over the objections of Arriaga and
a minority allied with him. The other delegates enacted measures that,
during the next half century, facilitated the greater concentration of
large properties in a few hands, and the simultaneous creation of an
impoverished mass of landless rural laborers with no realistic alternatives to hacienda employment.

The implementation of the laws of disamortization unloaded a
combination of blows on the pueblos. First, politically, the new laws
inhibited the role of the *cabildo*, or town council, as a representative
of community interests in outside litigation. Instead, when people
sought to defend their land they had to do so as individuals, which
undermined the autonomy of the pueblo and its ability to challenge
outside authorities like state officials or hacienda foremen. Second,
the new laws helped unravel the communal social fabric within the
pueblo by pitting neighbor against neighbor in a competitive scram-
ble for titles to previously common land and water. Third, by stripping the pueblo of its juridical identity and placing ownership in the
hands of poor, often illiterate individual peasants who could not afford
a lawyer like they could as a community, the Reform laws eliminated
their strength-in-numbers and made their communal lands easier
prey to outsiders.

The new laws had a cultural impact too. Most pueblos set aside
some common land for community income, and that terrain played an
important role. A pueblo could raise crops on that land for sale, or
lease the land to small rancheros or hacendados who paid rents. The
proceeds then went to fund community activities such as religious
festivals like saints' days and other festivities that provided an important cohesiveness to village life. The Ley Lerdo threatened those activities. Its attack on communal property also impacted the pueblos as an
assault on religion and the binding force of community observances

and celebrations because it gutted the source of funds for the local church.[47] So, if someone from outside the community who was leasing pueblo land denounced it, they acquired the right of first purchase, which meant that a pueblo that held land one day could easily lose it to the person they were renting it to the next. When that happened it impoverished a community by eliminating income that serviced events with social and cultural import. Those activities had traditionally brought people together and reinforced common bonds, shared beliefs, and community history. They also helped strengthen regional social ties that were intertwined with other aspects of life, like small-scale trade. The other thing they provided was a major source of organized recreation, and in the hard-working day-to-day existence of the Morelos countryside that mattered. So, the Ley Lerdo ended up increasing both corrosion from within the pueblos and pressure from without.[48]

Not surprisingly, the enactment of the Ley Lerdo coincided with a new wave of rural unrest, this time aimed at the Liberals. Although campesinos responded positively to certain elements of the Liberal agenda, especially the idea of greater local self-rule, they were quite capable of switching sides when local realities went against them. The ensuing Wars of the Reforma (1858–60), far from being simply a struggle amongst elites, brought the increased politicalization of the peasantry in Morelos, where an armed and agitated rural populace clamored to be heard. Álvarez had formed national guard units and distributed weapons to the rural population of Morelos twice, first to resist the American intervention and then to support the revolution of Ayutla. When the Liberals took office those units had remained under arms. The ensuing efforts to implement the Ley Lerdo aggravated already existing tensions in the countryside.

The Liberal Dilemma

The largest fault in the Liberal cause was that most Liberal leaders, with their elite backgrounds, failed to link social justice and the redistribution of land to the individual and political freedoms they espoused.[49] There was, therefore, an inherent contradiction in the Liberal position. Liberals, generally speaking, fell into two camps, "*puros*" and "*moderados*." Both wanted to attack the special interests inherited from the colonial period, like tobacco monopolies, military "*fueros*," and religious corporations, but they disagreed on how to alter those special interests. The Liberals had just come to power with the assistance of a rural population in the south that was poor, communalist, Indian, mulatto, and mestizo and was adamantly demanding some redistribution of land and wealth. Their elite opposition, especially hard-line Conservatives, despised them and referred to them as "*pintos*" and to Juan Álvarez as "an animal."

Whatever the disputes within the Liberal elite, campesinos focused their energies on issues involving land, water, and wages; "bread-and-butter" concerns, rather than the religious and military fueros and ecclesiastical properties that preoccupied those practicing statecraft. A clear conflict emerged between the groups, and it compromised the Liberal effort. Some leaders, like Álvarez and Arriaga, wanted to accommodate worker and pueblo aspirations, but the majority feared attacks on private property, class conflict, and general social disorder. Much of the Liberal leadership was leery of the desires of the rural population, susceptible to their portrayal in the darkest terms imaginable, and particularly vulnerable to the continually raised specter of "caste war."

The conflict boiled down to one between a populist brand of Liberalism versus a more elitist version. Popular Liberalism sought not only equality before the law, but greater social justice through the defense of local autonomy and agrarian communalism. Elite Liberalism stressed juridical equality but opposed any redistribution of wealth beyond that wasted in the "dead hands" of the church, lavished on the army, or locked in entailed estates. Urban Liberals generally sought the elevation of the bourgeoisie and promoted the supremacy of individual initiative. That approach was progressive because it facilitated upward mobility and offered a more permeable class structure. The program might have been helpful in the urban context by protecting child and women's labor during the harshest phases of industrialization, but it offered few tangible rewards to the working population of the countryside.

After the Liberal victory, rural workers throughout Morelos, probably expecting the support of the new government many of them had fought to install, demanded higher wages from the hacendados. Uneasy landowners in Morelos wrote to the new president of Mexico, Ignacio Comonfort, to express their concerns about disorder in the area. They worried that returning national guardsmen from the districts of Morelos and Cuernavaca might ally themselves with agitated campesinos and resume the struggle against the estates, as they had following the U.S. occupation. But the national guard was an eclectic mix. Some helped put down a Conservative-led backlash that broke out in the neighboring state of Puebla. Others, however, feeling abandoned by the Liberals, supported the Conservatives and early in the War of the Reform helped in the entrapment and surrender of a Liberal army under Miguel Negrete, as it attempted to march past Cuernavaca en route to the Pacific coast. Regardless of the shifting political alliances, hacendado fears of local militancy proved legitimate.[50]

Local Meanings of Ayutla

A month after the hacendados sent their letter, a group of hacienda workers and "common criminals" attempted to assassinate the captain of the rural security forces in Cuautla, and strikes broke out on the haciendas Cocoyoc and Santa Inés. Those incidents, which coincided with a more general demand for increased wages at the sugar estates around both Cuautla and Cuernavaca, led Cuernavaca's prefect, Alejandro Villaseñor, to ask Comonfort to send an army brigade to Cuautla.[51] The military commander in Cuautla traced the origins of the unrest to just before the victory of Ayutla, when Álvarez put more than one thousand weapons in campesino hands. After that a series of popular leaders emerged in local villages, including the reappearance of José Manuel Arellano of Tetecala. Landowners knew and feared Arellano because he had led armed bands in the attacks on haciendas in the Cuernavaca Valley in 1848. Now, he and others resumed local-level militant political activity. When Ayutla broke out, they called themselves military commanders of the general insurrection, but actually operated largely independently of outside authority, relying on the support of local villagers and hacienda laborers, which most of them were themselves. Rebuffed at the haciendas Atlihuayan and Santa Inés, they set fire to the cane fields there and at the hacienda Actopán near Tetecala. The crop damage from arson at Atlihuayan exceeded twenty thousand pesos. The blaze was limited to that estate, but its message reached further. The cane burning symbolized the economic damage that angry workers could inflict on estate owners, and although at a clear disadvantage, agitated workers and villagers were less intimidated by the hacendado's enforcers when they had Arellano and other armed guardsmen backing them up. Taking advantage of their temporary strength, they staged strikes and attempted to prevent others from working.[52]

The Liberal victory had initially excited hopeful villagers as well as hacienda workers. Villagers took over disputed lands from the estates and began to cultivate them "with their rifles on their backs." The Ministry of War in Mexico City responded to hacendado concerns about those actions and an impending "*guerra de castas,*" the "white" elite's ultimate fear, and ordered the army to confiscate all weapons in the hands of villagers and estate laborers in Morelos.[53]

The unrest in the countryside took on a violently anti-Spanish tone. Acts of violence and criminality, such as the murder of a hacienda *mayordomo* or other prominent Spaniard, were not viewed as isolated episodes at the time, but as part of a broader social conflict rooted in economic inequality and intensified by mutually negative images of "the other" that included deep ethnic and cultural antagonisms. The government ministry in charge of "public tranquility" received word in April 1857 that a Spanish hacienda employee had been murdered in the eastern district of Cuautla near Izucar, Puebla. Local authorities requested federal assistance because they lacked sufficient forces to pursue and punish the criminals and feared similar episodes would follow. They had reasons for their apprehension because this murder followed one of the more sensational crimes of the period at the hacienda Chiconcuac.[54]

The notorious incident occurred on December 17–18, 1856, when thirty armed men attacked the complex of sugar haciendas of Chiconcuac (see Figures 2 and 3), San Vicente, and Dolores, in the valley lying south of Cuernavaca. Pío Bermijillo, a wealthy Spaniard, owned the estates, and the attack became an international incident that demonstrated the relationship between national and local struggles. The episode began when an armed band kidnapped a Spanish employee, Victor Allende, outside the gates of Chiconcuac and then used Allende to try and gain access to the hacienda. When that scheme failed, they broke into the hacienda, robbed and looted the property, and rode to nearby Dolores, where they killed the unfortunate Allende during the night. The next morning at sunrise they smashed down the door of the big house of the neighboring hacienda San Vicente and ransacked the building. Bermijillo's family and staff who operated the estate ran and hid. The intruders searched for and found Juan Bermijillo, the nephew of the owner, hiding in the boiler room of the sugar mill. Realizing he had been discovered, Bermijillo broke and ran, but someone buried a machete in the back of his head. He stumbled across the patio gravely wounded and died in front of the *trapiche*, or mill house.[55]

The owner's brother, Nicolás Bermijillo, was the despised administrator of the hacienda. His hiding place under the waterwheel of the sugar mill was exposed by a vengeful Mexican employee. Three other Spanish employees and a Frenchman were hiding with him.

Figure 2. Patio of the hacienda Chiconcuac.

Spaniards in Morelos had earned a reputation among their Mexican employees as cruel and abusive and had a long history of acting with a sense of superiority toward their "*mozos*," enforcing discipline, and maintaining neck irons and the stockade. Bermijillo was pulled from his hiding place begging for his life. Desperate, he offered his tormentors a large sum of money to let him live, but they refused, dragged him to the front gate and shot him. After murdering the two Bermijillos, they killed two more Spaniards but spared the lives of another hacienda administrator who convinced the assailants that he was French, not Spanish.[56]

Figure 3.
Church at
Chiconcuac.

As news of the murders spread, panic swept the Cañada de Cuernavaca. Spaniards fled the countryside, flocking to the safety of the state capital. The ethnic overtones were obvious and it caused tremendous alarm across Morelos, in Mexico City, and in Spain. The

Spanish government vigorously protested to Mexican national authorities as rumors circulated of plans to kill all the Spaniards in Morelos. The Spanish government angrily pointed out that at least six officers under General Álvarez's command had been implicated in threats or actions against Spanish citizens in Mexico, and it tried to hold Álvarez responsible. Spain ordered five warships to bolster the armada at Cuba and prepared to protect the lives and property of its citizens in Mexico if the Mexican government would not.[57]

The murders took place in a national climate of instability and turmoil. No fewer than three Mexican governments had failed to provide security in rural Morelos for almost a decade. First, the defeat at the hands of the U.S. army had allowed general discontent to flare into widespread revolts. Then the Conservatives under Santa Anna failed to fully protect the haciendas from local insurrections by rebels and war veterans operating under the name of Álvarez. Finally, when the Liberals took over, they were unable to control the former national guardsmen and returning veterans of the revolution of Ayutla, whom Álvarez had armed and who were actively pressing their demands and hoping for government support. Hacendados felt that these central governments had provided insufficient security, so they created their own private armies and a confederation of mutual defense. But with hostile and potentially disloyal employees, and an armed and mobilized rural populace, that approach was less than satisfactory.

The Mexican government, like the Spanish, took a serious view of the murders at Chiconcuac and San Vicente. The animosity between Spanish-owned and operated haciendas and Indian, mestizo, and mulatto villagers and laborers in Morelos was real and old. Rebels and assassins had singled out and killed Spaniards in the lowlands before, and they would do so again. Those acts in general, and this incident in particular, symbolized a violent rejection of the caste nature of Morelos' rural society and the harmful effects the heightened commercialization of agriculture had on hacienda workers and pueblos alike. Spanish attitudes of racial and cultural superiority clearly aggravated the situation, and the highly varied ethnic population of the Morelos lowlands rejected their role as second-class citizens in their own country.

The identities of the perpetrators and victims at Chiconcuac and San Vicente said a lot about their local world. The men who committed the murders came from a marginalized cross-section of rural society. Two worked as hacienda employees for the administrator Nicolás

Bermijillo, and knew him. The main figure was Trinidad Carrillo. He lived on Pio Bermijillo's hacienda Dolores where he sharecropped some land. Carrillo's main accomplices were Camilo Cruz Barba, who worked as a *jornalero* (day laborer) on the hacienda Chiconcuac, and their friends, Inés López, who worked for wages at the nearby hacienda San Nicolás, and two others, Miguel Herrera and Nicolás Leite, who were agricultural laborers living in pueblos in the area and occasionally working on the neighboring haciendas.

Trinidad Carrillo's brother, Isidro Carrillo, headed Álvarez's national guard unit in Xochitepec. The townspeople there had a long, contentious relationship with neighboring haciendas, including Chiconcuac, and had repeatedly complained that Spanish hacienda administrators mistreated them. An earlier incident in 1852 had turned bloody when people from the pueblo killed some other Spaniards. The tensions at Chiconcuac began when Nicolás Bermijillo, acting as the administrator, seized a plot of land cultivated by Trinidad Carrillo at the hacienda Dolores. Bermijillo's brother, who owned the estate, had decided to upgrade Dolores and make more rational use of its acreage by raising more sugarcane. The Bermijillos took back the land they had been letting Carrillo cultivate as a sharecropper. From Carrillo's perspective, he and his wife had dutifully provided their services for the estate. His expectation was that the contract was long-term, as was customary, and maybe for life, with mutual obligations and responsibilities on both sides. The hacendado, however, felt no moral obligation and saw no deep betrayal when he kicked the Carrillos off the land. For the Bermijillos, the relationship was simply a matter of business and, as such, could be terminated at any time. They needed the land to raise sugarcane in order to increase profits; the Carrillos were incidental. The other factor that probably impacted the Bermijillo's decision was that Trinidad's brother, Isidro, was a national guard commander. National guardsmen had been active in challenging hacendado land claims in the area, so perhaps the Bermijillos considered Trinidad and his wife undesirable elements on the hacienda. Whatever the exact motivation, the Carrillos were evicted and had to find another place to live. They also had to leave behind whatever improvements they had made to the plot of land they tilled.

Presaging a pattern that would become endemic as a good number of the rural people of Morelos were transformed from peasants into workers during the last third of the nineteenth century, Trinidad Carrillo was displaced and suddenly found himself both landless and unemployed. His wife, Quirina Galván, was furious when the

Bermijillos repossessed the land and drove them from their home. The unrestrained rage she expressed when she reportedly said, "I will have no greater comfort than knowing that those Gachupínes have wallowed in their own blood," was apparently shared by at least a few other people in the area.[58]

Juan Álvarez was implicated in the crimes and accused of providing a climate in which they could occur. He defended himself against the charges and lashed out with a scathing indictment of Morelos's troubled rural society in his "Manifesto to the Civilized Peoples of Europe and America." Álvarez declared that he had nothing to do with anti-Spanish activity, which, he insisted, was conducted by local people who, although they used his name, were beyond his control. He pointed out, though, that Spaniards in Mexico had consistently supported the Conservatives politically and materially. They provided food, shelter, horses, money, and men, and in so doing had involved themselves in the destiny of Mexico in a manner beyond their rights as foreigners. Álvarez said that the deaths at the haciendas were lamentable but unsurprising, since the Spanish hacendados in Morelos continued to abuse and humiliate the rural people as they had done for years and therefore invited the violence against themselves. He concluded that the hacendados were responsible for creating the situation and had engendered the hatred of the populace because the greed of some hacendados knew no bounds. Álvarez wrote that many hacendados took over community and *ejido* lands and, with an "incredible lack of shame," claimed them as their own. Álvarez's "Manifesto" captured attention, but he merely wrote down what most rural people already knew: community appeals to the courts fell on deaf ears, and the usual reward for asking for what they felt was rightfully theirs was "persecution, incarceration, and disgrace."[59]

Responding to the gravity of the situation, the hacendados formed the Comisión Central de Proprietarios de los Distritos de Cuernavaca y Morelos, designed to defend their estates against "those forces which incessantly conspire against the properties of the esteemed hacienda owners and against the lives of their poor servants." The commission was a privately funded lobby intended to represent the interests of Morelos hacendados before authorities in Cuernavaca and the state legislature in Toluca. They requested changes in the way the rural police were organized in order to allow landowners a greater say in how they were selected, mounted, armed, paid, and deployed. Their lobbying efforts gave them greater input in the government's strategies to police the region.[60]

National leaders heeded hacendado concerns and moved to suppress a potential widespread rebellion in Morelos. The murders at Dolores and Chiconcuac were part of a larger pattern of social mobilization that united villagers and workers as it had in the 1840s. This time, though, it included veterans of the resistance against the U.S. invasion and the revolution of Ayutla. Those forces pressed an alternative vision of modern Mexico that challenged elite versions in multiple ways. Through their wartime sacrifices in the defense of their country, their contributions on behalf of the Liberals, and their continuing claims to inherited rights to the land, campesinos pursued their own interpretation of Mexican citizenship. They accepted elite Liberal notions regarding individual rights and property, but they also sought recognition of and respect for their communities.[61] They began to fashion their age-old ideals within the new language of the Liberal discourse and tried to combine the rights of citizenship with their traditional rights to land, water, woods, autonomous local government, and mutual aid.

During the 1840s and 1850s campesinos extended their vision to laboring conditions on the haciendas as well. They did not challenge discrepancies of wealth per se, but resisted the loss of political and economic independence of the pueblos and the poor treatment of estate workers. Zapata later reflected similar views in his revolutionary pronouncement of 1911, the Plan de Ayala, where he proposed a redistribution of wealth that allowed hacendados to retain their core lands, factories, cattle, horses, monies, and other assets, but demanded they return the fundo legal to the pueblos, partly redistribute what had once been common pastures and woodlands, and allow fair access to water. Although the 1850s agrarian precursors did not develop a national program like the Zapatistas did, their activities made clear that they also believed that the hacendados deserved to lose their assets if they did not accommodate elements of the new order that peasants, laborers, and even some Liberal leaders were trying to create. The public execution by garroting of Trinidad Carrillo and five associates on a special platform erected in front of the equestrian statue of Carlos IV at the *glorieta* of Bucareli and Reforma streets in downtown Mexico City, symbolized the larger official effort to choke off social unrest from below, just as before the Terror, the guillotine symbolized the decapitation of the leadership of the ancién regime.[62]

Competing visions coming out of the rapidly changing countryside offered sharp differences of what rural Mexico should look like. Elites articulated their proposals in plans, letters, and laws. The aspirations of the popular classes surfaced most clearly in court cases and in collective action, as they repeatedly clashed with both Conservative designs and fundamental parts of the Liberal agenda. The struggle in Morelos blended with a growing consciousness of events in the outside world brought on by the American invasion, the revolution of Ayutla, and rural working-class adaptations of Liberal ideology that conflicted with elite notions of how to organize life and work in rural Mexico. Mexico's great challenge was how to reconcile the two.

Chapter Four

CONTESTED VISIONS
Elite Discourse and
Agrarian Insurrection,
1856–1861

Regardless of their particular political ideology or social philosophy, Mexican elites pursued economic projects that threatened rural communities across the country. Government instability brought on by civil war and foreign invasion allowed sporadic resistance to spread in Morelos in the form of robbery, murder, and banditry and to take on greater social significance as they merged with larger national issues.

The Setting

When the Wars of the Reforma broke out, the area on the other side of the mountains south of Mexico City was dangerous. Yet the visiting Pal Rosty seemed unconcerned as he set out on horseback one morning in 1858 to explore the area. Rosty had fought as a Hussar in the 1848–49 Hungarian War of Independence, and when the war failed he had left that country. The conflict in Mexico left him undaunted as he rode southeast out of the Valley of Mexico toward the snow-capped peaks of the volcanoes looming at its southern rim.[1] He headed for what is today the state of Morelos, which, he had been told, was one of the most beautiful places in Mexico. He provided a detailed description of the physical landscape and recorded his experience. By midafternoon of the following day he was traveling along a trail through the pine-forested mountains that separate Mexico's central plateau from the semitropical southern lowlands. He rounded a bend and, glancing down through the branches, saw the verdant green of the Cuautla Valley spread out before him. He descended the trail, toward the expansive fields of sugarcane, which appeared to roll across the land like a "green sea." Two hours later, with the mountain pines and thin alpine air behind him, he found himself riding among the palms, fruit trees, tropical flowers, and aromas of the tierra caliente.

Ten years after leaving Hungary, Rosty was lugging his photographic equipment on three mules down a trail into rural Mexico. He was consciously emulating Alexander von Humbolt, another foreign traveler who had achieved notoriety with his written observations of the Americas almost fifty years earlier. Rosty made his mark as well. He took some of the first known photographs of Mexico, and his account of the journey painted a vivid picture of Morelos in the late 1850s.

As Rosty rode into the valley of Cuautla Amilpas, it was bustling with human activity and the sounds of insects and animals stirring in early spring. Birds sang and swooped by overhead, butterflies fluttered in the air, crickets chirped, and lizards scurried across the ground. The small, open-aired huts of villagers and hacienda field workers stood in the shade of orange, banana, and palm trees that offered some relief from the heat of the afternoon sun. Large colorful flowers covered trees and bushes, filling the valley with their fragrance. Rosty rode in the shadow of Popocatépetl, the giant volcano rising fifteen thousand feet above sea level. Surrounded by the colors and smells of tropical fruits and flowers and the rolling fields of sugarcane, he was struck with the natural beauty of the place and stopped to watch the setting sun cast its last light across the valley.[2]

When he left, Rosty followed a road going west. It took him past many of the area's large and beautiful haciendas with their imposing stone manor houses and sugar mills standing out against the green fields. They were surrounded by the thatched huts of agricultural workers who were "blacks, mulattos and zambos, all of them free." Rosty noticed that the worker's settlements on the haciendas constituted "actual villages" and that almost all the major plantations had their own churches.[3] As he neared the town of Yautepec, orange orchards appeared, watered by the many gulches and ravines that also irrigated the lands of the nearby haciendas. The locals proudly informed the stranger that the oranges there were widely considered to be especially delicious. Oranges were a mainstay of the local economy, and caravans of mules regularly hauled them and other citrus fruits up to Mexico City for sale.

Rosty rode on, westward, toward Cuernavaca. On the way he stopped at the hacienda Atlihuayán, just outside Yautepec, owned by a wealthy Mexico City merchant named Manuel Escandón. Although Rosty did not know it at the time, the Escandón family name would play an important role in the future history of Morelos. Leaving Yautepec, he passed through an arid zone of low-lying, rugged, and scruffy hills that separated the Cuautla and Cuernavaca valleys. As he reached a fork in the road the town of Cuernavaca came into view, but he turned his horse south, toward the haciendas in the rich valley below.

Despite the tranquil beauty of the countryside, Rosty was well aware of the social turmoil in the area. The violence in Morelos was related to, yet also distinct from, the conflict surrounding the Wars of the Reforma that were beginning to engulf the nation. After all, less than two years had passed since the sensation caused by the murders at Chiconcuac and San Vicente. The sugar estates were operating under the continuing threat of upheaval from neighboring campesinos, who continued to relocate or destroy hacienda land markers. Mexico's new Liberal government had failed to establish authority over independent-minded pueblo citizens and estate workers in the region, and the Conservatives were driving the Liberals out of Mexico City toward a government in exile at Veracruz. Under those conditions, no central authority exercised effective control in the country. The social tensions that marked Morelos for the past several years continued unabated.[4]

The War Within the War

The Liberal Constitution was promulgated in February 1857, and by March 2, Alejandro Villaseñor, still serving as the prefect of Cuernavaca, anticipated that state authorities would have difficulty enforcing compliance with the Liberal land laws. Carefully planned provisions for carrying out the Ley Lerdo and the constitutional

Article 27 that reinforced it were in place, but Villaseñor warned that resistance to its implementation could be expected. Responding to those concerns, Governor Mariano Riva Palacio had contacted the Mexican secretary of state's office, which assured him that the federal government stood behind the privatization process and urged him to carry the law forward, but to apply it gently.[5]

Trouble started immediately. The administrator of the hacienda Miacatlán, located southwest of Cuernavaca, warned the governor of a new organization that surfaced in February and was threatening to attack large landowners and seize their properties if they did not desist in their "denunciations" and occupations of village lands. Popular defiance surfaced with the first efforts by individuals to "denounce" pueblo land. With the memory of Chiconcuac fresh in everyone's mind, Miacatlán's administrator requested police or army support from the governor to insure the maintenance of order and "to keep everyone in his proper place."[6]

Although large landowners, their administrators, and government bureaucrats all worried about public reaction, they also pondered the seemingly limitless ramifications of the new laws. Both groups welcomed the legal innovations and the changes they sanctified, but nervously watched for signs of resistance. Landowner anxiety mounted as public hostility toward the new policies became palpable. Hacendados and government officials requested increased security and began to view all kinds of public gatherings, including religious parades and seasonal market fairs, as threats to public order.[7] Joaquín García Icazbalceta, an especially influential landowner whose extensive properties eventually covered most of eastern Morelos, revealed the concerns of many of his peers when he called for heightened vigilance during the coming "fair season" in March 1857. He called the fairs "reunions of thieves" and asked for an extra detachment of rural police for the upcoming event in Tepalcingo. García Icazbalceta recommended that the officers be quartered in nearby Jonacatepec and noted that the fair inspired so much dread in the "good" families of the area that most of them had all ready left.[8]

Whereas the hacendado dreaded and denigrated the upcoming event, hacienda workers and people from the small towns saw it as a major source of diversion, as evident in the following stanzas from the *corrido*, "The Fairs of Morelos":

> We're going to Tepalcingo
> to the fair of the three Fridays

that fair is a good one where
people come from everywhere,
from Puebla and Matamoros
and from the tierra caliente

You'll see a lot of raffles
from the buffets and the fruit stands,
you'll see restaurants by the rows
Like in all the other fairs,
or in any other fun place,
let's go, chatita, what are you waiting for?[9]

The hacendado's use of terms like "good families" and "thieves," provided a small glimpse of the mentality of the landed aristocracy and their acute awareness of the deep chasm dividing the social classes. Those differences were not only registered in material terms, but deeply embedded in the ways people of different social station, talked, thought, and felt about one another on a daily basis. Under the circumstances, hacendado fears of what would otherwise have been innocuous gatherings may have been well-founded, especially considering that the plot that later launched Zapata into the Revolution of 1910 was hatched at one of the annual Lenten fairs south of Cuautla.[10]

Despite their efforts to portray their workers as happy in their poverty, elites conceded the depth of the cultural gap in the countryside, as well as the level of popular opposition to the social and economic policies they sought to implement, when they called fairs and celebrations breeding grounds for collective disobedience. García Icazbalceta's request for a greater police presence and heightened vigilance also reflected his desire to demonstrate the ruling class's ability to maintain social control and impose their will despite widespread public opposition. Like the administrator at Miacatlán, he wanted everyone to know their place.

Meanwhile, the increasingly dispossessed rural citizenry, living in the crude huts described by the traveling Pal Rosty, chafed under their conditions while elites continued to live life at the other end of the social order. While García Icazbalceta fretted over the fair, the governor's son and future general and historian, Vicente Riva Palacio, enjoyed the company of other hacendado families at a lavish masked ball held at the home of his Aunt Bernarda. The contrast in lifestyles between the propertied classes living in fortified mansions and the disenfranchised living in dirt-floored shacks was stark.[11]

Juan Álvarez was sensitive to that fact and the animosity many rural people felt about it. He wrote to Governor Riva Palacio in mid-March 1857, expressing concerns about the growing alienation of public sentiment. He used the same reasoning that former governor Arrizcorreta had a decade before, advising Riva Palacio to urge the hacendados and public officials to exercise some restraint in their dealings with local pueblos and hacienda workers. Álvarez also called for the replacement of Villaseñor, the overzealous prefect of Cuernavaca, who he thought was aggravating old tensions. Álvarez suggested Riva Palacio "put a check" on the area's landowners, who, he felt, were running a "semifeudal" regime. He also reminded the governor, "The fight between the pueblos of the cañada and the haciendas is not new to you." He warned that if the hacendados continued to exasperate neighboring pueblos and "to attack their properties without respecting their titles of legitimate acquisition," and continued to refuse to "submit the disputes to just and definitive decisions, then no one could realistically... expect the results to be favorable." Álvarez believed hacendados would continue to trample on campesino and pueblo rights if the governor did not intercede. He worried that if government officials did nothing to address pueblo needs, it could spark a popular rebellion that rejected elite leadership entirely. Explaining that he had made promises to an agitated rural public that demanded action, he warned:

> More than once I have contained them; I have calmed
> them, I have assured them that the government would
> undo the wrongs committed against them, but if they
> see that time is passing and their injuries continue, per-
> haps they will not believe in my promises to find a
> binding resolution, and, dejected and enraged, they
> may commit a mistake which would prove the existence
> of a political plot to our enemies [the conservatives]
> and provide a basis for international reclamations.[12]

With the obvious allusion to a possible repeat of the kind of violence committed at Chiconcuac and the international furor it ignited, Álvarez counseled Riva Palacio to act prudently to avoid future "misfortunes" in the Morelos countryside.

Once again, campesino resistance had prompted Liberal leaders to seek a conciliatory posture and to temper the more egregious results of their own privatization program. Several factors were at play. Campesinos were threatening rebellion and trying to protect their patrimonies, but they were also being co-opted by the state. They adopted Liberal rhetoric, on the one hand, but they forced elites to address their particular concerns and include them in official policies, on the other. It was a special, if not unique, moment. The opportunity for campesinos to exert themselves was greater than usual because of the civil war. The Liberals needed at least some popular support to maintain power. Therefore, even though the rural population was being subjected to a broad, elite-inspired plan for national development, they were also participating in, and reshaping, the dialogue at many levels that forced would-be rulers to debate various strategies on how to deal with them.

All contending social groups, the Liberal elite, the hacendado ruling class, and the campesino population at large, alternately employed tactics of force or cooperation at different times. The state attempted to play a mediating role, although it generally acted in defense of private property. Sometimes national elites pursued a conciliatory approach that included a more gentle application of the policies and practices most resisted by the rural communities and working class. That was the approach advocated by Arizcorretta on the state level and by Álvarez as a national spokesman. Maximilian would later try that as well.

The political turmoil of the 1850s made a policy of co-optation problematic for both sides. As a result, the other, more common strategy involved government support for hacendado interests that went beyond simply maintaining the status quo and sought to implement policies that weakened pueblos and workers. Those changes were imposed through a biased legal system, harsh repression of individual and collective acts of resistance, and masked by lip service to the campesinos. Because of that, Álvarez was concerned that government intransigence would provoke an uprising by disgruntled peasants and workers who might pursue their own agendas outside of elite participation.

Álvarez also recognized the danger of bastardizing the long-term developmental goals of the Liberal privatization program. Although some idealistic planners intended from the beginning to empower campesinos as individuals, the danger existed that the Ley Lerdo would lead to the disintegration of pueblo communes and the loss of small private property to land-hungry hacendados, rather than to the creation of a rural middle class. Álvarez and a few other prominent Liberals, like Senators Arriaga and Ramirez, opposed those results and struggled against the further polarization of wealth in the Mexican countryside.

Pueblos in Morelos usually held the titles to farms, pastures, and woodlands as common property, but they allotted farming plots to individual families of the pueblo. As a result, individual usufruct, although not ownership, had come to dominate pueblo landholdings in the region. Most of their farms were undercapitalized and produced little beyond the subsistence needs of their tillers. The new laws intended to fundamentally alter the idea of property. Community-owned, but family-tilled land would become the individual property of the villagers who worked the plots. The laws of the marketplace would rule. The most successful among them would prosper by selling their farm surpluses to local markets, acquiring new lands, and increasing production for profit. The unlucky, lazy, or incompetent would be driven under by natural competition and end up working for their more successful neighbors, or they would move to where land, work, and wages were available, which in Morelos meant the sugar estates. The Liberals imagined that these mechanisms would stimulate a productive class of independent yeoman farmers that would provide the material basis for a new sense of individualism and the mentality necessary to realize their idea of national progress.

The Liberal approach, though, imposed a foreign model derived from very different historical experiences and therefore upset hundreds of years of traditional practice in Morelos. Villagers in the countryside quickly realized the negative realities of the new laws and resisted them. They may or may not have anticipated the potential long-term results of the Ley Lerdo, but, either way, they proved quite capable of deducing its immediate implications and took prompt action to meet the threat. Probably the most obvious problem was that the new laws meant that pueblo vecinos would have to pay for land they already used for free as part of their communal rights. Naturally, they resisted that. The other major danger, and the way the Ley Lerdo made its first impact on the pueblos, was that common pastures and woodlands that lacked specific individual tenants using specific plots of ground became nationalized and could be sold at public auction, or denounced by wealthy outsiders, including neighboring hacendados. The number of *denuncios* and cases of individuals trying to secure "*bienes nacionalizados*" soared. This process continued during the Porfiriato, impacting the pueblos harshly because it eroded what was left of pueblo lands.[13]

Confronted by pockets of local resistance, state builders and hacendados realized they were pushing a problematic proposition.[14] When angry villagers from the towns of Amacusac and Cuachichinola physically relocated the boundary markers at the hacienda San Gabriel, the message was clear. That hacienda was no stranger to hostile villager actions; back in the 1840s, the vecinos of Puente de Ixtla had entered into a heated dispute with the hacendado over who should run the local *tianguis*, or open-air market, which made up an extremely important part of the local economy. Based on those experiences, hacendados knew that greater dangers sometimes accompanied this sort of collective action, and they called for an augmentation of the police force.[15]

Reports reached Governor Riva Palacio's office from Cuautla, telling of popular agitation across the tierra caliente and warning that Spaniards there were in danger.[16] At the same time, bandits and "*pronunciados*" filled Jonacatepec. Government officials reserved the label "pronunciados" for organized political movements associated with the Conservatives. Anybody involved in local-level resistance that lacked a formal program or national goal, the government dubbed "bandits," or "*malhechores*." The governor received calls for help in protecting property from throughout the district.[17] "Bandits" invaded haciendas, including Tenango and Tenextepango.[18] Robberies increased, and the rising number of homicides accompanying them made many wealthier people worry about their personal safety both at home and on the roads.[19] The general breakdown of law and order and the deluge of citizen complaints forced both the governor of the state and the president of the republic, Ignacio Comonfort, to promise additional forces to impose tranquility.[20]

Perhaps most alarming to the governor were reports of public support for bandits in the district of Jonacatepec. Bandits there committed crimes and returned to their local communities, where they hid among the general population who protected them.[21] The authorities found themselves in a difficult situation. Bandits outnumbered the local police. They were also extremely difficult to catch because they enjoyed public support and safe harbor in some places. A profound unease on the part of officials and hacendados permeated the area, probably matched only by the anger that drove popular protest. Accustomed to a seignorial lifestyle, hacendados in Morelos complained that they could not even trust their own servants anymore.[22]

Banditry in nineteenth-century Morelos carried a social element that blended with other forms of resistance. Complaints by agricultural workers about the way they were treated on the haciendas, and peasant resistance to land and water usurpations through litigation, riots, and rebellion, merged with banditry to challenge local elite efforts at social control. Although they were very different forms of expression, all those activities disrupted the economic aspirations of landlords. The idea of "social banditry" implies that those engaged in it were doing more than simply committing random acts of crime motivated by self-interest and personal aggrandizement. Instead, I find it significant that official correspondence overwhelmingly stated that bandits came from local communities, hid there, and exerted a corrupting influence on the rest of the rural working-class population, as opposed to menacing or terrorizing them.

Government instability and reactionary activity against the Liberals allowed for the increasing banditry, lawlessness, and disorder on the part of Morelos campesinos. Peasants and workers took advantage of the situation, pressing their demands and taking the kind of un-sponsored action that Álvarez had warned might occur, although it was unsustained and lacked a declared agenda. Peaceful protest activities emerged too. For example, a political action committee appeared in Cuernavaca district to represent pueblo rights, while rural communities sent representatives to Mexico City to research land titles at the Archivo General de la Nación. But the widespread social banditry, anti-Spanish threats, robbery, murder, and assaults on property, drew the most attention and fueled fears of an all-out rebellion.[23]

Those violent outbursts were just the most obvious expression of a more constant and ongoing struggle that saw so many of Morelos's pueblos actively litigating land disputes, writing petitions to state authorities, and sending delegations to the archives during the nineteenth century.[24] The local authorities rarely sided with the pueblos, and after the passage of the Ley Lerdo, campesinos also forfeited their right to litigate communally. Stripped of legal rights that had helped hold them together in many disputes in the past, communal villagers became individuals with similar, but separate, claims in the eyes of the law.[25]

Destroying the juridical personality of the pueblo obviously left it vulnerable to outside incursions, but it also opened the door to a more insidious threat. A growing ethical and ideological dispute between communalist and individualist residents became a source of village strife. Wealthier vecinos sometimes saw the individual acquisition of land under the provisions of the Ley Lerdo as personally advantageous. Some may have viewed private ownership as the best way to escape poverty and backwardness. Poorer villagers, though, really had no chance to acquire anything through privatization because they lacked the resources. The story of privatization in Morelos, therefore, involved a widening hierarchy within the pueblos, on the one hand, and the piece-by-piece transfer of land from pueblos to hacendados, on the other. For the better off in the pueblos, the privatization may have represented freedom and opportunity, and many transfers were done legally. The ultimate effect of the laws of disamortization, though, was to allow the laws of the market to take over. Those with the most money got the most land.[26]

The results of the Lerdo law and Morelos's mid-nineteenth-century transformation lasted into the revolution. When Francisco Madero became president of Mexico after the fall of Díaz, he formed the Executive Agrarian Commission that sought to address the causes of the Zapatista rebellion in Morelos. Responding to interviews from the Madero regime's fact-finding commission in June 1912, the hacendado Luis García Pimentel offered a history of land transfer in Morelos in which he pointed to the process put in motion by the Ley Lerdo, and explained its legacy. As one of the largest landowners in the state, and one of the most articulate proponents of the special interests of that class, García Pimentel's vision of history reflected a social interpretation shared by other hacendados. That history provided the hacendado master narrative that explained how things got to be the way they were:

> The fundos legales, that were common property broken up into small parcels before the disamortization, are now the private property of the vecinos of the pueblos... the haciendas had nothing to do with this division....
>
> Before, the ejidos were held in common by all the vecinos of a pueblo, but the disamortization law affected them the same as it did the fundos legales, and the town councils of the pueblos divided a large part of the ejidos, calling them 'commonly divided lands' and the ejidos went on to become, in part, private property, ... and in many cases, the vecinos have sold parcels amongst themselves, and people from outside the pueblos have also acquired lands, including the

hacendados, but I believe they have always done so in accord with the law.... For my part, I have acquired pueblo lands on various occasions and I have my documents in perfect order and can prove the legitimacy of the acquisition.[27]

The conclusions of the Agrarian Commission appeared in an Informe by the head of the commission, Patricio Leyva, son of the first governor of Morelos and a candidate himself for that position in 1909. Leyva's job in 1912 was to explain the social bases of militant Zapatismo so that the Madero government could end it. The report he submitted offered an informed perspective on the history of the region based on a combination of personal experience, the previously mentioned hacendado surveys, and the access to information of a specially appointed government investigator. Despite the denials of the hacendados, Leyva found that the social revolution in twentieth-century Morelos *was* rooted in a deep agrarian problem that could only be understood in its larger historical context. His recommendations called for government recognition of local desires and a fundamental rethinking of the Liberal model of development in the Morelos countryside. Leyva believed that the Ley Lerdo and the general land privatization program of the preceding fifty-five years lie at the heart of the social problem that spawned the revolution in Morelos.

> The way in which the vecinos of the pueblos of Morelos have lived is not favorable for the development of individualism. Most of the inhabitants have seen the day-by-day growth of large properties through the absorption of small property.
>
> Most of the people of the pueblos of Morelos, through traditions, through custom, through their lack of education, through the local government's lack of protection of the small property owner, through the political power of the large landowners that puts in their hands all the means necessary to absorb the small land holder, through the absolute lack of a decent system of agricultural credit that would facilitate the resources necessary for their labors... [because of these things] they cannot be individualists, and have to opt for communal property because of the advantages

that it brings them; not least of which is the common defense of their interests.[28]

Leyva's thinking represented a continuum that stretched from Governor Arizcorreta to Ponciano Arriaga and Juan Álvarez, and to Leyva. The issues involved, though, only gained wider attention when repression failed to squelch armed insurrections and forced more enlightened members of the ruling class to consider alternatives. Leyva captured the essence of the problem and, although progressive relative to many members of the Mexican elite, he, Madero, and other state builders of the revolution still wanted the Morelos peasantry to accept small-scale private ownership. Leyva's work for Madero's commission represented an elite response to pressure from below, not a plan of social improvement conceived of and initiated from above.

Although it is difficult to document in a quantitative way, the Ley Lerdo provided a legal basis for the privatization of common lands from the mid-1850s through the Porfiriato. For example, when the Spaniard Ildefonso López denounced some land in Jojutla and Tlalquitenango in 1868, the vecinos of those places challenged him, saying that "it has come to our attention that Don Ildefonso López has denounced part or our lands." They pointed out that they had denounced the land themselves in 1862 in accordance with the Ley Lerdo and said that they would have done it earlier if the political chaos in the country had not precluded it. They managed to defend their holdings because they gave up communal claims. Instead, each person denounced a plot valued at eighty pesos a piece. The court decision in their favor held them up as a model, suggesting that all *terrenos de repartimiento* and fundos legales should be divided in the same way. The problem, though, was that when small holders faced hard times due to sickness, a death, drought, or some other misfortune, the circumstances might force them to sell the plot. When that happened, someone in the community could buy it, but a hacendado might too. As a result of falling prey to these kinds of market forces, pueblo holdings were whittled away little by little and hacendado holdings increased. By the end of the century most of the communally held land left in Morelos was in the higher northern elevations, not in the sugar-producing lowlands, and timber-rich mountain areas were being coveted by private investors.[29]

Hacendados were not the only threat. A series of denuncios in Yautepec demonstrated another problem the Lerdo law created.

Outsiders began moving into communities and purchasing nation-alized lands previously used by locals. José Serrano, Agustino Sayavedra, Rafael Rodríquez, and Albino García all came from Cuautla and denounced and received lands in Pueblo Nuevo, Yautepec, that had been parts of *cofradias* (a religious brotherhood or confraternity) there. At the same time, Mariano Romero denounced another plot that he claimed had belonged to the cofra-dia de la Virgen del Rosario and therefore had fallen under the rubric of nationalized lands, but the vecinos of Yautepec insisted that it belonged to the naturales of the barrio San Juan. These dis-putes all appeared in 1875, almost twenty years after the Ley Lerdo. They indicate two things. First, the initial efforts to apply the Ley Lerdo met with enough resistance that they were not fully imple-mented immediately. The Wars of the Reforma and then the French occupation followed soon after the law was introduced, which con-tributed to the delays until the late 1860s and early 1870s when the denunciations of corporate holdings began in earnest. Second, cases like these show that the effects of the law were not fleeting, but allowed for the continued assault on pueblo holdings for years to come.[30]

Some of the larger more ethnically mixed towns such as Jojutla, the largest and fastest-growing town in the hot lands of southern Morelos, experienced growing internal tensions. The introduction of rice paddies changed the local economy and probably contributed to the divisiveness. Some "indígenas" of the barrio of Nexpan accused the larger *ayuntamiento* (town council) of Jojutla of dispossessing them of their *tierras de labor* following the passage of the Ley Lerdo. They also complained that the ayuntamiento required them to pro-vide their labor services for the construction of the local school and then failed to pay them. The ayuntamiento did not deny the allega-tions, but responded with the countercharge that the barrio of Nexpan, comprised mainly of indígenas, was trying to take over all the good land in the area, even though they enjoyed ample access already. The barrio denied that, saying that their relationship with the town council had deteriorated so badly that, to their dismay, the ayuntamiento ordered one of Nexpan's *huertas* destroyed. The ayun-tamiento acknowledged the act and justified it by saying that the huerta lay outside the barrio's assigned land and that the vecinos could not have all the good land because they were unable to farm it all. The ayuntamiento then used the Liberal rhetoric of the day to level an increasingly common charge against communal land use, claiming that the indígenas of Nexpán represented an impediment to "fomento y progreso."[31]

Liberal ideas of progress and how to achieve it reached all the way down into local political power struggles. The Jojutla ayuntamiento echoed Mexican national elites when they complained that both native agriculture and attitudes stood in the way of the new national project of "growth and development." The complaints demonstrated that although ethnic identification could be overcome and different groups could at times find common ground, those cleavages persisted and sometimes fed intracommunity conflicts that were generally overshadowed by of the more violent encounters between vecinos and hacendados. The distaste that Jojutla's civic leaders expressed for the indígena barrio revealed the growing social complexity of larger towns in rural Morelos and the local power of mestizos, as well as the ethnic conflicts within communities that sometimes surfaced as they responded to new conditions. The increasing importance of rice cultivation and the rising commercial value of the land arond Jojutla heightened the tensions.

Some better-off villagers in Morelos acquired individual properties, and a number of small-scale farmers did emerge that way, but a far greater amount of land was transferred to outsiders with the money to purchase larger tracts. The resulting unequal redistribution of land exacerbated economic differences among pueblo residents and encouraged the arrival of additional unsympathetic outsiders. The principle of economic individualism jeopardized the needs of the larger community. The assault on communal property forced villagers to seek more work on the great estates in order to survive. Even though the laws were on the books and represented the intentions of the nation's modernizing elites, popular resistance, civil war, and another foreign invasion delayed a more widespread application of the disamortization laws.[32]

The citizens of Hueyapán, for instance, challenged the elite recipe for modernity by defending their claims the way most other communities did. They protested the denunciation of the rancho de Santa Cruz by an individual named Jacobo Sánchez, claiming that it formed part of their *común repartamiento*. Sanchez said that the rancho fell under the rubric of "bienes nacionalizados" because it belonged to a cofradía. Hueyapán sits in the mountainous northeastern corner of Morelos near the border with Puebla, and the villagers there said that each of them worked a small plot that they inherited from their parents who had "possessed it in the same manner" since "*tiempo immemorial.*" They continued to invoke traditional arguments and said that the privatization laws contained safeguards "for native Mexicans, such as us," which was true. But, they also tried to turn the new laws on their head and defend their communal title, saying that since they were already individually working their "*lotes,*" there was no need to go through the redundancy of seeking individual titles. Similarly, during 1865 and 1866, Doroteo Lazo represented the vecinos of Tezoyuca who protested that the haciendas San Vicente and Chiconcuac had unjustly acquired their land and water by using the Ley Lerdo to denounce them. And, at the same time, José L. García, the *alcalde auxiliar* of Texcala, asked the government to grant his pueblo more land because the fundo legal was inadequate to maintain the population.[33]

Everyone—hacendados, Liberals, Conservatives, and pueblo vecinos—realized that the pueblos had to maintain a significant portion of land if their self-sufficient lifestyle and local autonomy were to survive. The key to the remarkable cultural durability of communal villages in the face of spreading commercial agriculture over the years had been their ability to hold onto their communal entitlements. By the middle of the nineteenth century, though, the traditional pueblo stood marked for extinction.

The Paradox

Despite widespread resistance to the new order, the rural population did not act as a unified whole. Some aligned themselves with the Liberals; others supported the Conservatives, even though they had generally represented interests anathema to the rural working classes. The two main elite factions vied for campesino support as information reached Governor Riva Palacio in August 1857 that Conservative forces in Morelos were attempting to rally the indígenas to their side. That effort could be expected to meet with some success because of the widespread discontent generated by efforts to institute the new land laws.[34]

Campesinos were caught in a paradox. They were being squeezed by the Liberal reforms, but at the same time many of the hacendados in the area who had long-standing hostilities with neighboring villagers and records of advocating repressive social measures instead of seeking conciliation, were staunch Conservatives. Pío Bermejillo and García Icazbalceta were two of them. For example, October 1, 1857, one hundred armed men raided and sacked García Icazbalceta's haciendas of Santa Anna Tenango and San Ignacio. The local authorities failed to act due to a declared shortage of manpower and funds, although that hesitancy on the part of Liberal bureaucrats on the scene may have stemmed from García Icazbalceta's support of the Conservatives.[35] Even as these outbursts shook the countryside, it should be noted that most rural people remained aloof from them and still looked to hacendados like Bermijillo and García Icazbalceta for material security. They accepted a paternalistic relationship that offered shelter, access to a plot of land, the lease of plow animals, security during food shortages, and the possibility of small loans in hard times. Those benefits came in exchange for their labor, loyalty, and year-around service to the hacendado.

The multilayered changes taking place provoked myriad reactions at the popular level. As resistance to the government spread, the inability of authorities to maintain order was exposed. The negative impact of the Reform laws on the pueblos caused more campesinos to feel disillusioned and become attracted to the Conservative side. Others, remembering old wrongs, supported a popular Liberalism like that of Juan Álvarez.[36]

The Wars of the Reforma, 1858–1861

Conservative resistance to the Liberal Reforms, especially to the laws attacking church property, led to the Wars of the Reforma. Once the conflict reached Morelos, localized peasant unrest became a struggle within a larger arena. Events in Morelos reflected a mix of national politics with local conditions and history. "Bandits" in Jonacatepec and Tlaltizapan began attacking Spaniards in a way totally disproportionate to their percentage of the population. Most Spanish landowners had supported the royalists during the Independence Wars, the Conservatives after that, and then collaborated with the Americans during the U.S. invasion. That mattered to people like Juan Álvarez, who saw how national struggles merged with local conflicts. For most local folks, however, issues of national politics, while not irrelevant, were secondary to their more immediate concerns. Nevertheless, the two came together anyway as antihacendado and anti-Spanish sentiment repeatedly surfaced as the most important factors behind local banditry and rebellion because Spaniards retained their power and privilege, even as the fighting over larger national concerns raged. Although collective action in Morelos generally lacked centralized leadership and a larger national objective at this juncture, it belonged to a larger whole that encompassed those concerns.

Aware of their past and hoping for a better future, campesinos acted, above all, pragmatically. It would be a mistake to categorize their actions as simply reactive, or to assume that they were being manipulated by social superiors without knowing what they were doing. To survive, they had to be shrewd and they had to adapt. They resisted elite initiatives that disadvantaged them and offered their own alternatives that usually blended ideas they adopted from outside with their own goals and aspirations.

The varied human geography of Morelos and the uneven changes from the Liberal reform created a labyrinth of variables in the region. Social unrest became broadly related to the differences between the temperate highlands and the semitropical lowlands. The highlands remained more heavily Indian, retained more lands and woods, and enjoyed greater self-sufficiency than the valley communities tied to the sugar economy. Highland villagers profited from the sugar industry by providing the sugar planters with products, including wheat, woods, cloth, and seasonal labor. They received work, outside income, clothing, tools, tropical fruits, and other foods from the valleys in return.[37]

During the mid-nineteenth century, the national government reinforced unequal ethnic relationships within and between communities because it tended to accord more political recognition to ethnically mixed villages than to more heavily Indian ones. The *cabeceras*, or county seats, in Morelos featured a more heterogeneous mixture of people, more economic and social complexity, and more political power. Indian pueblos and local churches gradually receded as the centerpieces of social and economic life in the sugar-producing zones. For example, Jojutla was just emerging as an ethnically diverse and increasingly important political and economic center in the south of the state. The change came about for a variety of reasons related to commerce and increased rice production around the town that made it more prosperous. As a result, Jojutla eventually displaced Tlaquiltenango, the old cabecera, and became the most important commercial center in the region. Meanwhile, other communities in south-central Morelos, like San Salvador Miacatlán, San Gabriel, El Puente, and Temixco turned into industrial subsidiaries and sources of supplementary labor for the adjacent sugar mills and haciendas. Meanwhile, the *tiendas de raya* on the haciendas further diluted the importance of pueblo markets and weakened the communities by capturing much of the hacienda-worker trade.[38]

Even though they were more removed, mountainous temperate areas, including Tepoztlán, had old disagreements with hacendados and pueblo resistance was not limited to the sugar-producing zones of the tierra caliente. People in the highlands maintained a greater degree of autonomy and enjoyed a more balanced relationship with the haciendas, but found that the hacendados and other timber interests had their eyes on the forests that the pueblos had used for centuries. Their mutually beneficial trade relationships with the lowlands mitigated their differences with most major sugar growers, but their timber attracted attention while their linguistic and other cultural differences increased mutual suspicions.

A riot broke out on the heels of the Ley Lerdo in September 1857 in Tepoztlán. The rioters singled out the town's richest man, Don Felipe Gómez, and killed him. Officials in Yautepec, lying southeast and below Tepoztlán, feared that the rioting Tepoztecos would head their way to settle an old land dispute with the owner of the hacienda Oacalco. Yautepec officials noted the "bellicose character" of the Tepoztecos, fearing the episode would ignite an uprising in their own town. Memories of angry crowds committing murder and causing mayhem haunted Yautepec's politicians. Only one year had passed since a band of sixty armed men audaciously attacked Manuel Escandón's hacienda, Atlihuayán, just south of town. Local authorities and landlords saw each subsequent incident as part of a larger problem, and it made them nervous. A number of bandit gangs operating around Yautepec distressed "law-abiding people" and spread fear. Armies of "wrongdoers infest(ed)" Morelos. Anxiety and insecurity spread until they created a general state of alarm. Public officials felt obliged to move about with armed escorts. People lay restless in their beds at night, and the sounds of gunshots jarred them from their sleep as they listened to armed men on horseback ride through the darkened streets. Other violent outbursts shook Cuautla, Jonacatepec, and Cuernavaca, even though those places had plenty of soldiers and police there to protect them. The *gente decente* of Yautepec lived in fear, even as they plunged ahead in support of the transitions that was creating the social discord in the first place.[39]

The growing turmoil caused by bandit activity, riots, and the civil war divided the gente decente, the police, and the army, paralyzing their ability to deal with miscreants. "Immorality" ruled in Morelos from Yautepec, south. Robbery and murder were the order of the day. Yautepec's town officials shared a narrow analysis regarding the rampant lawlessness that absolved themselves and singled out "Spaniards" as the scapegoats.[40]

News of a large reunion of bandits at a nearby hacienda reinforced fears that the riots up in Tepoztlán could spill over into the Yuatepec Valley. The large number of bandits generated panic and a rumor, believable to many, that they intended to sack Yautepec. Between rioters, bandits, and pronunciados, tension permeated the Morelos countryside. The visiting Pal Rosty felt it in Cuernavaca and noted the disintegrating social conditions in his diary. Landlords, Spaniards, and the petite bourgeoisie felt it too, and they had no sense of confidence or security, as authorities maintained order with difficulty. People were being murdered every day and, as Rosty saw it, politics frequently served as an excuse for that crime, allowing people to act on their emotions and then try to legitimate them. He reached the same conclusion as Yautepec's local officials who believed that Mexicans were committing these crimes under the pretext that they hated the "Gachupínes" and wanted to exterminate them from the country.[41] That might have been true, but it was not just Spaniards who were victimized. "Criollos" and other foreigners were also killed and robbed, a fact that the foreigner Rosty naturally noted. During his three days in Cuernavaca, he saw six murder victims buried in a town of only fifteen thousand. One night he witnessed the arrival of a panicked priest from a neighboring pueblo who sought refuge in Cuernavaca because the people in his town had driven him out, threatening to kill him. The next night people from a nearby hacienda fled to the relative safety of the city in front of advancing pronunciados. Uneasy, Rosty left Cuernavaca late one night with an experienced mule driver to navigate the dangerous route back to Mexico City, hoping to slip through unnoticed by the gangs of armed men roaming the roads.

The nature of violent crime and the pattern evidenced seemed clear. It was as obvious to Rosty as it was to the subprefect of Yautepec and to García Icazbalceta, and it had been just as clear to Gabriel de Yermo and Lucas Alamán before them. Regardless of their causal analysis, they all knew who the targets of popular outrage were. Sharecroppers, peasants, and day laborers were not the ones who lay awake at night worrying about becoming the victims of collective violence in Morelos. Peasants and workers might be victimized by individual criminals or bothered for supplies, but most banditry and campesino militancy was directed against those who benefited from an unfair legal system and possessed what was viewed as ill-gotten gain. That group included Spaniards, some hacendados and their estate administrators who were widely perceived as cruel, as well as prosperous and arrogant shopkeepers, rich foreigners, abusive government officials, and others of wealth or authority. Civil unrest, banditry, and crime, although sometimes portrayed as random and unpredictable, grew because of the agrarian reform program and became a subtext to the civil war. The Reform laws sanctioned a land transfer that outraged sectors of the rural public. The emerging civil war removed the authority needed to control these sectors and created a space for their action.

Chapter Five

CIVIL WAR, THE FRENCH
INTERVENTION, AND
SOCIAL BANDITRY

Foreign invasions disrupted rural life in Morelos, but they did not stop the fundamental transition taking place from communal to commercial agriculture. The presence of French imperial forces during the 1860s added another element to the ethnic and cultural antagonisms that had characterized the region for years. Meanwhile, Conservatives violently opposed the alienation of church wealth as well as the imposition of Liberal ideology. They thought that the Liberals were attempting to break down social controls by instituting free trade and implementing the notion of a social contract based on the ideals of liberty, democracy, and equality, for which they believed Mexicans were unprepared. The Conservatives opposed a rationalist secular ideology and sought to maintain a greater degree of social hierarchy, including the caste system. Rejecting further dialogue with the Liberals, some Conservatives hoped to enforce their reactionary vision with a return to monarchy.

Conservative reaction against the Liberal reforms gave rise to an organized military effort under the Plan of Tacubaya that led to the first phase of the Wars of the Reforma (1858–60) and saw Conservative armies score major victories and dislodge the Liberals from Mexico City. The Constitution of 1857 called for the chief justice of the Supreme Court to be next in line for the presidency, so Benito Juárez, as chief justice under the Liberals, declared himself the legitimate president of the country and the standard bearer of the constitution. He and other Liberal leaders fled and established a mobile government in exile. The Conservatives quickly received the diplomatic recognition of Spain, and civil war ravaged the country for the next three years. The widespread fighting drew a cross-section of the rural populace into the fray as civic militias. The U.S. government eventually recognized Juárez and the Liberals. After three years of fighting, a victorious constitutionalist army reentered the Mexican capital on Christmas Day 1860. Officially the civil war was over, but in reality it was not.

The Liberal government was harassed on two fronts. Conservative generals such as Tomás Mejía, Miguel Miramón, and Leonardo Márquez kept up resistance. At the same time, many rural people in Morelos remained distressed because instead of receiving help from the Liberal government like they had hoped, they suffered continued land incursions that were encouraged by the government's policies. At the same time though, the discharge of the Liberal-leaning national guard units who had helped in the triumph of the constitution, resulted in some disillusioned former guardsmen joining bandit gangs that grew in central Mexico and became notorious in Morelos.[1] Many campesinos, feeling they lacked effective political representation, economically disadvantaged, and frustrated in the courts, turned to arson, banditry, and rebellion.

Bandits

Bandits in Morelos sometimes traveled in groups of one hundred or more mounted men. They came from the villages and haciendas and had friends and family in the pueblos and on the sugar estates who served as informants and provided shelter for them when they were on the run. Bandits operated throughout the region, exacting tribute from the sugar estates. Some hacienda managers had to pay the bandits so they could work their fields and send their cargo wagons to Mexico City unmolested. Bandits sometimes also demanded money from villagers and even levied tolls on the roads. They often outnumbered the authorities who were, therefore, less than effective in subduing them.[2]

Lamberto Popoca y Palacios tracked bandits across Morelos and claimed to know many of the leaders. He lived to tell about it, and when the Mexican Revolution broke out in Morelos almost forty years later, he wrote a book subtitled, "Ayer como Ahora," that compared the bandit activity of the 1860s with the Zapatista uprising of 1910–12. Popoca y Palacios labeled both groups as gangs of common criminals. His account was dramatic and some stories probably apocryphal, but much of his memoir reinforced the impressions of other contemporaries and coincided with archival information generated by personal correspondence and press reports at the time.[3]

Along with Popoca y Palacios, the general population in Morelos called the bandits "*los plateados*," or the men in silver, because they adorned their clothing with flashy displays of silver. The plateados often dressed in black, with pants slit at the seam fastened with silver buttons linked by silver chains. They wore silver on their belt buckles, on their jackets, and around the brims of their hats. They outfitted their horses in silver, with silver stirrups and pommel, and some prodded their mounts with silver spurs. Forty years later, Zapata sometimes dressed in the same way.[4]

Bandit leaders roaming Morelos's country roads in the early 1860s were well known. The most famous were Salome Placencia, who operated around Yautepec, Silvestre Rojas, in eastern Morelos, and Felipe el Zarco and his brother Severo. Placencia, who was from Yautepec, reportedly lived with his family on the *real* of Manuel Escandón's hacienda Atlihuayán. It was close to rugged country and to hideouts offered by the craggy mountains and steep ravines to the north around Tepoztlán, as well as to a succession of sparsely inhabited hills that offered a good retreat toward Puebla. The plateados became legendary and wreaked havoc in Morelos. They kidnapped hacienda administrators and held them for ransom, or blackmailed them in exchange for not destroying their crops and looting the haciendas. At the estates San Vicente and Chiconcuac, no strangers to violence, the plateados took the general administrator, Don Cipriano del Moral, hostage and exacted a ransom in exchange for not burning the sugarcane fields that stood ready to be cut.[5]

Banditry in Morelos had a social character that represented the widespread disaffection in the countryside. Bandits were criminals, though, and they were widely despised by the authorities, the hacendados, their administrators, the petite bourgeoisie in the larger towns, and by some permanent hacienda workers, townspeople, and campesino villagers. Despite that, bandits still represented one manifestation of a more widespread rejection of conditions in the countryside that fueled the discontent of a significant segment of the population who tacitly supported banditry. Trying to understand the intensity of the Zapatista uprising in 1912, Patricio Leyva looked back on the troubled social history of Morelos. He began with the year 1856 and the imposition of the Ley Lerdo and the general unrest associated with it, including the murders at Chiconcuac. Leyva said that "from then until 1867 the flag of the revolution protected all of the discontented in the state, leaving them organized as bandits designated with the title of plateados." No perfectly clear picture emerges, but banditry in Morelos was more a response to social injustice than it was basic crime.[6]

The Intervention

Instead of much needed political stability at this juncture, Mexico plunged into a deeper national crisis. After President Juárez temporarily suspended payment on Mexico's foreign indebtedness, France, England, and Spain rejected his actions and agreed to intervene to recoup outstanding debts incurred by the war-plagued Mexican government. They seized the customs house in Veracruz in December 1861, in order to confiscate Mexico's revenues from foreign trade and exact payment. The venture quickly exceeded its initial parameters though. The British and Spanish merely intended to collect a debt, but the French emperor, Louis Napoleon, attempted to install a puppet monarchy in Mexico. With the United States embroiled in its own civil war and unable to resist a European incursion on its border, the enterprise turned into an imperial invasion by France, like others conducted under Louis Napoleon in Southeast Asia at the same time.

Many Mexican Conservatives backed the invasion, and some leaders lobbied the French government, other European states, and the pope to help them defeat the Liberals and place a European aristocrat on a Mexican throne. Some even hoped that Mexico could be annexed to France, but the idea of installing a monarchy prevailed. The English and Spanish withdrew in early 1862, while French troops moved from the Veracruz coast up the central plateau towards Mexico City. The Liberal government prepared to defend itself in the name of Mexican sovereignty while the defeated Conservatives turned to the invaders.

The stunning defeat that Mexicans dealt the French at Puebla on May 5, 1862, in the famous battle known by its date, the Cinco de Mayo, sent the French army in retreat back to Veracruz. It then received supplies and reinforcements from an embarrassed French government. The victory at Puebla stymied the French advance for a year, but by June 1863, the Liberals were once again forced to abandon the capitol. The French occupied Mexico City and fanned out in all directions, seizing control of roads, towns, and provincial capitols.

Popular Defense

Local Liberal leaders throughout Mexico tried to rally peasants and rancheros to generate a popular resistance to the invasion. A pattern developed similar to the one that had surfaced in opposition to the American occupation fifteen years earlier. Many plateados in Morelos temporarily joined ranks with government forces and operated as guerilla armies. The plateados and other Morelos bandit gangs participated in the battles of "*la calavera*" and "*mal páis*," but lacking real military training and heavy guns, a professional army could readily disperse them in traditional combat. The plateados responded by doing what they did best, which was to carry out surprise attacks, ambushes, and nighttime raids. They joined local resistance leaders in nearby Puebla in a sustained armed struggle. The French military chased them when they found them, but the plateados were hard to catch. They disappeared into the hills, or became anonymous faces in the villages and towns.[7]

A change began to take place in Morelos and among the bandits themselves because the French invasion partially legitimized banditry and resistance. For example, the plateados took Yautepec in May 1862, and their flamboyant leader Salome Placencia was named prefect by Liberal leaders in Mexico City. Nervous town fathers in Yautepec rejected the move and called for his replacement. But in broad daylight on the town square in front of numerous witnesses Placencia shot down the man sent to take his post. He then fled on horseback through the streets with soldiers in pursuit. He returned the same day with more than three hundred men, and his opponents abandoned the town. So long as the bandits directed their activities against the French and other foreigners, especially Spaniards, and did not abuse the pueblos, they did not incite an organized reaction from peasants and workers in the Morelos countryside. They did, however, outrage the hacendados, and pueblos suspected of sympathizing or harboring plateados were punished harshly. Forces paid for by the hacendados burned the pueblo of Tecumán near the spring Las Estacas because the plateados sought refuge there.[8]

With the French occupation in progress, the plateados under Silvestre Rojas raided the wealthy Spanish-owned and French-administered hacienda Calderón, near Cuautla and southeast of Yautepec in late 1863. They stole 122 mules and an unspecified amount of silver from the tienda de raya. New levels of resentment for the French blended with the old anti-Spanish sentiment. The French administrator of Calderón, Señor Sourquet, naturally asked the local authorities to help recover his stolen property. As with much of the bandit activity in the area, authorities suspected that disgruntled hacienda employees had helped the plateados. They suspected two employees in particular because they had disappeared the day before the robbery, and because witnesses claimed they saw them with the bandits. But when it came time to track down the bandits the French administrator found, to his disgust, that diligent law enforcement was suddenly lacking.[9]

The military commandant in Cuautla initially replied to administrator Sourquet's urgent request for police action by saying that he could not divert men away from the town because the plateados posed a threat to the entire region, not just to one hacienda. Sourquet complained bitterly that the prefect of Cuautla was not doing his best to apprehend the "guilty parties."[10] Another twenty-four hours elapsed, giving the bandits, who relied on their knowledge of the back roads and woods of Morelos for survival, ample time to either disappear into the hills or ride to Puebla.

Sourquet's appeals to higher authorities finally brought the commandant to the hacienda at the head of seventy mounted men drawn from two sections of the Jonacatepec and Yautepec public security forces. That was an impressive detachment, but despite their numbers they did not immediately head off in pursuit. Sourquet noticed that the police did not seem particularly determined to apprehend the criminals. The Frenchman told them that the bandit gang fled south, but the commandant took his forces north.

Whether Sourquet was more dismayed or enraged one can only guess. He was totally frustrated, and when he finally requested to personally lead part of the men on a pursuit to the south, he was rebuffed. He notified the absentee owner of Calderón, a wealthy Spaniard living in Mexico City named Don Juan Alonso, of the situation. Alonso wrote and reminded the local authorities that he paid two hundred pesos a month to the "*fuerzas rurales*" for protection from "the bandits that infest[ed] the district," and he expected those forces to do their job.[11]

The social climate in which this episode took place was complex. The context, however, did not matter to the Spanish owner and the French administrator, both of whom expected the Mexican police force to energetically pursue the marauders. The imperfect police performance hinted at the local commander's reluctance to serve the two foreigners. Yet, higher-ups sent seventy mounted men to protect the hacienda, which meant that somebody was willing to help them and wanted the perpetrators caught. The fact that the bandits received aid and shelter in the countryside also meant that they had at least some support there. The failure of the police to try to track them down probably meant that not only did they not feel like helping Sourquet and Alonso, but also that they may have even felt some solidarity with the bandits, at least given the particulars of this instance.

Another wealthy Spaniard, Ignacio Cortina Chávez, owned the large hacienda Tenextepango, lying in the southern part of the Cuautla sugar valley, and he also ran into trouble with the plateados when he contracted to lease his hacienda to José Leonardo Pereda and José Aguayo. The parties signed the six-year lease agreement in the summer of 1866. Señor Aguayo agreed to assume the role of administrator of the hacienda, but upon his arrival he found the hacienda occupied by "the bandits known as the plateados."[12] The bandits brazenly prevented him from taking over the hacienda and remained headquartered there, denying him all the rights and responsibilities he had agreed to assume as the renter. Fearing for his life, Aguayo left. It appeared to him that the hacienda had been overrun for "quite some time" and was in the permanent hands of the bandits. Government officials, despite all their resources, found it impossible to dislodge the plateados even though they knew they were there. Aguayo returned to Mexico City and appraised the absentee landlord, Cortina Chávez, of the situation on his property. The bandits' open defiance of both the property owners and the state challenged and upturned the more traditional social relations of power between rich and poor, hacendado and campesino.[13]

Bandit activity during the 1860s caused hacendados so much trouble that they and other "comfortable" citizens, like the leaders of Cuautla and Cuernavaca, agreed to privately fund an even more specialized and, they hoped, responsive, rural police force. The fear of rural crime was so pervasive that local officials in Cuautla and some of the smaller towns raided their municipal treasuries in order to support extra police. That decision came in response to the brazen disregard for authority, including a daring jail break late on a rainy night in

October 1864, when three men armed with pistols and daggers scaled the wall of the jail in Tetecala, overpowered the guards, and freed twenty prisoners, including Crispin Rojas and Genaro Arellano. Crispin Rojas shared the last name of the plateado leader Silvestre, and Genaro had the same name as the locally famous national guard leader Manuel Arellano, known for defending the pueblos during the U.S. invasion.

Official responses to banditry were mixed. The sometimes ambivalent attitude of local officials toward a wave of rural violence that was linked to the guerilla effort against the French occupation may have demonstrated where they stood on the issue of the civil war. Some officials in Morelos passively resisted assisting Sourquet in the apprehension of the plateados, while others sided with the landlords and, under intense pressure, opted to serve the interests of the French.[14]

Maximilian von Hapsburg, the archduke of Austria and cousin of Louis Napoleon, arrived in Veracruz in May 1864 and, after a triumphant tour of carefully selected towns, the Conservatives crowned him emperor of Mexico. The Liberal government had been dispersed and its army routed, but the war was really just beginning. The presence of French armies, the new imperial authority, and Maximilian's frequent personal presence in Cuernavaca imposed a superficial sense of order on Morelos. But the waves of land litigation, public disturbances, and banditry continued. Although distinct modes of expression, they were all manifestations of the ongoing transformation taking place.

Life and Work on the Haciendas

Despite major disruptions caused by civil war, foreign invasion, and social upheaval, many sugar haciendas managed to perform quite well. The haciendas San Miguel Treinta and Zacatepec offered an example of the changes taking place during the 1860s. The Treinta occupied the southern reaches of the Cuernavaca Valley near Tlaltizapán and Jojutla, and increased its production of sugar by five thousand loaves between 1864 and 1865. The Spanish owners, Cándido Guerra and Alejandro Arena, added one thousand cones for drying and crystallizing the sugar to the three thousand they already had. Arena also owned the nearby hacienda Zacatepec, which increased production from twenty thousand to thirty-three thousand loaves of sugar during the same time span. Greater capital investments, like a new irrigation canal, expanded the amount of productive land and fueled the increases in production, and, more importantly for the hacendado, profits. Zacatepec generated 18,394 more pesos in income from sugar sales in 1865 than it had the previous year. Besides raising and processing sugarcane, Arena's workers cultivated orchards of coconut, orange, and coffee trees and planted twenty-nine banana trees imported from Costa Rica.[15]

Hacendados had good reason to push modernization forward. Although Arena spent fifty thousand pesos on labor costs and material improvements, he regained 36 percent of his investment in the first year and increased the overall value of his estate. He purchased new equipment for the *casa de calderas*, where workers installed new filters, storage tanks, and a crusher for the cane fiber. Arena not only improved existing lands through irrigation projects, he also bought a new tract of land called Chicomocelo and annexed it to the estate. Although the exact size of Arena's property is not clear, it is certain that he was expanding and modernizing the industrial operations. Hacendado successes in those regards, especially territorial expansion, increased social tensions across Morelos.[16]

Despite increased employment opportunities on the estates, people often resented the change in lifestyle and loss of independence caused by hacienda growth. The process involved more than changing material conditions. Work on the sugar haciendas ran in cycles, with long spells of unemployment when hacendados cut their work forces radically. The hacienda Acamilpa, just northwest of the town of Tlaltizapán, for example, employed about twenty-five people for irrigating fields and planting seeds during the month of March but only retained three workers for this task in December. The number of gañanes (day laborers) also varied widely, ranging from seven to thirty, depending on the season. Some workers earned cash wages, but only seasonally; they still had to find other work for part of the year. Workers from independent pueblos hoped to maintain their small plots of land and the limited degree of self-sufficiency they provided. The changeover in land tenure, though, made that option a fading one. A more likely outcome was seeking access to land from a hacendado. The result was that increasing numbers of people left their villages and moved onto the estates. As haciendas like Zacatepec and Treinta expanded and acquired more fields, they surrounded nearby villages, limiting the ability of settlements to absorb natural population growth. Hacendados compounded the problem by continuing to claim that pueblos such as Anenecuilco, for example, were not really pueblos but were merely hacienda settlements that had forgotten their origins.[17]

Morelos had a relatively dense population, but resistant Indian villages offered enough of an alternative to hacienda labor that hacendados periodically complained about labor scarcity. This may have led to some debt peonage in the region, although little archival evidence of this exists in hacienda records. However it did result in the paying of scrip instead of cash on many haciendas. It seems that with time, the use of debt decreased as dependency on the haciendas resulted from their rising domination of land and other resources and there was no need to hold a peon in debt.

Independent villagers enjoyed greater freedom than hacienda dependents. Seasonal work on the haciendas had grown in major proportions, attracting laborers from nearby settlements with diminished resources and from mountain villages with naturally limited agricultural possibilities. A system emerged in which some people became *capitanes* who recruited landless or land-poor villagers to migrate as a group to the haciendas for seasonal work as jornaleros. Population growth, combined with the loss of land resulting from hacienda expansion, increased competition for work within the pueblos. The haciendas emerged as the most viable alternative and attracted increasing numbers of people from pueblo populations that were outstripping their old fundos legales.[18]

The changing conditions left some pueblos unable to pay their head taxes. As early as the 1840s, the leaders of the town of Mazatepec in southwestern Morelos told the tax-collecting authorities in Cuernavaca that they could not make their tax payments in cash, and Anenecuilco had the same problem. Many vecinos from Mazatepec worked on the hacienda San Salvador Miacatlán, where the hacienda paid them in scrip redeemable only at the company store. Mazatepec, although nominally independent, had become economically reliant on the hacienda for jobs. As a result, the pueblo's ability to function as an independent political unit was in danger.[19] Although scrip payments were common, the hacendados did not pay all of their employees in chit monies. Salaried employees, like administrators, received their pay in cash. During the 1860s the owner of the hacienda Acamilpa paid most of his employees their weekly salaries in cash. That arrangement included the administrators, mechanics and industrial workers in the mill, domestics and clerks in the big house, as well as the carpenters, gardeners, and cowboys. The pay for the lower-status field workers, however, who lived in the shacks that formed the settlements on the estate, and their counterparts from the neighboring pueblos, was a mixture of currency and scrip.[20]

On the other side of Morelos, at the hacienda Acamilpa, *macheteros*, or cane cutters, earned two reales a day; *cargadores de caña*, the transportation workers, were paid four reales a day; *trapicheros*, or mill workers, received three and a half reales a day; and *volteadores*, the men who worked with the finished sugar turning it into loaves, made three reales for their day's work. These positions were all seasonal, and many of the people who filled them, like those who came in groups from outside villages, worked for a time and then left. Others, however, remained on the estate the year round.[21]

The relations of production on Morelos's sugar haciendas were changing during the latter half of the nineteenth century. The stratified and alienating nature of estate work, and the uncertainty of alternative options, translated into a new social hierarchy whose impact reached well beyond the boundaries of the estates. On the sugar haciendas, only administrative personnel, skilled workers, and a few resident laborers had any stability or security. As employers, many hacendados felt they met their obligations to their employees' needs when workers were injured, needed child care, or were weakened by disabilities, illness, and old age. Those hacendado services replaced the mutual assistance communal villages traditionally practiced. But what the hacendados saw as their own beneficence did little to actually improve conditions for workers, who experienced poverty, illiteracy, economic dependency, and short, hard lives. Meanwhile, only upper-strata personnel on the estates could count on work all year.[22]

Administrators and some privileged permanent workers had a personal stake in the successful operation of the hacienda and were more closely associated with the hacendados than with the employees. Administrators in Morelos earned as much as 160 pesos a month while day laborers at the same hacienda received between two and four reales a day. The vast economic differences often meant ostentation on one side and, almost always, penury on the other. Deep resentments divided Morelos's workers from their employers and labor bosses. Those conditions reinforced two separate and often antagonistic lifestyles and cultures.[23]

As a result, the administrators of large estates such as Acamilpa, Calderón, Treinta, and Zacatepec shared the aspirations and views of their employers vis-à-vis the ethnically, culturally, economically, and socially distinct workers. Hacienda administrators, like the owners themselves, were often Spaniards or criollos, and since they were responsible for the smooth functioning of the estates, including enforcing work discipline, workers often saw them as arrogant and abusive, and they despised them for it. Disgruntled hacienda workers and marginalized dependent residents on the estates joined with resentful independent villagers defending their patrimonies to create a constant undercurrent of social and political tension. That situation fed the antihacendado behavior for which Morelos was notorious.[24]

The Junta Protectora

Much to the chagrin of the church and other Mexican Conservatives who supported the French intervention during the 1860s, Maximilian failed to offer Mexico a declaration of Conservative principles, nor did he annul the Reform laws. Instead, he instituted a series of measures intended to ameliorate the condition of campesinos and win popular support in the process. He outlawed corporal punishment on the estates and most debt peonage, and he reinstated the right of communal property ownership. He also decided that some rural communities lacking ejido lands should receive them. Maximilian created a review board, the Junta Protectora de las Clases Menesterosas (Protective Council of the Needy), to deal with disputes over land use and rights involving community property. Pueblos inundated the junta with land claims. Most of them told the board that their lands had been usurped, especially following the Ley Lerdo, and that they were trying to reclaim what was rightfully theirs.[25]

The pueblo of Atlacholoaya, about five miles to the southeast of Xochitepec, appealed to Maximilian and the Junta Protectora, insisting that they had a "natural right" to the land and water within the town limits as marked by their ancient titles. They informed the junta that they had lost much of their resources to the neighboring haciendas of Treinta Pesos, Chiconcuac, and El Puente. As a result, those haciendas totally surrounded the village and stifled its ability to grow. When the members of the junta read the following story from the "*vecinos indígenas*" from Atlacholoaya, it gave them a view of the larger process taking place in the Morelos lowlands:

> These small parcels must sustain the individual
> families comprising the town, and they have bad
> consequences because they are not really sufficient,
> but the town itself must get its wealth from the labor of
> every one of its vecinos and their families and to satisfy
> other debts and social functions from the products of
> these miserable plots of overworked land. Naturally, as
> a result, seeking a better situation, some individuals

> break from the whole of the community to look for a
> more comfortable life, pursuing various avenues, and
> in the meantime their generation grows and the land
> gets broken up into smaller pieces, and there is no real
> place for the natural growth of the population and the
> progress of the town.[26]

The statement allowed the junta to visualize the life of a pueblo as its vecinos saw it. They considered it an organic, living, consuming, and producing thing, and like the people living in the Morelos countryside, it had to struggle to survive. Their assessment of local conditions included a variety of variables such as demographics, civic responsibility, and the ability to maintain a community both financially and in accordance with customary and still desired practices. It proved a difficult task.

During the U.S. invasion of the late 1840s, the vecinos and "*alcaldes*" (mayors) of Atlacholoaya had relocated some land markers accompanied by the commandants Don Manuel Arellano and Don José de Leon, who backed their action. This was the same Manuel Arellano who commanded a national guard unit under Juan Álvarez. After the American withdrawal and the dispersal of the guard units, the hacendado moved the markers back. But the French presence and a renewed breakdown in central authority inspired the vecinos to again try to relocate the boundaries where they believed they belonged. When they did, a skirmish broke out and the hacienda guards at Chiconcuac shot and killed three vecinos and wounded others. Nonetheless, the townspeople still hoped to reassert their prerogatives and looked to the Junta Protectora for verification of their land reclamation under Arellano. The junta ruled that the people were indeed entitled to some of the land they had repossessed to meet their fundo legal. The junta explained that their ruling was intended to protect the "*clases menesterosas*" from the hardships they would incur without the land and to avoid a long legal battle.[27]

The Unified Pueblos

The socioeconomic transformation underway and the breakdown in state authority brought new developments in the sugarcane-growing valleys south of Cuernavaca. The towns of Xiutepec, San Francisco Izacualpan, Tesolucan, Xochitepec, Acatlipa, Cuentepec, Teclama, Alpuyeca, Ahuehuecingo, and Atlacholoaya joined together in a large joint protest against land and water dispossessions incurred at the hands of hacendados in their area, including the owners of Chiconcuac and Temisco. Residents of those pueblos resented the land takeovers and the destruction of their crops, but the fact that hacendados and their administrators punctuated their actions with verbal abuse and ethnic slurs added insult to injury. Many pueblos harbored bad feelings from the past, but reached new levels of outrage because they felt degraded by hacendado efforts to hang onto vestiges of the old caste hierarchy that treated the vecinos like second-class citizens.

The unified pueblos represented a large and important geographic and cultural space running the length of the Cuernavaca Valley. They included various ethnic groups from different communities coming together to voice their opposition to what they considered the excesses impacting all of them.[28] Their coalition demonstrated that the mentality in the commercialized sugar zones of Morelos was not just "local" or inward-looking in nature, but was more broadly based and inclusive.

People in Xochitepec, for example, like the other pueblos, identified and thought of themselves as members of their own community and recognized their own local leaders and history, worshiped their own patron saint, and participated in their own fairs and local politics. But they also saw beyond their local boundaries and recognized they shared a common condition with their neighbors, and that allowed them to view each other as fellow citizens and act as joint litigants. At this removed date, we can only judge them by their actions. Their actions indicated that they realized that the changing world in which they lived affected more than their particular pueblo, and that they shared a common experience with others throughout the area. Submitting a petition with other pueblos during the mid-nineteenth century required a high level of interaction and mutual trust. Some pueblos may have preferred not to encumber their cases with that of others who may not have had as strong a legal position since rural communities frequently encountered contested status as pueblo or ranchería. The ethnic composition was an important factor to any claim. Hacendados had effectively argued that many would-be pueblos were really just settlements of mestizos and mulattos living on the private property of the hacienda and had no previously recognized rights to the land, and sometimes they were right. Complicating issues of ethnicity and the historical origins of a hamlet was the fact that some recognized pueblos lacked, or had simply lost, documents and land titles. Thus, joining forces had its risks.

The ethnic diversity of the unified pueblos revealed the changing social composition of the area, and a growing level of consciousness.

Xochitepec, for example, was more than 40 percent mulatto, 35 percent Indian, and 8 percent mestizo during the 1860s.[29] Cuentepec, Alpuyeca, Acatlipa, and Ahuehuetzingo, by contrast, were predominantly Indian. Despite their ethnic differences, all four joined the vecinos of Xochitepec. Their alliance overcame ethnic divisions and recognized that as vecinos and workers they confronted similar obstacles that transcended local concerns and divisive labels based on race and caste that had been imposed from above.

Campesino awareness extended well beyond the physical boundary markers delineating local space and encompassed a larger community that was not just imagined, but recognized.[30] The joint appeals to Maximilian's government also demonstrated a recognition of changing power relations at the national level, as well as their awareness of who could help them by limiting the negative influences on their everyday lives. In that sense, vecino efforts at organized self-defense mirrored those of the hacendados. Large landowners had often banded together because they recognized their own shared class interests and its ethnic overtones. They formed a privately funded mutual defense league of 364 carbine toting, mounted rural policemen to safeguard their social positions and to support the armed guards that each hacendado drew from among their loyal hacienda employees.[31]

The pueblo appeals to the Junta Protectora showed an appreciation of national power and meant that Maximilian received tacit recognition from at least some campesinos. At the same time, however, resistance to the French intervention also surfaced in the form of the plateados and others in Morelos. The situation was volatile and complex, with some pueblos in the countryside willing to recognize a foreign government for pragmatic reasons. Even though some of the philosophical elements of Liberalism attracted them, such as the *idea* of a decentralized government and more local control, the *reality* of land dispossession via the Liberal reforms appealed much less, and thus the villagers were willing to try their luck with the junta.

Although they squabbled amongst themselves, pueblo vecinos expected outsiders to respect their land grants from the colonial period. They believed that the old titles constituted "natural" or even "sacred" rights. Those rights formed part of their self-identity as "children" of their village, informed their sense of history, and gave a feeling of permanence over time. Pueblo vecinos often viewed encroachments on their entitlements as threats not only to the living inhabitants of a pueblo, but also to the legacy their ancestors left for them. They also tended to view attacks on traditional land entitlements as threats to despoil their children and future generations of their just inheritance. When pueblos entered litigation and said the land was "rightfully" theirs, they meant it in a moral sense more than a legal one.[32] Their lawyers expressed the convictions of their clients, sometimes with eloquence, but villagers and workers themselves demonstrated the depth of their commitment through their own actions like strikes, riots, cane burnings, and, ultimately, revolution. Those acts revealed, in a direct way, the values and goals given verbal expression in court documents.

Hacienda expansion, facilitated by the laws of privatization, exacerbated problems for independent villages by worsening tensions over land and other resources and caused pueblos such as Tesollucan, Acatlipa, and Izacualpan to outgrow their fundos legales. People living in these three settlements, like many others in Morelos, found themselves hemmed in with little chance to increase their farmlands and accommodate growth. Acatlipa, for example, was surrounded on all sides by the hacienda Temisco. By the mid-1860s, Temisco had encroached so much that it even included the graveyard next to the church in the center of town.[33]

Acatlipa's vecinos tried to meet the needs of a growing population with a shrinking land base. They repossessed some disputed land from the hacienda Temisco by planting it. The administrator of Temisco, Don Manuel Fernández, seemed to allow the repossession to go unchallenged, but he was only biding his time. He waited until the villagers cleared and planted the soil, and then appeared one day with a band of armed men. He ordered the freshly sowed bean fields destroyed, and the stone wall that the villagers had erected to mark their boundary leveled. The assault caught the villagers off guard, rendered their labor wasted, their fields ruined, and the food source that they needed destroyed.[34]

The vecinos appealed to the local authorities who refused to help and, instead, allowed the hacendado to recover the fields. Local officials condemned the pueblo vecinos as "perturbadores del orden publico," and dismissed them as criminals.[35] The townspeople became outraged at the entire matter, which they viewed as unjust and corrupt. Aware that other communities faced similar situations, they united with other pueblos and turned to Maximilian and the Junta Protectora for justice.

Acatlipa's actions demonstrated that pueblos sometimes instigated land disputes through efforts to repossess and occupy lands. The primary difference between their actions and those of the hacendados though, was that they usually took theirs because they felt that the land had been unjustly usurped from them at some point in the past. From their perspective, all they were doing was setting matters straight again. The French intervention provided the vecinos an opportunity to assert themselves because war made state support of the hacendados more tenuous. Pueblo vecinos recognized that fact and acted on it.

Acatlipa's case offers a good overview of the pattern of agrarian conflict during the period and the emotions involved. The vecinos told the junta that when the laws of disamortization took effect, the hacendado of Temisco seized "all the best lands" that the town was leasing to him and then suddenly claimed that he was the legitimate owner. The Lerdo law sanctioned his actions. This episode demonstrated some of the effects of the Ley Lerdo and the implications for the future. The pueblos, vexed in their efforts to defend their lands, resentful of the connivance of local officials with hacendados, and angry over general attitudes and treatment, protested the manipulation of the Ley Lerdo and took advantage of elite divisions to try to get back what they had lost. Frustrated and desperate, the vecinos of Acatlipa became so agitated in fact, that their lawyer ended one of his petitions by warning that without a "careful" and "just" ruling a "bloody uprising" could result. His statement did not ring hollow because it resonated with past events in the region and echoed similar warnings from Arizcorreta and Álvarez before him.[36]

At the time of the dispute, Acatlipa, like many pueblos in Morelos, was paying rents on lands which they claimed were actually theirs. This was common practice and represented a growing pattern in the state, exemplified here and at Atlatlahucan.[37] It was galling in and of itself, but became unbearable when the hacendado raised rents and imposed a new fee that he knew the vecinos could not afford in what the vecinos described as an effort to "destroy" the town.

In 1912, Ramon Corona, acting as representative for Morelos sugar hacendado, Ignacio de la Torre y Mier, son-in-law of Porfirio Díaz, attempted to deny that the haciendas had spread at the expense of the pueblos, but admitted that the haciendas Temisco and Calderón had purchased in cash and in the most correct manner, piece by piece, the total extension of "Acatlipa" and "San Pedro." His statements helped demonstrate one way that hacendados acquired previously inviolate pueblo holdings, and they showed the practical results of the Ley Lerdo. Back in 1866, the hacendado also tried to physically isolate Acatlipa by blocking the road the people used to communicate with their *cabecera municipal*.[38] A host of factors complicated the seemingly simple struggle over land and had long-lasting consequences.

The general proceedings involving Acatlipa coincided with the case brought by vecinos of Xochitepec. That pueblo's lawyers produced copies of the towns original land titles bearing the signature of Viceroy Luis de Velasco, who had granted the community "dos sitios de estancia para ganado menor" with detailed boundaries of their land entitlements. Xochitepec had been despoiled of a large amount of that land since, and the villagers felt that their "natural rights," and even their right to exist, were under attack. They wondered why the courts ignored their rights as citizens even after they produced their "primordial" land titles.[39]

Laws change, but pueblos in Morelos constantly fought for what they considered their "natural rights," above and beyond what was legal at any given time. Hacendado efforts to despoil communities, both before and then under the auspices of the Ley Lerdo, sometimes went beyond the law too, even though they had the courts on their side. The situation was fluid. The same pueblo and the same people might fight against the Americans or the French, attack haciendas, and present their activities in Liberal rhetoric one day, and then recognize Maximilian's government through their appeals the next. Villagers defended the nation, supported Liberal principles, and fought invading armies, but they were also very pragmatic. When they felt abandoned by the Liberal promise, they sought help where they could get it.

The pueblos of Xiutepec, Xochitepec, Acatlipa, Cuentepec, Ahuehuezingo, and others exercised a common, long-recognized strategy when they asked a central government to curb local abuses. Perceived mistreatment at the local-level had led to appeals to the central government, whether Royal or Republican, for centuries. That continued during the French intervention, as summarized by the legal counsel of the united pueblos in 1866: "As the representative of these towns I would like to say that they are convinced that the local authorities not only do not do anything on their behalf, but, on the contrary, when the pueblos try to recover lands that have been usurped from them by the hacendados the authorities create obstacles, and [by taking matters into their own hands] the case could arise that these pueblos become 'pertubadores del orden publico.'"

Community appeals to higher authorities regarding local abuses did not mean they were willing to give up local autonomy. An important change was taking place though. Pueblos in the colonial and early independence era had turned to central authorities mainly in hopes of remedying *local* problems, and they displayed little concern about larger regional issues. During the mid-nineteenth century, though, a widening consciousness emerged as villagers and rural workers became increasingly aware of their shared condition. That awareness encompassed a larger regional social space and provided a popular home-grown basis for modern nationalism. Local problems became tied to wider issues, the Liberals achieved their military victory against the French, and the pueblos engaged in the ultimate pragmatism and went with the winner. It was only then that their "nationalist" character began to coalesce. The most important part of that development was the interjection of campesino demands into the national dialogue and the part it played in shaping popular ideals of nationhood and justice. Their demands that the government recognize those ideals and meet its responsibility to its citizens represented the next difficult step in the making of modern Mexico.

Chapter Six

APATLACO AND THE MORELOS COUNTRYSIDE
Defining Citizenship and Creating a Nation

The uneasy transition from peasants into workers during the nineteenth century caused people to look back to an idealized image of the past. Changing conditions forced people to make choices between inherited communal values and a new way of life that emphasized commercial exchange over self-sufficiency, wage labor over collective farming, private property over the ejido, and the rights of the individual over the community. Campesinos accepted contemporary ideas concerning equal rights and citizenship, but they chafed under the harsh realities of land alienation. The cultural divide between themselves and their employers dampened the desire of many to assimilate into the new order.

When the residents of the small village of San Pedro Apatlaco petitioned the district court in Cuautla in late September 1864 to recognize

their settlement as a legally incorporated pueblo, the story they told illustrated the larger process going on all around them. They said their hamlet stood on the same ground where, for hundreds of years, their ancestors before them had lived and died. None of them could remember exactly when the settlement first appeared, but they were certain it was a legally constituted pueblo because the stone ruins of a colonial church still stood in their midst. Over the years, a growing agricultural and industrial sugar complex, called the hacienda Cuahuixtla, had surrounded that church, the community it was built to serve, and its attendant fundo legal (see Figures 4 and 5). The hacienda's presence extended beyond the loss of the fundo legal to the culture it supported. People from Apatlaco no longer *knew* that they made up a pueblo, they only thought they did, based on the remains of a crumbled old building.[1]

Throughout nineteenth-century Mexico people realized the integral role the church played in determining pueblo status, with all the rights, responsibilities, and privileges that recognition had entailed ever since the Spanish Crown issued land grants to settlements that accepted Christianity, built a church, and gave residency to a priest. However, those early colonial settlements had been comprised of Indians, and as the recognized inheritors of the land, they received

Figure 4.
Ruins of the sugar mill
at the hacienda
Cuahuixtla.

guaranteed access to water, woods, and fields sufficient to meet their needs and sustain their towns, even as their larger civilization was laid to waste.

Three hundred years later, Apatlaco stood in the heart of the steadily commercializing Cuautla sugar valley, just a few miles away from Emiliano Zapata's hometown of Anenecuilco. Many rural people in the area were descendants of African slaves, and townships of mulattos and mestizos had sprung up on or near the haciendas. As non-Indians, their communities did not predate the Spanish arrival and lacked the official status and protection awarded their Indian neighbors. By the mid-nineteenth century, many no longer carried any knowledge of their settlement's colonial legal status with them. Yet many rural workers living in hacienda settlements shared the ideals of the nearby independent pueblos. Those pueblos stressed local autonomy, peasant agriculture, and community integrity. But as the century wore on, those traditional aspirations became coupled with more modern calls for fair pay and better working conditions on the haciendas. That development reflected the concerns of a protoindustrial rural citizenry gradually changing into an agrarian working-class that was becoming increasingly dependent for their survival on the jobs available on the great estates.[2]

The Case and the Context

Sitting on the outskirts of the hacienda Cuahuixtla, Apatlaco, like other rural places in the Morelos lowlands, had literally become surrounded by the lands belonging to a vast sugar plantation. The absentee owner of Cuahuixtla, a Spaniard and wealthy Mexico City merchant and future railroad promoter named Manuel Mendoza Cortina, and his Spanish administrator Gumisindo González, considered Apatlaco nothing more than a squatter camp of undesirables living on the hacienda real. Mendoza Cortina had González divert the water that Apatlaco depended on away from the community, hoping to drive the people from the land and punish them for the independent attitude they expressed by petitioning for pueblo status in the first place. The water sustained their plots of corn and household gardens, and when González redirected it their crops were left to wither in the sun, and their independence with it.

Maximilian, the would-be emperor of Mexico, stepped into these local concerns as he sought to earn support for his government from the peasantry. The people of Apatlaco took advantage of the French intervention and acute domestic elite factionalism and submitted a petition to the Junta Protectora explaining that the administrator of the hacienda Cuahuixtla had conjured up "the new and barbaric idea

Figure 5.
Ruins of Cuahuixtla.

of throwing us off of our own land and from the places where we were born, and where our fathers, grandfathers and most remote ancestors before us were born, lived, and died."[3]

In order to achieve this malicious end, González first took away the water that "served for all the uses of life, [and] killed with his own hands" several head of cattle. When his efforts failed to make the people leave, González ordered them to collect their farm animals and possessions, take their families, and vacate their homes within ten days, or face eviction by force. People at Apatlaco did not want to move and, instead, sought government protection from the actions of the hacienda administrator.

Local concerns in Apatlaco outweighed abstract ideas about nationhood and nationalism. The residents chose to petition the Junta Protectora, thereby implicitly recognizing Maximilian and French authority in Mexico, yet still claiming their rights as Mexican citizens. They knew that seeking pueblo status would anger the hacendado and administrator, so González's threats worried them. They also knew they needed protection and asked the junta for it, saying, "as we now have proof of his violent character and have suffered many vexations, we do not doubt that he will follow through with his threats." Apatlaco's petition offered the junta a clear image of hacienda life as they knew it in the Morelos lowlands during the 1860s:

> The servants of the haciendas of the hotlands are divided into two classes; some still come from distant pueblos, work all week in the fields, and leave on Saturday to return the following Monday. For others the hacienda provides housing so that they are always there and there is no lack of labor services. The houses that are given to this second class of people are what is called in the tierra caliente *"el real"* and in the *tierra fria "la cuadrilla."* We of Apatlaco form in common, a pueblo and *we are self-governing.* Our plot of ground, or fundo, although within the hacienda is distinct of that part called "el real."[4]

The document bore the signature of resident Carmen Quintero, who would reappear many years later as a local elder watching the torch of resistance be passed on to Zapata in Anenecuilco. Other names stood out on the document too, including that of Joaquín Rubín, who signed for all those who did not know how to write.

The people of San Pedro Apatlaco faced a situation that had become increasingly common in the Morelos lowlands. They responded in a manner that many hamlets chose when confronted with the superior power of a wealthy hacendado. Following a tradition born in the colonial period, they went to the courts for protection against local abuses. But from the mid-nineteenth century on, pueblo efforts met increasingly hostile court rulings as the emerging coalition of landlords, local politicians, and Liberal economic policies began to weigh more heavily against them.

González not only deprived the vecinos of water and killed some of their cattle, he also confiscated 108 other animals, locked them up in a hacienda corral, and refused to return them unless he was paid one peso for each animal. Most hacienda jobs in Morelos paid between one to four reales a day, so the amount he was demanding was substantial for poor people. González justified his actions by charging that the animals trampled hacienda crops, costing the hacienda money. Apatlaco took the case to court, asking that the confiscated cattle be returned, the five head González slaughtered be paid for, and the water be allowed to reenter their *"solares"* because they had enjoyed its use since "tiempo immemorial."[5]

The vecinos submitted their petition in September, and on December 5, 1864, Francisco del Castillo, the Juez de Primera Instancia for the district of Morelos, ruled in favor of Mendoza Cortina and Gumisindo González. The district judge found that the Apatlaco appellants had failed to fully substantiate their claims to the land and that their petition contained a fundamental contradiction. The legal reasoning of his ruling reflected a larger pattern being applied in the Morelos lowlands in the wake of the Ley Lerdo. The judge said that Apatlaco could not claim, as they had done in a creative attempt to use the new laws privatizing communal land holdings to their own advantage, that each of them held a small individual plot of land in conformity with the Ley Lerdo, and at the same time call themselves a communal "pueblo." Apatlaco's approach reflected a larger strategy in which communities tried to protect themselves and justify their claims by appealing to both old practices and new regulations. The judge decided that the people of Apatlaco could not "file a group action and at the same time claim to be separate individuals."[6] The ruling that the vecinos of Apatlaco could file individual claims against the hacendado, but could not litigate as a community, was critical and posed a serious, ongoing problem for all rural communities in Morelos.[7]

The residents of Apatlaco had to decide how to approach the issue, and it became a test of solidarity within the community. As individuals, different people probably had stronger cases than others for property titles to the land they were tilling based on ancestry and ethnicity, on how long they and their families had lived in the area, and other variables. Some people's personal claims would be more persuasive than others, providing the temptation to make individual appeals. A poor agricultural worker, though, could not possibly afford to compete with a rich hacendado and his army of attorneys in a long, drawn-out legal case. As the case moved forward, various opinions and opposing views of what a pueblo was, both legally and conceptually, emerged. What happened at Apatlaco revealed a lot about rural Morelos at the time, including the perceptions of the rural populace, the position of the hacendados and their administrators, as well as each group's respective relationships with the lower and superior courts, with local politicians, and the central government.

The ideas and actions of people living in communities like Apatlaco did not simply come in response to structural forces imposed from outside. They involved the individual experiences, feelings and perceptions of the people living in them, which, taken together, helped shape their collective identity. Society was hierarchical, but the dominant classes did not sustain themselves by force alone. There was a subjective order to rural society that was held together by at least some voluntary adherence from the various groups to the dominant ideas and structures. By the mid-1860s, the dominant ideology was Liberalism. But that meant different things to different people. During an age of rapid change marked by the privatization of rural properties, a general, usually latent, resistance to the dominant culture was endemic. Although they may appear merely practical at first glance, the concerns of the peasantry and rural workers held broader political implications since their group interests usually contradicted the programs of the landed aristocracy and new rural bourgeoisie. Challenging the status quo invited repression from landlords, rural police, or even government troops, and could lead to imprisonment, impressment into the army, or death.

Despite the risks involved and the open threats from the administrator González, the people of Apatlaco decided to act together. Of course, the fact that individual litigation cost more than impoverished subsistence farmers and laborers could afford to pay on their own made a collective case the only real option. Even so, legal fees could bankrupt an entire town. Compounding matters for the vecinos was the fact that the public registry at the time did not list San Pedro Apatlaco as a legally recognized pueblo, which severely limited the possibility that their lawsuit would succeed.[8]

Nonetheless, a few days after receiving the lower court's ruling in favor of Mendoza Cortina, the residents of Apatlaco sent a delegation of five village representatives to Mexico City to seek out a capable lawyer and a notary public in order to declare their intention to continue the litigation as a group. They pledged the mutual contributions of their future earnings before the notary public in order to finance the litigation. It would be an uphill battle. They were competing against the resources of the owner of one of the largest haciendas in Morelos. Due to his encroachments on village entitlements, Mendoza Cortina had plenty of experience fighting court cases against pueblos. He was engaged in legal disputes with almost all of his neighbors at some time or another, including the pueblo of Anenecuilco and the area's head town, Cuautla.[9]

Hegemony and Force

While community representatives pledged their solidarity and commitment to stand together, the crisis back home deepened. González rode into Apatlaco early one morning supported by an escort of armed guards from the hacienda and the special forces of Morelos's *seguridad pública.* The seguridad pública was a private mounted police force hired and paid for by *"los señores hacendados"* to combat the bandits that roamed Morelos at the time. Not always successful in fighting bandits, they functioned far more efficiently and with greater enthusiasm when confronting unarmed pueblo folk. The *juez auxiliar* of the judicial district rode with González at the head of this contingent of armed men, lending greater legitimacy to what they were about to do. His presence also revealed the larger web of shared interests and attitudes between hacendados and many local-level political and judicial officials.

As they rode into town, González's men encircled the house of a vecino, Manuel Berdín, and set it on fire. While the house went up in flames, they began to hack down the fruit trees growing in his yard. After destroying Berdín's house, they moved toward Vicente Quintero's. Quintero and his brothers were community leaders at the forefront of the ongoing struggle with Mendoza Cortina and González. A body of armed men stood watch while others chopped down Quintero's fruit trees and set his house on fire too. Vicente Quintero was not home at the time; he was in Mexico City meeting with a lawyer, but his wife and children were there and they fled their burning home for the shelter of Carmen Quintero's residence. That was a mistake. Carmen Quintero's signature stood out as the first one on the original *amparo de restitución* submitted by Apatlaco. González had his men leave the home a smoldering ruin. With González, the judge, and the forces of the seguridad pública watching, the other hired men finished their work at Apatlaco by cutting down the community's modest orchard and burning the crops of Paulino Quintero before setting his house on fire too. The Quintero's were not alone though. González and his men torched forty-seven other homes and left the town in ashes.[10] This was not merely a personal or family grudge between the administrator and the Quinteros. The vecinos of Apatlaco were being taught a lesson about what happened to people that challenged hacendado rule in Morelos (see Figure 6).

The leaders of Apatlaco had expressed their fears of the harsh reprisals that might come in response to their legal action. Anticipating trouble, they specifically asked for protection from the administrator in their previous petition because of his well-established record of abusive behavior, including the shooting of their cows, which proved to them his "violent character" and left them worrying about what else he might do. Their fears materialized in the form of the rural police and the hacienda's armed guards, who forced them to watch helplessly as

Figure 6.
Rural hamlet with
typical thatched
dwellings, nine-
teenth century.

their meager worldly possessions went up in smoke. The alliance of
the hacendado, the rural constabulary, and the judge, as well as their
willingness to use violence, was not new, and the events in Apatlaco
were not unique. But each successive incident hurt the recipients, violated their sense of justice and morality, and further embittered them
to the system that allowed it.[11]

Gumisindo González expressed no remorse for his actions.
Instead, he pointed out that it was his duty as hacienda administrator
to be responsible for the conduct of the residents of the hacienda.

González, like the prefect Villaseñor before him, believed that those responsibilities included the meting out of punishment and the dispensation of rewards. González personified the paternalistic and racist attitude of many nineteenth-century Morelos hacendados and administrators who viewed their Indian, mestizo, and mulatto employees as dependents in need of others with superior intellect to watch over and guide them. That social outlook had a long history in Morelos. Despite the abolition of official forms of caste hierarchy and the most blatant methods of exploitation like slavery and the encomienda, the sentiments that had created them persisted. Ethnic and cultural prejudice played a significant role in rural Morelos into the twentieth century, and they aroused deep animosity.[12]

Commentaries by both Joaquín and Luis García Pimentel, whose family owned the large and profitable sugar hacienda, Tenango, in eastern Morelos, offered an insight into the attitudes of some elites at the time. The younger Joaquín held the opinion that the Indian "has many defects as a laborer, being as he is lazy, sottish, and thieving." His older brother shared his views. The opinions of the García Pimentel's echoed the writings of earlier Mexican intellectuals of the 1830s and 1840s, including rivals such as Lucas Alamán, José María Luis Mora, and Lorenzo de Zavala, who, despite their differences, espoused cultural and ethnic elitism.

Gumisindo González translated attitudes into action. He acknowledged the havoc he wreaked on Apatlaco and admitted that his men destroyed four thatched-roof adobe houses, as well as the forty-seven "chozas," where most people lived. Residents of Apatlaco, like most rural folk in Morelos, lived hard, short lives in shacks on the fringes of the estates, and they died in similar quarters. Labor on the sugar plantations was notoriously tough.[13] Their hardships, though, were not the administrator's concern. What bothered him was a court order directing him to refrain from destroying any more homes in Apatlaco. Reflecting widely held elite attitudes, González complained that his actions fell perfectly within his rights, and he pointed to a state law passed in 1863 granting hacendados the authority to evict anyone from their land that they wished.

That provided the legal support for the raid on Apatlaco, which was carried out in the morning when most of the men were either out in the fields, working at the hacienda, or away as part of the delegation sent to Mexico City. When González and his forces arrived they found what they had expected, mainly the women working at home. The commandant of the rural security forces, Manuel Díaz, ordered the women rounded up and taken away. The vecinos later claimed that González imprisoned the women at the hacienda, but he denied that charge, saying he did not want them around, not even in his jail. He told the court that he took them to a field at night and released them near a road a few hundred yards from the fringes of the estate. But, even if that was true, it still meant that he had kept them against their will for the whole day, since the raid and roundup took place in the morning. Mendoza Cortina offered no apologies, saying instead, "Everybody knows what kind of women they are." He justified his treatment of the wives and mothers of Apatlaco by saying that they were women of "bad character" and that, in fact, "among the women referred to are found those of the families of bandits Severo and Felipe el Zarco and those of the family of Pablo Amado. These women are in effect evil presences on the estate because of the clandestine relationships which they must necessarily have among themselves while stealing material goods."[14]

Besides revealing interesting class and gender assumptions, González's testimony inadvertently exposed the form that bandit activity often took in rural Morelos. His complaints about the amicable relations that bandits enjoyed with some of the population living on the haciendas and in the neighboring pueblos was telling. Felipe el Zarco and his brother Severo were locally famous bandit leaders, and it was common knowledge that they and others received food, lodging, rest, and support from the local populations. People in the hacienda ranchería settlements and citizens of legally independent pueblos often offered the bandits refuge, without which they could not have operated.[15]

González's testimony coincided with other complaints of pervasive bandit activity and of an alarming degree of public support that frightened authorities and landowners. Ignacio Manuel Altamirano, in his famous novel *El Zarco, the Bandit*, set in nineteenth-century Morelos, in and around the town of Yautepec, portrayed various aspects of banditry familiar to everyone living in the area. Altamirano paralleled reality with his depiction of who supported the hacendados, how hacendados dealt with their employees, who helped the bandits, what the bandits demanded, and what they did. The following passage tells the point of view of Nicolás, a fictional blacksmith and one of the loyal salaried employees of the valuable hacienda Atlihuayan— later owned by Pablo Escandón—the unpopular governor of Morelos who was driven out by the revolution. Altamirano has Nicolás tell an old widow in Yautepec how the hacienda combated the ever-present danger of bandits:

> As the bandits have always relied on having spies
> among the estate hands and the villagers, we began by
> turning out anyone we suspected of being in league
> with them. Now, all our people are loyal and the estate
> is armed. The worst that the plateados can do to us is
> to burn the cane fields, and we keep close watch at
> night to guard against this as much as possible. The
> bandits have demanded money from the owner of the
> estate and have threatened to burn down the big house
> but he pays them no attention.

Altamirano lived through the time about which he wrote, was a staunch Liberal who fought against the French intervention while Apatlaco was fighting for recognition, and was an astute student of his society. His novel hit directly on the main elements mentioned in newspapers and official and personal correspondence of the day that reported bandit sympathizers in the villages and haciendas, bandits extorting money and burning sugarcane fields, and hacendado efforts to combat alleged bandits and their supporters.

Altamirano captured the essence of the prevailing social climate. Like Altamirano's fictional hacendado, the real-life owner of Cuahuixtla, Mendoza Cortina, sought to evict the people of Apatlaco whom he labeled as bandit sympathizers. Mendoza Cortina complained in his testimony before the court that the residents of Apatlaco posed a "constant threat to the security of the hacienda, causing much damage, not the least of which [is] perverting with their bad example and advice, the honorable workers of the estate."[16]

The large sugar estates employed a mixed labor system that created a varied rural society. Some dependent estate workers, referred to with the denigrating term of "mozos" by the independent-minded people of Apatlaco, reenforced the social relations that the hacendados wanted to instill by accepting the prevailing practices of the estate managers. Like Nicolás and the loyal workers depicted by Altamirano, they formed part of the hacienda armed guard, and at hacienda Cuahuixtla they joined with the public security forces to enforce estate discipline on the people of Apatlaco. Mendoza Cortina contributed fifteen men, and the same number of horses and carbines from Cuahuixtla to the fuerza rural of the district. The total force was made up of 364 men who helped sustain the developing patterns of social control and furthered hacendado efforts to achieve hegemony.[17]

Other campesinos, however, sought to distance themselves from the control of the hacendados and to challenge the administrator's efforts at labor management. They sought better wages and conditions, and many towns within the borders of the hacienda real strove to function as politically independent and economically self-determining communities. They harbored certain independent aspirations, supported and generated antihacendado activity, and actively pursued their goals through the courts, where they hoped to find some justice. Apatlaco's experiences, therefore, offer a close-up of a larger landscape and the changing social contours of the sugar valleys of the Morelos lowlands.

Part of Apatlaco's particular conflict with the hacienda, in addition to the classic issues of crop land, water, and pueblo status, revolved around the use of pasture lands. Like arrangements elsewhere in the region, the owner of Cuahuixtla charged the residents a fee for pasturing their cattle on what he claimed to be hacienda land. The vecinos of Apatlaco refused to pay the fee. The standoff reflected divergent views. Villagers in Morelos routinely maintained that pastures had always been, and should remain, common lands. Meanwhile, the hacendados pursued a steady process of enclosure.

Hacendados engaged in a constant battle with villagers, many of whom were also part-time estate workers who, being weaker and enjoying very little protection from the law, often carried out a silent, anonymous struggle. Sometimes the latent conflict came out in obvious cases of sabotage such as nighttime attacks on irrigation works. The general, everyday struggle is hard to document from this distance and has usually been neglected by historians in favor of more dramatic and well-documented events. But the essence of daily, low-level, and ongoing social tension surfaced in seemingly mundane comments such as Mendoza Cortina's about the "bad advice" the women of Apatlaco offered to other hacienda workers.[18] Hacendados considered that sort of thing a problem as they tried to maintain social order through strict work discipline, economic pressure, and social and psychological mechanisms such as the selected dissemination of education and religion. Ultimately, though, those day-to-day strategies rested on the threat and occasional use of force.[19]

Hacendado Perspectives

The events at Apatlaco revealed the attitudes of people from different social strata in the changing social landscape of nineteenth-century Morelos. Representing a common hacendado perspective, Mendoza

Cortina asserted the rights of private property, insisting that no "pueblo" of San Pedro Apatlaco ever existed. He claimed that Apatlaco was merely a cluster of people living on the hacienda real where he allowed the "*operarios*" to live. They remained there only through his "tolerance," since he had the right to do whatever he wished on his own property. Beyond that, and providing more insight into how hacendados often viewed things, Mendoza Cortina defended the behavior of his administrator González, calling the destruction he caused "minimal" and assigning the damages a monetary value amounting to less than fifty pesos. The hacendado's belief that he could pay for whatever injuries the administrator caused, and his designation of a strictly financial worth to the trees, crops, animals, homes, and worldly possessions of the people who owned them, revealed his general contempt for the families of Apatlaco. The sentiments voiced by both sides reflected more widely held landowner and campesino attitudes of the day. Mendoza Cortina's statement about the Apatlacans residing in the part of the hacienda devoted to the living quarters of the "operarios" was a useful indicator of the limited rights which that category of hacienda laborer held in his view. Lacking even the most remote claims to pueblo status, most "operarios" found themselves with few social guarantees and in an increasingly dependent relationship with the hacendado. That, perhaps, helps explain the lack of debt peonage in Morelos and the low levels of debt owed by workers. Apparently, there was no real need to tie workers to the estates, even though labor shortages were occasionally reported. The ongoing process of land transfer left dispossessed small holders with few options other than to seek labor opportunities on the estates.[20]

The psychological impact of the proceedings at Apatlaco, and the social statement they made, must have had a profound effect on the inhabitants there and on the rest of the hacienda. What transpired made salient the campesino's lowly social standing, lack of power within the prevailing system, lack of worth in the eyes of the hacendado, the administrator, and the local authorities, all of whom comprised the dominant elements in rural society. The violence of the administrator, the feudal-like assumptions of the hacendado, and the complicity of the police and courts vividly demonstrated the prevailing social hierarchy to all concerned.

Apatlaco also revealed that the social conflict in the Morelos countryside extended beyond the obvious material competition over land, water, and woods. Landlords and civil authorities were trying to enshrine a dominant ideology and realize the hegemonic control that would flow from its general acceptance. That acceptance required widespread recognition of established symbols of authority that would encourage obedience and the toleration of prevailing social relationships. Campesinos continually challenged those efforts though. The struggle comes out most obviously over material conditions, but the conflict included clashing worldviews, ideas of justice, and understandings of what things were worth and why.

At the practical level of this particular case, the hacendado clearly believed that the fruit trees cut down and the homes burned could be measured in money alone. But to the campesino family that owned very little, their value went beyond that. The trees took years of care, and the fruit they bore provided an important and independent supplement to a very basic, but widely practiced diet. For the hacendado, a wooden shack was relatively worthless; but the family living in it had made the rudimentary structure a home like that of their neighbors and many other hacienda workers in Morelos. Rural communities had long prized their self-sufficiency, their independence, and their autonomy. Those things were not necessarily measured by money, but by the widespread belief that they were fundamental rights.[21] Hacendados had a different vision, and the state played a mediating role between the two sides. Ultimately, when conflicts burst to the surface, they usually did so over specific issues of property, treatment, or wages, but those particulars existed within the larger whole.

Since they had trouble convincing much of the rural populace that their vision was just and good, hacendados often resorted to coercion. For example, Mendoza Cortina justified using the seguridad pública on the people at Apatlaco by complaining that general lawlessness in the area forced him and fellow landowners to support the force with a *"fuerte contribución"* of three hundred pesos a month. He also maintained his own private security that he claimed cost him an extra six hundred pesos a month. That kind of ongoing commitment to defending hacienda properties reflected the polarized nature of the society the hacendados were creating.[22] Despite the heavy outlays for law enforcement, they routinely expressed fear of various segments of the rural working population around them. Instead of modifying their own behavior, most hacendados felt that the best way to guard against the threat from below was with increased police powers and legal rights for themselves.

Especially important, and understandable from the hacendados' perspective, was the right to determine who lived on their haciendas, and to be able to evict the unwanted. One problem with that approach was that many estates surrounded legitimate pueblos. Mendoza Cortina justified his general stance on this matter, and his administrator's actions in particular, through appeals to the law. But his statements revealed deep and pervasive class antagonisms that elites usually tried to conceal by focusing instead on individual vecinos, bandits, disgruntled workers, or rancherías claiming to be pueblos. All were attempts to marginalize or delegitimate them by singling them out and labeling them malcontents or criminals. Mendoza Cortina voiced concerns shared by many landowners in the tierra caliente about their property rights and the threat posed by communal claims saying, "This risk will run in all actions, if this right is not protected, the threat is—so to speak—at the door, because the people of the countryside have become agitated to an incredible point and nothing is more common than attacks against property."[23]

The episode at Apatlaco was one example of changing cultural attitudes and the development of a more inclusive rural working-class perspective that was taking shape. For example, ethnic distinctions between Indian, mulatto, and mestizo began to blur at the same time the categorization separating dependent hacienda residents and independent villagers began to change too. Recently displaced villagers moved onto the haciendas, but they maintained some of their previous independent outlook. Like migrants everywhere, they brought their social values and habits with them. In this case, it meant that they tried to re-create village life on the fringes of the estates. Because of that, the hacendados saw them as an insidious threat.

As a more inclusive rural working culture began to emerge, the distinctions among the lower rungs of the social ladder also became less marked and less easily made in ethnic terms. Socially and culturally defining bonds such as indigenous languages and religious practices persisted, but they were weakened by a new social structure that was forming in direct relation to the demands of hacendados and merchants, who were themselves responding to larger developments in industry, commerce, and export agriculture. The new political economy pointed toward the beginning of a class, rather than caste, society. The ultimate outcome remained unclear in the nineteenth century, but the transformation took place because of the capitalization of the countryside, and people tried to accommodate the changes the best they could.

Apatlaco reflected that, and so did Mendoza Cortina. He offered a perspective consistent with an older feudal mentality that claimed it was the hacendados' "duty to be vigilant of the conduct of their veci-nos." His stance reflected hacendado images of their social role and that of "their" dependents. Their image of the patrón had deep histor-ical roots stretching back to the sixteenth century. Although colonial labor systems were gone, the social attitudes that supported them were not.

Confident of their social standing, Mendoza Cortina and Gumisindo González complained to the prefect of the district that they were not receiving enough official assistance to deal with the "squatters" and that, in fact, the prefect was impeding their expulsion by not ordering an armed force to evict them once and for all. Mendoza Cortina revealed a common hacendado sense of entitle-ment. He not only wanted, but expected, immediate state support even while the case remained under review. Hacendados in Morelos had learned to assume that the government and the courts would rein-force and legitimate their power.

When the people of Apatlaco responded, they spoke for them-selves and for the particular situation they confronted, but many ham-lets in rural Morelos found themselves in similar circumstances. Apatlaco's rebuttal to Mendoza Cortina's claim that he could do what he pleased with the people of his finca, burn, tear down, and destroy whatever he wanted and expel whomever he chose said in part:

> One cannot help but feel that the days of feudalism
> have been revived and that Mendoza Cortina believes
> himself to be the lord of a castle: with the rights of life
> and death over all its inhabitants, who give thanks
> every day he lets them continue to live. Now you see
> why it is no surprise that on the hacienda Cuahuixtla
> they have the stocks, and that they use this instrument
> of mortification which for years now has been banned
> by our laws.[24]

Their rejection of pretensions of nobility, special privilege, and cor-poral punishment was significant because it hinted at the changing attitudes of peasants and agrarian workers who had long been defined by a caste system as legal dependents, and it reflected the beginnings of the emergence of a free labor ethic. Their statements also resonated with those of some Liberal leaders such as General Juan Álvarez of Guerrerro, Senator Ponciano Arriaga of San Luis Potosí, and former governor Arizcorretta of Mexico State. The changing times affected everyone, including campesinos, Maximilian, the Conservatives, and the Liberals, despite all the contradictions between them. Divergent ideas and needs from different levels of society became intertwined and contributed to a contested, but emerging ethos.

Campesino Perspectives

People in Apatlaco understood their precarious position and argued along legal grounds, hoping to gain legitimacy in the eyes of the state. But even though it was a legal case, they repeatedly returned to moral issues and ideas of fairness and of right and wrong. Their views offered a glimpse of what many rural people thought their society should be like. Uncovering their perspective reveals the origins and historical continuities in the political evolution of Morelos, especially the roots of what was to become Zapatismo.

The vecinos of Apatlaco felt that those on the bottom rungs of society were treated with less concern than "barnyard animals." According to Apatlaco, while the administrator took special pains to insure the health and well-being of the hacienda's cattle, he called "the *citizens* of Apatlaco mere hacienda inhabitants, something akin to serfs] which were in his view lower than the animals." The vecinos of Apatlaco said that to hear the hacienda owner talk, one would believe "that we were born to suffer in silence without the right to make a complaint, to ask for the correction of an abuse to the injustice and violence with which we are treated. That is the spirit of Mister Mendoza Cortina." A generation later, when Zapata went to Mexico City to train horses for a wealthy Morelos planter, he famously remarked that the horses there were cared for better than most people in Morelos. The feelings coming out of Apatlaco in 1864, and reiterated by Zapata, conveyed something larger than a lament. Those sentiments were widespread on the eve of the revolution, when workers found it believable that some hacendados intended to brand them.[25]

As the vecinos of Apatlaco saw it, Mendoza Cortina's behavior was retrograde. They regarded themselves as Mexican citizens with corresponding rights and obligations. The hacendado's intransigent position on property rights was expected, but his total disregard for their "natural" rights reached back to archaic pretensions of nobility, and indicated to those at Apatlaco his evil spirit. When the courts rejected their claim and actually condoned the abuse they had suffered, the next step for Apatlaco, and others living in similar circumstances, was to condemn the entire political system, not just the men who caused them the immediate harm. But such a radical leap would not come for many years. It required the erosion of economic growth and the total bankruptcy of the cultural hegemony of the elite. That situation eventually materialized by 1910, and it led to the disintegration of the voluntary adherence of the rural working population to major elements of the social code. But, until then, campesinos in Morelos continued to seek the protection of the federal government against local abuses. So long as rural workers and villagers accepted some dictates of the new Liberal ethic and benefited from them in some manner, they pursued that path. One particularly conspicuous element in the application of Liberal ideology in the case of Apatlaco was the use of the term *ciudadano*, used by enlightened Liberals to describe themselves since the French intervention.

Apatlaco's experience resonated with other resistance movements before and after it. It blended into a larger picture punctuated by the murders at Chiconcuac, the riots in Tepoztlán, the takeover at Tenextepango, and widespread social banditry. Most bandits came from haciendas like Cuahuixtla and communities like Apatlaco, and many of their actions constituted resistance against the socioeconomic process underway, and a flagrant rejection of a prevailing attitude of landowner superiority that was becoming more widely challenged by the general population.

Hacendados like Mendoza Cortina were seldom visible in Morelos. Most lived in Mexico City. When they did visit their haciendas they arrived in comfortable horse-drawn coaches and later in private rail cars, stayed in their formidable, fortresslike country manor houses, rode fine horses, and held elegant parties. The plateados represented a counterstatement. They came from humble origins on the hacienda settlements and from the pueblos, but they countered elite displays of wealth and refinement with their own ostentatious dress and manner. Hacendados and their administrators enforced order with armed and mounted men and talked of keeping people in their place. The plateados demonstrated open defiance by riding on horseback dressed in elaborate clothing, carrying guns, defying the law, and doing daring deeds. They represented a stark contrast to the barefoot or sandaled campesino dressed in rough white cotton with backs bent toiling in the hacendado's fields.[26]

When confrontations over property arose, elites often characterized rural citizens, like those of Apatlaco, as socially deviant and criminal. Local authorities joined the hacendado in treating the Apatlacans as outlaws for challenging the landowner and, implicitly, for challenging the larger land-tenure system. The behavior of those who resisted, like the Quinteros, exceeded the immediate local issue of the deprivation of water and the seizure of cattle and spilled over into an affirmation of an alternative ethos. Perhaps they felt empowered by the new Liberal discourse of citizen's rights, to which they adhered. But they offered a radical version of those rights; one that served their cultural and material interests, and they extended it to include the restitution of property on the basis of need, tradition, and what they thought was fair.

Survival Strategies: Seek Justice or Obey the Law

As the legal maneuvering proceeded and the rulings continued to favor the hacendado, Apatlaco's strategy took an important turn. The vecinos began to abandon formal laws and appealed to the court's sense of fairness based on what was morally right. They asked the court consider their rights as citizens and to consider the prerogatives that they *should* have, not even as a pueblo anymore, but simply as people living off the land who had been there for a very long time. Their argument transcended the contemporary laws. They did not want to be judged strictly by what some temporal rules might say, but wanted to know what official society thought was just. When the judge rejected their legal claims, they basically abandoned their efforts to be recognized as a pueblo, a prized status that carried with it the right to a designated amount of communal property. Instead, they argued that regardless of their status, it was tremendously unjust to throw them off the land on which they had lived for so long just because they had wound up on the wrong side of the current hacienda administrator. They wondered if the court felt justice would be done:

> If today the idea occurred to the owner of Cuahuixtla to bring one hundred families of poor *Spaniards* and give each one a small plot to farm, with the condition that they be workers for the hacienda and help in tilling the fields; at first these families do not have anything; but eventually the woman buys a hen; later a little lamb, further down the line a pig, a cow, a donkey; she has planted an avocado seed, a banana, and a mango tree, and has taken pleasure in watching these plants and animals grow, along with the children she has borne there. Her children, when their parents die, continue in the same manner, and so do their children, and the children of their children, because this is the natural

progression of humanity. And after one hundred years
when their great-great-grandchildren are living on
what is today the hacienda Cuahuixtla, is someone
going to come and tell these families "get out of here,
take your animals, uproot your trees or leave them
behind, because we do not want you here anymore, we
want you gone, and what we want is the law?"[27]

Apatlaco specifically substituted *"españoles pobres"* in their portrayal of village life and, feeling equal to "Spaniards," asked for equality as citizens.[28] Based on the ethnic makeup of most rural
communities in the Morelos lowlands, the document coming out of
Apatlaco served as a strong commentary on the issues of the time.
Their rhetorical question revealed a keen sense of who they were, and
who they were not. The question being addressed was simple: Would
a group of Spaniards be treated differently than the residents of
Apatlaco themselves were being treated? Was society officially racist?
Would the authorities not find it unfair, or even outrageous, to treat a
hamlet of one hundred hardworking Spaniards in the same manner
that they treated the people of Apatlaco? Issues of ethnicity, cultural
identity, and equality were not lost on people in the Morelos countryside. The sting they felt as second-class citizens in their own country
appeared in their statements about their society, and by demanding
that it change they represented a forward-looking and progressive
influence on Mexico.[29]

Ideological Precursors

The conflict at Apatlaco demonstrated the adaptation of Liberal ideology and how the lower classes fed off of, and transformed, political
dialogue in Mexico. That interaction resulted in a contentious political discourse between elites and the working classes. Ultimately, the
issues underlying the tensions of this period burst to the surface in the
agrarian revolution in Morelos. That movement sought a major redistribution of land and wealth and offered a political vision based on
local autonomy that included an end to dictatorship through effective
suffrage and no reelection of the president. The disputes of the mid-
nineteenth century anticipated those revolutionary goals.[30]

Meanwhile, the growing domestic demand for sugar and potential of exports encouraged commercial expansion by the hacendados,
and state-sponsored land-privatization programs helped the estates
attain the higher levels of sugar production that they sought. Those

circumstances clashed with campesino efforts to protect and perpetuate pueblo communalism and the independence of their communities. The new rural working class combined the defense of community with a seemingly contradictory desire for individual freedom, mobility, and opportunity based on Liberal ideology. The castelike system still existing on the estates, though, and the lack of other viable labor alternatives, the company store, scrip payments, and sharecropping constricted the Liberal promise. People were frustrated at Apatlaco, for example, because it seemed like the caprice of the hacendado took precedence over promised political rights and obliterated time-honored practices like seasonal employment and access to land and water. What happened at Apatlaco demonstrated that some people working on the haciendas sought to escape the more feudal social relations on the estates, but also expected to maintain some of the mutual obligations and understandings between landlord and peasant about access to land in exchange for labor and other benefits.

The prevailing social climate left rural workers vulnerable on all fronts. The fact that the administrator of Cuahuixtla went unpunished for his acts reflected that situation. The vecinos of Apatlaco suggested that perhaps the reason González was immune to punishment had something to do with the fact that the district judge had "such intimacy with the administrator that they carry on almost like brothers."[31] Unlike villagers and workers, González came and went from the courthouse with his hat on his head and a pistol in his belt. In addition to that, the judge and his family frequently arrived as special guests at parties and receptions held at the hacienda, riding in a carriage pulled by fine horses and a chauffeur sent by Gumisindo González. The vecinos wondered if that kind of a relationship stood in the way of the judge's partiality, especially since the administrator was a known "arsonist." The situation violated their sense of justice as guaranteed by a social contract between the governing and the governed, in which all citizens are honored by the recognition of their inalienable rights.

Not surprisingly, the judge's initial ruling granted the hacendado a full victory in all respects and included the additional burden that the people of Apatlaco pay all Mendoza Cortina's court costs as well. Apatlaco appealed to a higher authority, but the Ministry of Justice in Mexico City maintained Mendoza Cortina's right to evict the vecinos of Apatlaco. They did, however, order him to pay for the property damages caused by the overzealous González. Mendoza Cortina attempted to dismiss the entire matter, saying "that in the entire district of Morelos there is no pueblo known by the name San Pedro Apatlaco, they have invented and continually repeated this name in the hope of convincing someone, someday, that it is a pueblo." Mendoza Cortina's rejection of Apatlaco's pretensions inadvertently acknowledged that a colonial-era pueblo still carried special standing and legitimacy even after the Reform laws. In the short run, Apatlaco got burned down and the people lost their case. But Mendoza Cortina was right. Apatlaco did continue to hope of convincing someone, someday, that it was a pueblo. The revolution of 1910 gave them their chance.[32]

Together, Gumisindo González and Mendoza Cortina demonstrated the harsher possibilities of Liberal economic ideology, which Porfirio Díaz would realize more fully later. Their attack on communal property, combined with already existing imbalances of power and the continuance of archaic social relations in the countryside, created fresh abuses. Somewhat ironically, the elitist mentality that staunch Conservatives, such as Lucas Alamán, had supported, came to the fore quite effectively in the corrupted Liberalism of the nineteenth century. The Conservatives had justified their segregationist beliefs that Indians and other castes be denied juridic equality with the transparent excuse that those groups had to be looked out for and watched over because if treated equally they would be more easily exploited. The Liberal land laws made the Conservative's insincere concerns a reality. The laws dictated that the bulk of new opportunities afforded by Liberalism went to those with economic resources, which meant mainly those of European descent or cultural heritage. The results exacerbated cultural cleavages in the countryside, and the government and courts increasingly insured those outcomes.

Both sides in Morelos, the owners of the great estates and the communally oriented campesinos, argued in defense of their interests in a transitional society. Each had one foot in the past and one in the future. For their part, the people of Apatlaco expressed their particular needs and concerns within the context of the larger cultural, economic, and social changes taking place. The hacendados defended the traditional and semifeudal cultural, political, and social powers enjoyed by the Spanish landholding elites of the colonial era. At the same time, though, they demanded the application of modern Liberal economic principles based on the rights of the individual, but mainly in conjunction with the protection of private property, the advancement of capitalism, the establishment of limits on governmental interference from taxes and regulations, and guarantees against communalist challenges from below. They demanded order and struggled against crime, especially banditry and robbery, as part of their search for stability, a favorable business climate, and an expanded recognition of property rights.

The rural poor, by contrast, adopted those elements that favored them and fought those that disadvantaged them. They often expressed their feelings in actions that spoke louder than writings or proclamations. They looked to the past when they cited the ancient traditions of the legally endowed pueblos in their efforts to defend their communities, autonomy, and way of life. But they also embraced the future and demanded equal juridical rights, the powers of full individual citizenship, and economic participation offered by nineteenth-century Mexican Liberalism.

Maximilian walked into that volatile situation. He took a political gamble in his struggle for the control of Mexico and lost. The special commission he established to provide minimal protection to pueblos, and the policies he designed to alleviate some of the hardships on the lower classes in the countryside, caused many large landowners to drop their support of him. He then failed to gain sufficient backing among Liberals, some of whom had flirted with the empire but eventually rallied around Benito Juárez. Because of Maximilian's conciliatory attitude toward the pueblos, the popularity of the empire faded among landholders, even though most had initially welcomed it as a protector of property and privilege.

Paradoxically, only hard-line Conservatives supported Maximilian despite his apparently genuine efforts to ameliorate the conditions afflicting the agrarian poor. When the French government withdrew its military support, his remaining army was defeated, and Maximilian was captured and executed in June 1867 on a hill above Querétaro. His death caused shock and stirred criticism in Europe. The execution, though, made the point that Mexico would not tolerate efforts at reconquest at a time when European powers were colonizing large parts of Africa and Asia. Juárez and the triumphant Liberals then attempted to restore peace and order to a Liberal Mexico governed by civilians. Apatlaco offers a microcosm of events in nineteenth-century Morelos and presents a useful case for examining the contradictory processes under way in rural Mexico during the nineteenth century, which, unresolved, exploded in revolution in 1910.

Chapter Seven

POVERTY AND PROGRESS, 1876–1910

Carved out of the state of Mexico in 1869, Morelos made up an area contiguous with the old administrative district of Cuernavaca and the third military district during the French intervention. Over the objections of the planters in Morelos, President Juárez nominated General Francisco Leyva for governor against the hacendados' choice of General Porfirio Díaz, one of the heroes of the battle of Cinco de Mayo and the general resistance against the French. The planters had attempted to impose their rule on the region off and on during the politically tumultuous years following the U.S. occupation, but with the emergence of the Juarez regime, they were once again confronted with a central authority that could threaten the semifeudal social relations they had long sought to maintain. Because of its efforts to reassert federal authority, the constitutionalist government represented a rival structure to the home rule the hacendados wished to practice in Morelos.[1]

Hacendados supporting Díaz for governor ran an advertisement in June 1869 in the Mexico City newspaper *La Iberia*, backing him and a slate of candidates from the landed families of the region. But Juárez chose Leyva, and the planter class jockeyed with the new governor and the reimposition of central authority. Following the wars and social strife of the previous two decades, the planters hoped for a stable regime that would maintain peace and order so they could profitably operate their enterprises and enjoy their country estates. They viewed Leyva's government with apprehension, in part because he had difficulty providing adequate security, but mostly because he sought to raise taxes on the sugar haciendas and had been associated with Álvarez, Arellano, and the militancy of the national guard and its anti-hacendado activity in the past, including the assault on the hacienda Chiconcuac in 1856.[2]

Despite the antagonism of the landed elite, Leyva served as governor of Morelos as long as Juárez held the presidency. But Juárez faced his own difficulties. Rival Liberal forces under Miguel Negrete, operating along the Puebla-Morelos border in 1868, sought his ouster for violating the principal of no reelection. Some pueblo citizens in Morelos supported Negrete, who supported Díaz, because both leaders had promised to help the pueblos retain their ancient land titles. As a result, local agitation over land disputes in places like Villa de Ayala and Jonacatepec merged with the wider effort to overthrow Juárez and "restore Constitutional guarantees." When Juárez won the presidential election in the fall of 1871 over Sebastian Lerdo de Tejada and Díaz, Lerdo went back to being chief justice of the Supreme Court, and Díaz opted for rebellion. Díaz found some support in eastern Morelos, but Juárez's death in mid-July 1872 brought an end to the movement.[3]

Lerdo became president in accordance with the constitution and kept Leyva, who continued to fund the operation of the state government through taxes on the sugar haciendas that represented "the wealth of the state." The total value of agricultural properties in Morelos in 1873 amounted to 13,150,000 pesos, with the sugar haciendas and mills accounting for about 12,000,000 of that. When Leyva's term ended, his successor, Governor Francisco Pacheco, reported that twenty-eight haciendas were raising sugarcane, and that the eight major mills manufacturing sugar employed about twelve thousand operarios, who earned about 1,720,000 pesos a year. The twelve pesos a month that sugar workers in Morelos's rural factories took home meant their wages exceeded those of any other rural employment in Mexico, except for the industrial job of working in a mine. As a result, people came from the states of Puebla, Mexico, and Guerrerro seeking

Figure 7. Workers outside a hacienda sugar factory, nineteenth century. Image captures the industrial and agrarian aspects of sugar production.

work, prompting Governor Pacheco to remark that the mills had become major magnets for labor (see Figure 7).[4] Sugar was not the only important agricultural enterprise in Morelos though. Rice cultivation was introduced into the irrigated hot lands in 1843, near Tetecala and the valley of Jojutla, and timber and fruits represented important enterprises in different subregions of the state, but sugar still ruled.

When the Mexican government contemplated granting a railroad concession to the Pennsylvania Railroad in 1872, the company conducted a commercial analysis to measure the quantity and value of goods being transported in the area to determine the potential profitability of the project. They found that the volume of crops shipped from the greater Cuernavaca Valley to Mexico City via mule in 1871 totaled 1.5 million *arrobas* of sugar, five hundred thousand arrobas of corn, and one hundred thousand barrels of *aguardiente* (a low-grade, rum-like drink). The numbers illustrated the large market for Morelos's agricultural products outside the state, as well as the high level of commerce between Morelos and the central valley. The established economic activity, as well as the future potential, attracted the railroad to Morelos. The railroads did not create the commerce, but they did expand it significantly.[5]

Predictably, the government tried to exact its share of the wealth, levying an 11 percent tax on the sugar haciendas in 1874. By that time it was apparent that Díaz was going to have difficulty ever being elected president, so he launched another rebellion, this time to overthrow Lerdo. Díaz seized power by force in 1876, interrupting the peaceful transfer of the presidency in Mexico and making the 11 percent tax Leyva had charged, the highest the hacendados in Morelos would have to pay for the next forty years.[6] Despite his earlier promises to the pueblos, Díaz proceeded to instill a political climate that supported hacendado rule across Mexico, stifled pueblo autonomy, and promoted economic growth through commercial agriculture and raw-material exports. As a result, land consolidation and pueblo deprivation continued in Morelos, with profound social consequences for the region and the nation.

Sugar and Progress

Díaz set about pacifying villager resistance to the elite version of Liberal progress in Morelos and across the country. The Porfiriato (Díaz's rule from 1876–1910) brought sustained economic growth for many years. Political stability helped make that possible and so did a model of development geared to attracting foreign investment and stimulating exports in mining and agriculture. During Díaz's reign, Morelos underwent a form of rural industrialization that drove real estate values there higher than anywhere else in Mexico except the nation's capital. Relative social stability improved the conditions for business. By 1881 commerce and travel between Mexico City and Cuernavaca, considered extremely dangerous only twenty years earlier, flourished because of the expansion of the sugar industry and greater safety on rural roads. For example, in 1881, 151 stagecoaches carrying 3,263 passengers went between those two cities, as did 35,920 mules and 40,376 donkeys hauling sugar and other tropical products, along with 23,445 people on foot, all being passed by about thirteen thousand riders on horseback. More than fifteen thousand head of cattle added to the traffic as they were driven through the low mountain passes on their way to Mexico City slaughterhouses.[7] Commercial agriculture grew so that by 1910, agricultural products displaced silver as Mexico's main overseas export earner. Meanwhile, technological innovations in the sugar haciendas led to huge increases in production, and major improvements in transportation enabled producers to supply a growing domestic market that Díaz protected from foreign competition with high tariffs.

The apparent economic prosperity and political stability of the Porfiriato, however, veiled the social costs accompanying it. The sugar estates subsumed entire pueblos as they expanded, and hacendados tried to make their control of resources translate into control of people too. All the major hacendados established hacienda schools and maintained hacienda churches to provide rudimentary education and social indoctrination to their workers. The combination worked to justify the prevailing social order to dependent laborers living subservient lives on the estates. Despite hacendado efforts at social management, the system of domination that emerged did not stop rural workers from developing a sociopolitical vision distinct from elite alternatives.[8]

The concentration of wealth in Morelos became more extreme during the Porfiriato, even at the top. Larger haciendas annexed smaller ones, while others dropped out of operation all together. For example, twenty-eight families owned about forty haciendas and controlled half of the territory of the state in 1880. By 1909, only eighteen large landowners remained.[9] Smaller haciendas and mills were abandoned, or absorbed by larger more productive enterprises operating on a greater economy of scale. Haciendas like Mapastlán and Xochimancas decayed, and some, like Apanquetzalco, vanished entirely as the oligarchy tightened.[10]

Raising sugarcane was the single most profitable pursuit in Morelos. But the sugar industry also stimulated other local business activities, and the concentration of land ownership allowed the hacendados access to a variety of crucial natural resources within the boundaries of their properties. The main ancillary product from sugar was aguardiente, and thirty-two distilleries manufactured it for local and regional consumption. Outside of endeavors related to sugar production, people could find work at one of the five breweries, one of three cigarette factories, or in small mining operations. Thus, other activities existed, but they offered limited employment alternatives. The profitability of sugar was what motivated hacendados to take over pueblo lands, wrest control of their subsistence fields, expand their fields devoted to the cash crop, and transform a large portion of the rural populace from a partially self-sufficient peasantry into a wage-dependent rural proletariat.

Due to a paucity of sources, it is difficult to document the acre-by-acre expansion of the sugar haciendas in Morelos, but their growth marked the period from 1860–1910 and did not stop until the revolution ended it. At that point, in 1910, only about 13 percent of the surface of the state remained as communal pueblo land. Most of that belonged to pueblos in the mountainous northern parts of the state and included forests and pastures with little agricultural value. Commercial timber interests began to encroach there by the end of the Porfiriato, bringing some of the conflict that had marked the sugar regions to the mountains.[11] Other evidence, particularly increases in sugar production, rising values of the estates, land litigation, complaints of labor shortages, and changing demographic patterns indicate the impact that the loss of common land and water had on rural society.[12] For example, back in 1864 the hacienda Santa Inés, in the municipality of Cuautla, was valued at three hundred fifty thousand pesos and had about 2,575 hectares of land planted in sugarcane and produced about seventy-two thousand panes of sugar and sixty-four thousand arrobas of honey. By 1900, Santa Inés's value reached five hundred fifty thousand pesos, cane covered about 3,240 hectares of irrigated land, and workers processed the cut cane in two mills on the estate, producing approximately 1,874,072 kilos of sugar and 1,139,180 kilos of honey in 1900–1901. Production continued to go up for most of the decade. That increase did not represent land acquisition alone, which continued but had largely been consolidated by the early Porfiriato. It mainly reflected the hacendados' concentrated focus on increasing sugar production that was made possible by technological innovations and putting more acres under irrigation, and facilitated by government complicity in the commandeering of other resources besides land, especially water.[13]

Santa Inés fit a general pattern across the state. Other haciendas, like Cuahuixtla, rose in value from an estimated three hundred and twenty thousand pesos in 1864, to one million three hundred thousand in 1900. Morelos's sugar haciendas produced 9,912 tons of sugar in 1864; 21,493 tons in 1898–99; and reached their apogee at 52,230 tons ten years later. Those fantastic increases resulted from geographic expansion, improvements in transportation, innovations in the productive process, increased irrigation, and the social stability provided by the Díaz dictatorship.[14]

The expansion of privately owned export-oriented agribusiness onto communal lands where people are raising staple crops in a subsistence based agrarian society usually generates hostility and resistance from those disadvantaged by the change and earns support from those who benefit. The process does not generally lead to social tranquility and stability. Cash-crop economies are inherently unstable, and so are the societies shaped by them. It is ironic, then, that the achievement of stability in Morelos coincided with the expansion of the sugar estates and dramatic increases in sugar production, even though that meant significant losses in pueblo patrimonies.

Díaz's ability to pacify the countryside resulted, in part, from the brutality of the rural police under the command of future governor Manuel Alarcón, and in part from expanding employment on the estates. When the revolution brought the Porfiriato to a violent end, hacendado Luis García Pimentel reminisced in June 1912, "Until the beginning of 1911, a perfect peace, perfect tranquility and perfect security reigned in the state, maintained by the Government with a body of Rurales." Others did not find it so perfect, however. Writing one month earlier and in the midst of the Zapatista uprising, Patricio Leyva, son of the former governor Francisco Leyva, referred to the troubled social history of the area:

> It is public knowledge that General Leyva carried out large massacres in order to pacify the state, and later, with peace restored, there were executions during the administration of Coronel Alarcón that probably reached into the thousands. That is how the social unrest that has existed in this region has been suffocated for many years, without bothering to find out its origin nor to seek its solution, because it cannot be that executions were a real solution.

Despite the appearance of calm in Morelos, it was an imposed "peace." Resistance to the changes being wrought by the hacendados continued throughout the Porfiriato, but in muted form.[15]

The Díaz regime pushed land privatization forward across Mexico, which caused the number of independent pueblos in Morelos to drop from 118 in 1876 to 105 in 1887, even though the population had increased slightly. The particularly contentious zone around Cuautla, home to Apatlaco and Anenecuilco, saw Villa de Ayala decline from about two thousand inhabitants in 1900, to one thousand seven hundred fifty in 1910, as people were driven from their pueblos onto the estates. Most pueblos held onto their fundos legales that made up the center of town where the civic buildings and peoples' houses were. Many vecinos, though, had to hire themselves out as day laborers, or they left their pueblos and moved onto the haciendas as sharecroppers and tenant farmers because the haciendas had acquired most of the farm and pasture land. Once on the estates, the landless wound up providing labor services in return for rental arrangements that allowed them to plant their crops on hacienda land in order to feed themselves.

The experiences of future Zapatista coronel Carmen Aldana of Tepalcingo offer a glimpse of the times. Born around 1880, Señor Aldana spent his youth working as a labrador with his father and brothers sowing their milpa of pueblo land with a yoke of oxen his father rented from the hacienda Tenango. His father paid the hacendado ten *cargas* of corn (one carga was 181.6 liters) for the use of the oxen. Like most Morelos campesinos, the Aldana family raised corn, and if the crop was good they sometimes sold a small amount, "una carguita," (a small load), to neighbors who had no land. But, even though the family was fortunate to have access to their pueblo's communal land, when he was a young boy, Carmen Aldana also had to go work on the hacienda when the foreman demanded it from "all the *ajihados*" (literally, god-children). When asked how much he was paid, which included working "one day with the ox team, to plow or scatter seeds," Señor Aldana replied, "nothing, that son of a bitch that was in Huitzilac would say 'you're going to work over there, but for free' and he would send us away to the hacienda, as we were already cowed." The hacienda representative in Huitzilac was a man named Don Lupe, and if someone refused to work, he had the police come and throw them in jail in Jonacatapec. But, for Carmen and his brothers, who had access to pueblo land, free labor services were only an occasional obligation. Others, though, were less fortunate than the Aldanas.[16]

Agapito Pariente and Lorenzo Vergara, contemporaries of Carmen Aldana, were both born the sons of landless "peónes" on the hacienda Tenango, and they, like their fathers before them, became hacienda "peónes" too. They lived lives familiar to many, including the 892 other resident laborers on Tenango in 1900.[17] They woke before the sun rose and worked from six A.M. to six P.M. for fifty centavos a day, six days a week. They paid five or six cargas of corn for the use of the hacendado's oxen when they needed to till their own semiarid plots that the hacendado allowed ranchería residents like them to farm. In addition to gaining control of the state's natural resources, the planters created a ready labor force out of the people they dispossessed.[18]

Despite that widespread pattern, the influential hacendado Ignacio de la Torre y Mier of Tenextepango said he did not know of any haciendas that "had absorbed any pueblos, with the exception of Temixco and Calderon, which paid cash and bought, piece by piece, the total extension of the pueblos of Acatlipa and San Pedro." Another important hacendado, Manuel Araoz, saw the process the same way and explained that

> it should be said that the haciendas of San Juan,
> Santa Cruz, Chuachichinola, La Luz and the vast
> tracts dedicated to cultivating sugarcane and rice,
> called the "Llano de Tlaquiltenango" and the "Llano
> de Higueron" were formed exclusively from lands
> that used to be common lands, by acquisitions at just
> prices and under free contracts they have slowly and
> surely been uniting these tracts until they formed the
> ones mentioned earlier.[19]

The sugar estates continued to expand by acquiring pueblo ejidos and suffocating small villages, but they also surrounded major towns. For example, by the 1890s, Jonacatepec, the most important town in the southeastern portion of the state, had almost stopped growing because the hacienda Tenango hemmed it in on all sides. Even a significant town like Cuautla was totally surrounded by haciendas and sugarcane, which grew right up to the edge of the urban center. Medium-sized ranchos also began to disappear as land ownership became increasingly unequal. There had been fifty-three ranchos in 1876, but only thirty-six remained in 1887. The Ley Lerdo and the Liberal effort to create a class of small independent yeoman farmers failed, at least in Morelos.[20]

Hacendados and their administrators understood what was happening to both pueblos and small farmers, and it coincided nicely with their rising needs for labor. Their cultural attitudes exacerbated the material conditions as they also took pride in being Spaniards, distinguishable from their Mexican workers. Other upper-middle-class educated Mexicans also recognized a difference and granted them a kind of noble status. Cecilio Robelo, a well-known engineer and the author of a descriptive account of the geography and people of Morelos, described Tomás Ruíz as a "Spanish gentleman, known throughout the state, and one of the most respected cultivators of cane." Ruiz served as the administrator of the large and productive hacienda Zacatepec and told the state government in the early 1880s that to "achieve greater sugar production it will be necessary to form larger haciendas with sufficient labor." He also said that ongoing technological improvements in production and the consolidation of larger estates would be futile without sufficient labor power.

Figure 8. Irrigation canal and bridge, nineteenth century. Note the inflow of water at left. Water disputes increased as large landholders built canals to irrigate their own fields and diverted water away from pueblos and other smaller-scale landholders.

Hacendados felt a real need to insure a supply of dependent, or at least readily available labor. Thus, taking over land not only led to dispossession, it created a landless labor force as well.[21]

The men working on the sugar haciendas performed specific tasks according to a tight time schedule, especially during the zafra, or harvesting of the cane. Pueblo vecinos who moved onto a hacienda experienced some fundamental changes, even as they tried to hold onto elements of their peasant lifestyle. Instead of growing subsistence crops for himself and family on inherited communal lands that were passed on from father to son, a worker answered to the clang of the work bell on the hacienda, took orders from the foreman, and worked in the fields raising a cash crop under the eye of an overseer, on somebody else's land for somebody else's profit.

Hacendados devoted the most well-irrigated land to sugarcane and left less favorable lands dependent on rainfall for their workers' plots of corn (see Figure 8). Because they were relegated to marginal lands with insufficient water, no real system of *colonos* (small-scale farmers raising their own cane and selling it to the mills for processing) developed in Morelos, as it did in some other sugar-growing regions of Latin America, such as Cuba or Brazil. As a rule, hacendados opposed the independent cultivation of sugarcane by pueblos or campesinos and, as a result, the raising and marketing of the region's most profitable product was totally dominated by a few powerful individuals who were mainly absentee landowners living in Mexico City.[22]

Peasants into Workers

Driving people off the land and onto the haciendas was the first step in their conversion from peasants into workers. Even though they had to leave their communities to seek employment, campesinos in Morelos maintained their ties to the soil as they became part of an incipient rural proletariat. All hacendados kept large tracts of unirrigated land, called tierras de temporal. They leased out small plots to the campesinos of nearby communities, which the tenants worked for their own subsistence. Workers then paid the hacendado three to six cargas of corn for the use of the land and occasionally provided free labor in the fields.

Lorenzo Vergara's father lived in a ranchería settlement on the hacienda Tenango where the hacendado allowed him to work a piece of land and rent a team of oxen for five cargas of corn. Some of his neighbors, like future Zapatista Plácido Amacende Pérez of Tepalcingo, were better off. His father had access to a plot of land where Plácido worked when he was a boy. When there was no work to be done on their own land, they sometimes gathered firewood to sell in Jonacatepec. Señor Amacende Pérez reported that others, the "*peónes acasillados*," who lacked land and had to rent from the hacienda performed tasks like creating the borders and rows for the rice paddies and served one day a week with the oxen, plowing or seeding, or cleaned and repaired irrigation ditches, bridges, and water works in return for access to their small plots.[23]

Hacendados devoted only a small fraction of their operations to sugarcane cultivation, but the forests, pastures, irrigated, and unirrigated lands formed an integrated unit. They disposed of their resources in different proportions depending on the ecological peculiarities of their properties, but their overall goal remained producing sugar and making money. The forests provided the wood and charcoal that fueled the furnaces in the mill house, the unirrigated outlying fields grew corn and other consumables that fed the workers living in the clustered shacks, and the pastures fed the grazing cattle, oxen, horses, and mules. The draft animals hauled the wagons loaded with cut cane and carried other hacienda products to nearby markets and railheads. All the parts of the hacienda played important roles in the productive process and formed a secondary source of income themselves.

As hacendados continued to claim open or ejido land, more campesinos had to pay fees to pasture their animals on hacienda lands and for the right to gather dry wood for the charcoal that they sold, or used for heating and cooking. Luis García Pimentel inadvertently revealed the extent of hacienda expansion by 1912, when, in an effort to make himself and other hacendados appear magnanimous, he said the pueblos near his properties had always received excellent and just treatment, "especially in the times of Sr. Dn. Manuel Alarcon y del Teniente coronel Dn. Pablo Escandón, who obtained from me considerable concessions in favor of the pueblos, such as the reduction of rent from their corn crop, donations of water, corrals for their cattle etc."[24] What the hacendado was saying, apparently without realizing it, was that his haciendas had taken over so much pueblo and public lands that the vecinos of neighboring pueblos now had to come ask him for permission to graze cattle in the pastures, or receive "donations" of water, the source of which were rivers and springs that had been part of the public domain and had fallen under the control of the estates. The fact that pueblo vecinos had to rely on the good will of a hacendado to lower rental rates on the land where they raised their corn indicated the extent of hacienda expansion and that not only the hacienda workers but also the once independent pueblo vecinos had become dependent on the whims of the hacendados.

The sugar harvest took place during the dry season, from December to May, with a workforce paid mainly in cash. Generally, the campesino's workday was from sunup to sundown, lasting from about six in the morning to six in the evening, with a one-hour break for a meal and some rest. The day began with the administrator's assistant, *el segundo*, calling roll in the predawn and shouting out the names of the cane cutters, where they would work that day, and with which cart driver. The cane cutters wore loose-fitting homespun white shirts and trousers fashioned out of locally grown cotton. They worked in groups of ten or twelve and moved through fields of green cane that towered above their heads. A hacienda captain on horseback watched over them and was responsible for the production of their teams. The cane cutters swung their machetes at the base of the tall cane plants, severing them, and at regular intervals workers paused to heave the long cut stalks to the cane loaders, who stood on the flat beds of the mule carts and stacked the cane into piles for transport to the mill (see Figure 9).[25]

Cane cutters and other fieldworkers lived in wooden shacks on the hacienda real, or were recruited from the nearby communities. When he was eighty-one years old and being interviewed in 1973, former Zapatista cavalry captain José Lora Mirasol recalled growing up in Jonacatepec, where his father was a bricklayer. When José was only seven, his father was killed along with about two hundred others in a major accident while building a bridge at La Cuera for the hacienda Calderon. The hacendado compensated the widows and orphans with pensions. José received fifteen pesos. With his father dead, the young José began working at the hacienda Santa Clara to support himself. Luis García Pimentel owned Santa Clara and claimed that the treatment of workers before the revolution "in all the haciendas could not have been any better, because in addition to the magnificent day wages they were paid, the workers and peónes on the estates are provided with doctors, medicine, schools, religious services, as well as pensions for the elderly and invalids, and for the sick and for the orphans and widows of the workers."

The benevolence of the García Pimentels and the fifteen pesos meant to replace his father did not keep José and the other workers on the estate from going to sleep in chozas on beds made out of sacks. The crude structures lacked wooden chairs or any other comforts, but provided the most common home for many resident families. Men from villages further away, who were recruited by field captains and attracted by the seasonal work and relatively high pay, lived in these shacks until they went back home. The demand for labor during the zafra brought men into Morelos from Guerrerro and Puebla. Afraid of labor shortages at critical moments, some hacendados contemplated importing workers from Asia.[26] During the zafra, seasonal laborers mingled with hacienda dependents on the estates, where temporary workers earned anywhere from three to four reales a day (thirty-eight to fifty centavos), which was paid out before sunset on Saturdays.[27]

Few workers on Porfirian Morelos sugar haciendas were debt peons, though the practice was prevalent in other parts of the country, especially the North. On the eve of the revolution, Morelos sugar workers complained about being paid in scrip redeemable at the company store, but not about debt. Agapito Pariente, for example, grew up on some marginal land on the hacienda Tenextepango. Like most hacienda peónes, his family paid the hacendado five cargas of corn for that right. When he was seventeen, Agapito began to supplement his family's income by working at the haciendas Chinameca

Figure 9. Workers unloading carts of cut cane inside hacienda walls, nineteenth century.

and Tenextepango. Both haciendas had their own tienda de raya (company store), where they sold him goods by docking his pay and keeping a record of his transactions. Two main classes of resident peon prevailed, those who worked in the fields like Señor Pariente and those who worked "inside the hacienda." The latter were paid more and treated better.[28]

Born in 1895, in San Miguel el Grande, Miguel Dominguez Peña joined the Zapatista rebellion at a young age, and his story reflected a broader pattern. His father had no land, so the family was forced to go to the hacienda Tenango and ask permission to till some marginal land there. The hacendado charged the usual five cargas of corn, two *tareas* of unpaid work in the cane fields of the hacienda (one tarea equaled three-quarters of an acre) plus help in bundling one hundred bales of hay." Not everyone from San Miguel had the same kind of rental agreement with Tenango. Some enjoyed access to pueblo lands; others had to rent from the hacienda, and some were "peónes de la hacienda," who Señor Dominguez said were more submissive and humbled and were more permanent fixtures on the estate.[29] The demand for labor during the zafra, and the difficulty of the job, with backs bent constantly under the heat of the tropical sun, with only a large straw sombrero for protection, made wages in the cane fields of the Morelos lowlands higher than agricultural pay elsewhere in the country. The pay varied from twenty-five to seventy-five centavos, depending on the hacienda and the age and experience of the worker. Meanwhile jornaleros in the Mexican Mesa Central scraped by on only eighteen to twenty-five centavos a day.[30]

Work on a sugar hacienda resulted in stark divisions. Privileged employees like the administrator, the sugar master, and the segundo formed a well-compensated salaried group. The administrators of major haciendas formed part of the local elite. Their social activities included interacting with other people who held important positions, such as judges, engineers, police chiefs, and even governors. Their allegiances were to the hacendado, not to the workers, the "peónes acasillados," the rancherías, or the pueblo communities. Estate administrators were recognized as the representatives of the hacendado. They were responsible for maintaining worker discipline and for the profitable functioning of the haciendas. Salaries for administrators ranged from fifteen hundred to three thousand pesos a year.

Besides the huge discrepancy in income, status, and lifestyle between management and the mostly illiterate, dependent peónes, there were clear ranks within the upper echelons. The second-in-command earned between five hundred and one thousand pesos a year and the sugar master somewhere between four hundred to eight hundred pesos, depending on the hacienda. The larger more prosperous operations employed an extra assistant to the sugar master who made about three hundred pesos annually. These men constituted the most important and loyal employees of the estate, with administrators living on the haciendas in special quarters with house servants waiting on them in a situation reminiscent of the colonial era. García Pimentel was aware of the "friction and bad feelings that in many cases was due to the clash of the races that work in the state, the Spanish or white, and the indigenous; but it is certain that there has been no systematic abuse on any hacienda." Despite the hacendado's claims, Morelos, in the late nineteenth and early twentieth centuries, still echoed with the servitude and paternalism of a rural society built on Indian tribute and black slavery.[31]

Other more or less permanent employees participated in the elaborate operation of making sugar. Mounted *guarda tierras* patrolled the fields armed with guns and made sure bandits and other marauders did not burn or disrupt the harvest. The assistant administrator, or el segundo, watched over the *macheteros* (cane cutters), accompanied by the *guarda cortes*, who made sure the cane cutters and fieldworkers kept their machetes swinging and did not

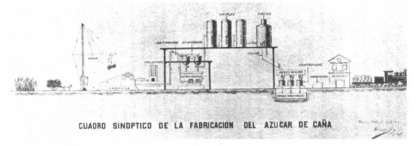

CUADRO SINOPTICO DE LA FABRICACION DEL AZUCAR DE CAÑA

Figure 10. Diagram of sugar-making process from cane standing in the field to sugar weighed and sacked for transport.

eat or steal the crop. Although most were not bound by their debts, work for hacienda dependents took on a form of forced labor. If they did not work, they were expelled from the estate, and since their was no other land available, they had to meet the labor obligations the hacendados imposed.

The macheteros in the fields cut the cane, and the *carreteros* piled the cut stalks high onto mule-driven carts. A couple of men then walked along behind the wagons as they made their way to the mill and picked up any cane that fell off. They unloaded the cane at the mill house and weighed in their work with the scale operator who recorded the name of the head machetero and from which part of the hacienda the load came. The cane cutters and cart drivers repeated the process all day until the sun set. The value of their work for the week was based on the weigh-ins and determined every Saturday by the *purgador*, who oversaw the draining of the sugar of impurities.

Making sugar out of cane was a long and arduous process that required a rigid division and specialization of labor around the mill.[32] The trapiche, or mill house, had to work day and night during the five-month harvest, so administrators divided their mill workers into teams that worked in six-hour shifts twenty-four hours a day. They changed every time a team completed its tarea, or work shift. The jobs in the mill house were heavy and dangerous and performed in withering heat. The *guarda-trapiche* was in charge of the smooth operation of the mill and supervised the workforce of *molederos* who fed the cane into the crushers. He also supervised the other men in the boiler room and around the mill and machinery. After the cane was crushed, the juice squeezed out of it flowed down a canal to waiting cauldrons. A *bagacero* took the refuse fiber (*bagazo*) from the cane and piled it onto carts to be taken outside, dried in the sun, and then stored as fuel to

Figure 11. Inside a Morelos sugar factory, nineteenth century.

feed the furnaces later (see Figures 10 and 11).[33]

Once the crushers extracted the juice from the cane plant, the syrupy substance entered a canal watched over by a *canalero* who cleared the path of debris and contaminants as the juice rolled its way to the *espumadera* (filter boxes). Passing through the filters, the product went to the *caldero* who boiled the whole brew. The *caldo* (strained cane juice) was then checked for sweetness and taken from the fire at just the right moment before the final group of workers in this sequence of specialized tasks, the *banqueros,* had to remove the hot syrupy caldo and pour it into forms to dry. According to the administrator of the hacienda Miacatlán, "For the *banco* you want strong men because it is a heavy job and, above all, they should be dexterous, because if they are not they are very likely to burn themselves."[34] Working in a Morelos sugar mill was exhausting, dangerous, and characterized by fatigue and overwork during the harvest.

Once the cane became raw sugar, a *guarda-melado* took note of the quantity of the outgoing sugar to make sure none turned up missing. The sugar master watched over the entire process to see that everyone did their job properly and at the right moment. The sugar master and his segundo looked after the whitening of the sugar, while a third official made sure that "the peónes work[ed] with order and did not waste time."[35] The sugar master's task was considered something of an art, and finding a good sugar master was crucial.

Administrators divided workers into two general groups according to ability and experience. Those they deemed "more intelligent" made up the first group and worked in the more industrialized aspects of production when the mill ran around the clock six days a week. They rested on Sunday. When the sugar-making operations stopped, the people who worked in each part of the mill cleaned their area. All the while other permanent employees did their jobs, including the men responsible for keeping the fires stoked, the blacksmith and his assistant, the mechanics who repaired the machinery, the workers who cleared the irrigation ditches, and the cowboys and ranch hands who tended the herds in the pastures. The administrator's job was to coordinate the activities of all these people. His trusted position usually only came after years of service to the hacienda, filling positions like assistant to the sugar master and foreman, although some who came from Cuba obtained the position because their reputation preceded them. It was important that the administrator be familiar with all aspects of the hacienda and have close knowledge of both agriculture and industry.[36]

Most workers received their pay by the week, and wages varied by task and skill. Some workers were paid a daily wage, others by the job. Child labor was widespread, with many children beginning their working lives at about age ten Those over ten years of age generally received a set amount per day. Women worked preparing food, but none worked in the cane fields or in the mills. The temporary laborers were all men or boys who worked with no guarantees and earned their pay piecemeal.

Cultural and linguistic differences accentuated the marked social distinctions on the estates because many of the administrators were Spaniards. The well-connected hacendado of Tenextepango, Ignacio de la Torre y Mier, expressed a widely held sentiment: "It is important to understand that field workers in the warm climates of this country are extremely apathetic and unfortunately, for the most part, excessively viscious." Those age-old prejudices helped insure that social and political advancement in Morelos failed to keep pace with economic growth during the Porfiriato. Thus, despite relatively high wages, the workers' share of what they produced was going down relative to rising hacendado profits. Coupled as that was with pervasive contempt and racism, many rural people resented it.

Little hope existed for social mobility or to improve one's station in life in the Porfirian Morelos countryside, because where people started out in life was usually where they ended up. José Lora, for example, went to work at age seven on the hacienda Calderon, where he slept on a dirt floor in a wooden shack. Señorita Luz Cordova, by contrast, was a daughter of the Escandón family of Atlihuayan and took piano lessons as part of her grooming to become a cultured woman. While boys like José Lora were laboring in the fields on her family's estate, she demonstrated her piano playing for the visiting governor of Morelos and a small entourage in the hacienda's main house in August 1885. Cecilio Robelo, one of the state's leading engineers, accompanied the governor on his tour of Morelos. He called Atlihuayan "one of the finest estates, because of the quality and amount of sugar and alcohol, and its magnificent residence, crowned by a soaring viewing tower, it is a exquisite mansion one would never want to leave, mainly because of the grace and cordiality of its residents." At the same time that Cecilio Robelo was admiring Luz Cordova, and the gallantry and cordiality of his hosts, the neighboring campesinos were litigating because their lands were being taken from them. Workers on the estates would later complain that during the Porfiriato they were beaten when they worked too slowly, that they were cheated at the tienda de raya, and that the estate administrators generally treated them like either animals or slaves.

While the owners and mansions of the haciendas of Morelos impressed *licenciado* Robelo, much of the religious imagery and cultural aspects of the campesino countryside repulsed him. He wrote in his journal:

> I wanted to talk about the images of some of the
> saints that we have seen being worshiped in the temples, and about the religious practices that I have had
> occasion to witness in certain pueblos; but I decided
> to wait to see if this phenomenon was reproduced in
> other places. And that is what happened...the images
> of Jesus Christ venerated with the name "Santo
> Entierro," are in general, the images of a black sugarcane worker; their facial features are quite ugly, and
> they apply a large amount of black balm [to the
> images] regularly. Every year on June 24th, the people
> of the pueblo of Coatelco submerge a statue of John
> the Baptist in the lake all night long, in order to
> prevent the lake from going dry.

Licenciado Robelo's aversion to these religious images underscored the cultural divide in Porfirian Morelos. Although they were all citizens of the same nation, their worlds were as different as if they were separated by the sea.[37]

It was a time of interesting juxtapositions in general. The main urban centers had barbers who still bled people when they complained of certain ailments, resulting in accidents and deaths, while the newspapers reported the progress of the railroad and the increasing telegraph network in the state. Newspapers also offered scientific sections on topics like how cyclones are formed and cultural segments that included excerpts from French history and philosophy and reports on the symphony's performance in Cuernavaca. Most of Mexico's technological and cultural advancements failed to improve the lives of the average campesino, though, and most remained illiterate.[38]

Born within a year of each other, Carmen Aldana and Emiliano Zapata were raised in different pueblos, but both worked their father's pueblo lands when they were boys. By the time they grew up, neighboring hacendados had acquired large parts of their pueblos' lands, including their fathers' family plots that were supposed to be their inheritance. When the hacendado de la Torre y Mier took over communal lands used by the Aldanas and other vecinos of Tepalcingo and incorporated them into the hacienda Tenextepango, the Aldana family suddenly found themselves having to pay a rent of five cargas of corn to till land they considered to be rightfully theirs. Years later, when asked where the family took their rent payment in the era before the revolution, Señor Aldana answered that they took it to Tenextepango. His resentment when he said "we took the land rent over, and there those sons of bitches, those high-class gachupínes" was matched by others who lived through the Porfiriato in Morelos, many of whom later became Zapatistas. Zapatista Brigadier General Manuel Sosa Pavon, for example, recalled how the Spaniards and landlords "castigated the Indians, and how unjust the Spaniards were with our race. The Spaniards, the rich, run the haciendas, the general administrator of Tenextepango was a Spaniard, and all the haciendas around there were run by Spaniards." The prevailing inequity in Morelos fueled animosities that became seared in people's memories and came spilling out as they recounted their lives years later. Most people offered little open resistance during most of the Porfiriato, though, because they feared the consequences.[39]

Because of the latent hostility permeating rural society, some campesinos believed that the authorities were watching them. Men the authorities designated as troublemakers often wound up being sent away to work on road gangs carrying rocks. Others found themselves conscripted into the army, or sent into what amounted to slave labor in Quintana Roo. Miguel Dominquez Peña, for example, came from a poor family that lacked pueblo land and rented from the hacienda Tenango. He claimed that he could not even trust the priests at confession because they would tell the administrator when someone confessed to doing something like stealing a small piece of sugar from the hacienda, then the police would come and take the person away during the night.

Serafín Placencia from Villa de Ayala worked on several haciendas in the area and offered accounts similar to those of his fellow Zapatistas. Señor Placencia recalled older ingrained hostilities when he called both the hacendados and the priests of Morelos "gachupínes." He also said that the "peónes acasillados" of the haciendas were obligated to work six days a week for the hacendado, and if they failed to do that, the police arrested them. Constant fear of repression hung over rural society and discouraged resistance.[40]

Technology and Society

The 1880s marked an important turning point in the history of Morelos. Hacendados began to import more modern machinery from Europe and the United States and improved their techniques for producing sugar, which changed the nature of work. Before that, Morelos had lagged behind advances being made in other sugar-producing parts of the world and archaic methods prevailed. As an indication, in 1870, only one-third of the products from the twenty-eight active sugar mills was actually sugar, totaling 9,912 tons. The remaining 16,893 tons were molasses. Thanks to the greater sophistication of the techniques employed, by 1898 output in sugar relative to molasses improved to 27,493 tons of sugar to 23,602 tons of molasses. By 1908–9, the mills were turning out 52,230 tons of sugar and only 19,345 tons of the molasses by-product. That represented a colossal leap in the quantity and refinement of the sugar and in the ultimate reward: profits.[41]

Morelos, though, was an enclave economy. Increased sugar production depended on imported foreign-built machines, and profits depended on markets outside the region. The rate of technological advancement differed at every hacienda, but all the major hacendados had purchased the imported machinery and updated and modernized their mills by 1910.[42] The hacienda and *ingenio* known as San Vicente serves as a good example. Located in the district of

Cuernavaca, two hundred meters from the San Vicente stop on the Mexico, Cuernavaca, and Pacific Railroad, the hacienda was one of the major sugar producers in Morelos. Three different haciendas—San Vicente, Chiconcuac, and San Gaspar—made up the complex. A German-made rail system linked them together, with mules pulling carts loaded with cane on iron rails to the ingenio. This "steel road" measured twelve kilometers, and an offshoot of the main railroad linked the train station to the mill. Seventy-five platform cars of German construction carried the sugar to the station where new hoisting cranes unloaded it. The hacendado-businessman Delfín Sánchez owned the San Vicente complex and had helped bring the railroad to Morelos. After his death his widow became the absentee owner of this vast operation. She traveled from her home in Mexico City to visit her country estate, and she arrived looking out on the shacks of her peónes and other workers in the fields from the window of her luxury passenger car made in France.[43]

San Vicente was a fully modernized industrial operation. The trapiche's eight-cylinder crusher extracted the juice so thoroughly that it left the bagazo dry enough to pass directly into the furnaces for fuel without being dried in the sun. The trapiche could mill thirty-five thousand arrobas of cane every twenty-four hours. Modern apparatus like centrifuges, filters, and a press with evaporators, plus a second boiler to purify the cane juice, produced crystallized sugar. The machines ran on steam, were built in French factories, and yielded a high-quality sugar in vastly greater quantities than had been possible before.

The hacienda Zacatepec, near Jojutla in the south, was another modernizing mill run with foreign machinery and producing increasingly vast quantities of sugar. Production at Zacatepec went from 708,797 kilos of sugar in 1899 to a huge 5,393,953 kilos in 1909. Today, the complex is the largest producer of sugar in the state. The hacienda Cuahuixtla, near Cuautla and Apatlaco, made similar advancements. Foreign technology and major capital investments allowed hacendados to transform their estates into modern agribusinesses. But the haciendas needed workers. According to Governor Jesús Preciado's report in 1887, sugar production, because of "its industrial nature requires innumerable hands" and provides "a secure source of subsistence to a great number of the vecinos of the state." The governor also pointed to the United States, Mexico's largest trading partner, and commented that among those enjoying Morelos's sugar were customers in "the neighboring republic to the north, confirming its deserved reputation so that we can be assured that if not superior to (sugars) of other countries, it can compete with them."[44] The governor made two important points: first, a large number of people depended on the sugar industry for a "secure source of subsistence," and second, the ability of Morelos sugar to compete abroad was of increasing importance because booming production threatened to outstrip domestic demand. Although he could not have predicted the results of the Cuban war for independence, or the so-called Spanish-American War, any reliance on the U.S. market still presented a risky gamble because of Hawaiian sugar. If Mexican production outran domestic demand, the governor's hopeful prognostication about Morelos sugar being globally competitive would meet a critical test. It was the same test that eventually faces all one-dimensional cash crop- and raw material-producing economies everywhere. Failing it could have dire consequences, including jeopardizing the "secure source of subsistence" of much of Morelos's population.

As the Morelos sugar industry moved into the modern age, it seemed like all that hacendados with sufficient capital needed to do was raise enough cane to keep their new machines busy. That, however, required more land and water first. Hacendados responded by ordering the construction of ambitious water-transport systems to bring their drier fields to life. Investments in irrigation, along with prior commitments in developing the railroad and technology, turned Morelos into a network of rural factories. Workers for Ignacio de la Torre, for example, built a canal that doubled the irrigated surface area of his huge and profitable estate, Tenextepango, that sat to the southeast of Anenecuilco, Apatlaco, and Villa de Ayala. The results justified the effort. The hacienda produced a very respectable 2,652,159 kilos of sugar in 1903, but by 1909 production increased to 4,177,688 kilos.[45] Likewise, Luis García Pimentel invested $166,000 in the construction of tunnels, canals, aqueducts, and dams to divert water over sixty miles from where it flowed in the Cuautla River.[46] The water making its way to Tenango helped the growth of other family-owned properties, like the hacienda Santa Clara, but it also fueled disputes with villagers who wanted to use that water too.

The Railroad

The Díaz regime brought more change in thirty years than the Morelos economy had seen in the last three hundred. Along with the new technological advances in production and a more stringent work regimen, the railroad proved a big boon to business. Responding to a questionnaire from the Secretaría de Hacienda in 1887, hacendados south of Cuernavaca complained about the poor conditions of the roads their pack animals had to travel when transporting sugar from the lowlands, up through the mountains, and back down into Mexico City. The costs of this antiquated practice consumed 25 percent of their total productive outlay each year.[47] That bite, they said, concerned them more than anything.

A railway linking Mexico City to the large and wealthy haciendas around Cuautla had been built in 1881. Envious hacendados in the Cuernavaca Valley were elated when the last stake of the Mexican Mesa Central was finally driven in 1892, connecting Mexico City to Cuernavaca, and down to Puente de Ixtla. At Puente de Ixtla the Interoceanic Railroad connected with the Cuernavaca line of the Mexican Central. A loop of the Interoceanic also linked Cuautla to Puebla by 1902. The Interoceanic ran all the way to Veracruz and connected the Mexican interior to the world. The first decade of the twentieth century saw the Morelos branch of the Interoceanic carrying "large freights from the sugar mills around Cuautla and other portions of the state."[48]

Interestingly, the railway reaching Cuautla, in the heart of Morelos's richest sugar-producing region, was built eleven years before the one linking Cuernavaca, the state's capital and largest urban center, to Mexico City. It was typical of Porfirian efforts, which placed growth, exports, and markets above the general public and their daily needs. The construction of the railroads presented very real opportunities for personal advantage to both Mexican and foreign entrepreneurs. Morelos hacendados like Delfín Sánchez, investor in various haciendas, actively participated in bringing the railroad into the state and shared financial interests with some of the most powerful men in the country, including General Manuel González, who served as president of Mexico for four years and was an ally of Porfirio Díaz.[49]

Díaz himself had presided over the ceremony inaugurating the earlier-built Cuautla Railway, and the notables of the state had stood with him, including large-scale landowners and major stockholders in the rail company, individuals like Mendoza Cortina of the hacienda Cuahuixtla, García Icazbalceta of Tenango and Santa Clara, and Delfín Sánchez, the son-in-law of Benito Juárez, along with other sugar producers and investors in the railroad.[50] Despite an inauspicious beginning where a bridge collapsed causing a train to fall into a gorge, killing 149 people and injuring another 112, the gross profits per ton of cut cane grew by more than 100 percent from the day the railroad opened to the outbreak of the revolution, so it was viewed as a major success.[51] By 1888, most Mexican stockholders sold out to British investors who had helped sponsor the venture; thus, the British assumed control of Mexico's Interoceanic Railroad. From the hacendados' perspective though, the main goal had been accomplished and the most lucrative parts of Morelos were linked to Mexico City and beyond. The revolution in transportation in Morelos was only one part of a process taking place throughout the country. The amount of track laid across Mexico climbed from 1,073 kilometers in 1880 to more than 12,000 kilometers by 1898.[52]

The Mexican railroad system reflected a series of well-planned investments intended to facilitate the country's import and export trade. In what was seen as a mutually beneficial relationship by the Porfirian government and foreign investors, the railroads were built linking places of production, or potential production, to major urban centers and ports, while simultaneously opening up those centers to foreign manufactures coming the other way. A look at a map of the railways constructed by 1884, demonstrates the overall pattern of linking resources and markets quite clearly. The ports of Veracruz, Guaymas, Progreso, and later, Tampico were all linked to major urban centers where some foreigners hoped to sell imported goods, and others hoped to invest in extractive industries. The Mexican government encouraged both activities, because it hoped to tap the wealth of Mexico's natural resources by promoting foreign investment. The railroads in northern Mexico ran north to south, linking Mexican ores, timber, and agricultural products to U.S. markets. Mexico City dominated the center of the country and sent its arms of track reaching out into the countryside to pull in food and crops for sale to the city. The capital also served as a conduit on the way to the coasts and overseas markets.

A growing national economy and new job creation in export-oriented activities across the nation had uneven effects in Morelos. The local impact of the Porfirian model of development was that the sugar industry generated fantastic profits for a few, but did not promote domestic industrialization. The Porfirian model also failed to create a healthy market of middle-class consumers in Mexico. Morelos provided a classic case of economic growth that created great wealth for some and unstable, low-paying jobs for most. The result was socially retarding. It led to little autonomous development, no middle-class market creation, and little domestic innovation. The failure was national in scope. The problem was most acute in regions like Morelos that depended on the performance of one main crop, or in the North, which depended on markets in the United States.

Meanwhile, as the nineteenth century turned into the twentieth, Morelos's hacendados acquired an estimated one-half of the total territory of the state. Caught in the struggle between the communal villages and the haciendas, small properties, including urban houses and garden plots, as well as small ranchos, survived but on only about one-fifth of the total surface area of the state. That situation was magnified by the fact that the hacendados controlled the best, most well-watered lands.[53] Morelos produced by far the most sugar in Mexico and its beautiful haciendas were famous as the most mechanized and productive in the country. At the turn of the century, the state ranked third, trailing only Puerto Rico and Hawaii, in the global production of sugarcane.[54] At the time, those successes seemed to hold few social costs for elites, who perceived themselves as uplifting the nation and dragging the recalcitrant Mexican peasantry, kicking and screaming, into the modern age.

Chapter Eight

SOCIAL COSTS OF OVERPRODUCTION AND THE ORIGINS OF THE MORELOS REVOLUTION

Potential profits from greater sugar production during the Porfiriato fueled land grabbing by hacendados, while pueblos tried to defend their lands in the courts but met constant defeat. The expanding plantations drove campesinos from their land and absorbed them as seasonal wage laborers. Increases in the amount and value of sugar being produced indicated the advances of the sugar industry, while villager-hacendado disputes over land and water, and worker-hacendado disputes over wages and treatment, reflected the human costs of progress based on the Porfirian model of absentee-owner, export-oriented economic growth. The process aggravated social tensions, but the model worked so long as the hacendados could employ the people they displaced. As if to prove the point in 1884, the *Mexican Financier* deemed Morelos "one of Mexico's most progressive states where peasants are not so restless because they are being hired at higher wages."[1]

Like other parts of Mexico undergoing rapid modernization during the Porfiriatio, modern transportation and technology revolutionized the sugar-producing zones of Morelos, but social advancements lagged. At the García Pimentel's hacienda, Tenango, the redheaded administrator, Fernando Segovia, nicknamed "The Radish," physically abused workers, including kicking them. Although Segovia had a reputation for harshness, Señor José Epitia Ruiz, who worked at Tenango, recalled that the Pimentels themselves sometimes brought their peónes clothes from Mexico City and provided a doctor when someone fell severely ill. The Pimentel's behavior reflected an old, semifeudal idea of reciprocity and mutual expectations between workers and employers on the estates.

Employer-employee relations on haciendas in Porfirian Mexico remained governed by unwritten codes of conduct that were left to the personalities and whims of the hacendados and administrators, not by social guarantees and codified responsibilities enforced by the laws of a modern state. The hacendados' sense of responsibility, although paternalistic, hierarchical, and, ultimately, degrading, sometimes made an otherwise intolerable situation more bearable for some dependent hacienda laborers who might feel personal affection for a benevolent hacendado, although rarely for an administrator.[2] Not everyone at the Pimentel's haciendas Tenango and Santa Clara was satisfied with the system, though, and elsewhere in Morelos, the "hacendado Español," Mendoza Cortina continued to run a notoriously "feudalistic" enterprise at the hacienda Cuahuixtla. Commenting on the prevailing conditions in Morelos, the newspaper, *El Hijo del Trabajo*, commented, "It is not without reason that we have been repeating that since Leyva, there is no government there but that of the Spaniards."[3]

Working to maintain the distribution of wealth and power in the state, hacendados and politicos resorted to repression when challenged. The state government, for example, considered a law suspending individual "guarantees" for certain classes of criminals. Bandits or *salteadores* who robbed trains or coaches, interrupted commerce, and disturbed the public order would face the death penalty. The harshness of the proposed punishment relative to the crime showed the real face of the Díaz dictatorship and revealed the polarity in the countryside.[4]

El Cronista de Morelos reported the murder of "el segundo del campo" of the hacienda Hospital in June 1884. Authorities accused Lino

Sánchez and Antonio Carreón, two estate workers, of the crime. Security forces captured the two men and were taking them to Cuautla to appear before a judge, but shot them to death on the way for allegedly trying to escape. Attempted "escape" was an increasingly common cause of death for criminals and bandits. But it could also apply to common laborers or campesinos unfortunate enough to be charged with committing crimes against people of power and property. The accused were routinely denied legal proceedings under Díaz's rule.[5]

Although riots and rebellions diminished under Díaz, other acts of collective resistance continued, and dissident views came from sources other than the impoverished countryside. For instance, one month after the murder of the second in command of the fieldworkers at hacienda Hospital, and the subsequent police murder of his alleged attackers, an anonymous note appeared on a post in downtown Cuernavaca. The broadside denounced Governor Carlos Quaglia and other functionaries of the city. No one knew exactly who wrote it, but, whoever it was, he was literate and urban. The newspaper, *El Cronista*, only four pages on average, ran over one full page of articles condemning the posted note, the cowardice of its authors, the harm it could cause, and discussed the mutual suspicions it created in the town. The fact that the flyer was anonymous indicated the fear of persecution for open dissent that hung over Porfirian Morelos. It also revealed that significant dissatisfaction existed in some urban quarters, while the concerned response from the pro-government newspaper demonstrated official awareness of public resentment, as well as their efforts to channel it in a more easily controlled direction.

Urban discontent surfaced among middle-class and working-class groups in Porfirian Mexico. In May 1892, the Díaz government crushed a political rally of students and workers in the Zócalo in Mexico City who were protesting the president's continual reelection. The pro-government newspaper, *El Progreso de Morelos*, condemned the Mexico City paper, the *Monitor Republicano*, for its anti-reelection rhetoric. Rural issues became integrated with these more urban-based proletarian concerns due to the energies of dissident journalists, on the one hand, and organizational efforts like the First Indian Congress of 1878–79, on the other. The First Indian Congress included representatives of the pueblos indígenas of the states of Mexico, Morelos, Hidalgo, Michoacán, Veracruz, and the Federal District. They went before the national congress in 1878 to increase awareness of the usurpations of their lands and the miserable wages they received on the estates. The Cámara de Diputados declared itself "incompetent to undertake this issue." But the Indian Congress met again a year later, in March 1879, to study how best to defend their lands and rights. Developments in Morelos were being watched and written about by others outside the state, including the Mexico City press.[6]

Implementing a united strategy on a regional scale, nine pueblos in the district of Jonacatepec, including Jantetelco, Chalcatzingo, Tetelaya, Telixtac, Amacuitlapilco, and the cabecera of Jonacatepec, all of which had become totally surrounded by the hacienda Santa Ana Tenango of the García Pimentel family, wrote a letter to Porfirio Díaz in July 1886. They asked him "como un buen padre" to personally intervene on their behalf to protect their village land rights. The supplicatory manner in which they asked Díaz for help was common of pueblo petitions in that period and reflected the social climate in which they were written. Nevertheless, given the time in which it was crafted, the broad-based petition demonstrated the awareness of the vecinos of those pueblos that they faced a common problem, and like other unified pueblos before them, they chose to act collectively. Nothing tangible came of their efforts, however.[7] Five months passed, and the lack of official action on their behalf led to the appearance of a "*gavilla de malhechores*" (band of criminals) near Jonacatepec that was spreading political proclamations and threatening the sugar haciendas. The governor at the time, Jesús Preciado, wrote Díaz to inform him that state troops were pursuing the gavilla. The nervous governor told the president, "I fear that the appearance of this group of individuals making up this gavilla ... in these same towns and related haciendas, could very easily take on an alarming character given the level of excitement which the indígenas reach when dealing with land.... Considering this, and the fact that all the haciendas are in the zafra, we must consider the grave prospect of a fire in the cane fields on one or more of the haciendas at this moment."[8] Governor Preciado then asked Díaz to send the rest of the third battalion from Guerrero (thirty of whom were already in Morelos to put down a separate rebellion of indígenas near the hacienda Tenango). Díaz told the governor to try to make do with the forces on hand, but he promised that if the crisis deepened he would send troops from Mexico City. The gavilla appeared again in January in the pueblo of Axochiapan, in the same district. It was obvious to the governor that resentment over land usurpations by the hacendado of Tenango and Santa Clara gave rise to this gavilla. One of Morelos's former governors, Carlos Pacheco, reminded the concerned parties that the pueblos involved had been trying to reclaim the disputed land through the courts for the last twenty years.[9] Frustrated in their efforts, the pueblos finally turned to extralegal means. Concerned state officials asked Díaz for permission to allow troops to pursue the gavilla into Puebla because they were too hard to catch in Morelos, since they received protection from the general population and then disappeared into the barrancas and backwoods to plan future attacks.

One year after the vecinos of the nine pueblos sent their letter to Díaz, people throughout the district of Jonacatepec were actively germinating ideas of "revolution."[10] They were not alone, and the unrest was not limited to that area. The hacendado and administrator of Cuahuixtla, near Cuautla, had their own difficulties. Someone robbed the proceeds from the tienda de raya by hijacking the hacienda mule convoy and stealing the mule carrying all the money.[11] The authorities suspected complicity on the part of the mule drivers because they found two of them far from the robbery, unscathed and getting drunk. Despite the various problems he faced, Governor Preciado assured Díaz that he was doing all he could to safeguard "the hacendados and whoever traveled" on his roads. The facts that hacienda employees aided bandits in their crimes against the estates and that villagers harbored fugitives alarmed the authorities and brought back memories of the plateados and the campesino violence of the 1860s.[12]

Christmas Day 1889 saw another armed group emerge. This time they appeared on the outskirts of Cuautla and included vecinos of that town. Usually vecinos supported insurgents with food and lodging, or by feigning ignorance about the whereabouts of a wanted bandit. The civilian population's lack of cooperation with the government insured freedom of movement for the gavillas, allowing them to elude capture. Local authorities in Cuautla uncovered the rebellious group there when they apprehended the night watchman at the north end of town as he met with three armed men, two of whom carried copies of a revolutionary political plan drawn up over a year earlier.[13] The episode at Cuautla came on the heels of another troubling case involving a rural schoolteacher named Antonio Neve, who ran a school that had no children in it. Instead, the students were all adults whom Neve was "indoctrinating" with ideas of rebellion. Whether he had any effect is unknown, but the governor claimed Neve's students had begun to "forget their duties as citizens." The governor decided to open another school to combat the negative effects caused by Neve and his ideas.[14]

The hacendados and political leaders of Morelos appreciated the value of education as a means of socialization and control. The elder Luis García Pimentel, owner of Tenango, stressed the need for schooling on the haciendas and insisted that his hacienda school held as much importance as the "trapiche and the casa de calderas." He felt that "without good teaching there are not good people," and he swore to fight those teaching false history like "so-called Liberal historians for their perverse ends." Despite the emphasis hacendados claimed to place on schooling, the hacienda schools apparently did a miserable job of actually teaching people how to read and write. Most of those who lived and worked on the haciendas as children and attended the hacienda schools in Morelos remained illiterate until the revolution.[15]

Along with education, García Pimentel felt it was crucial to provide a good Christian example to workers on his hacienda. He counseled his son and heir to give alms to the poor, especially children, because it would fortify his soul and pay for his sins. The hacendado's concern with charity, although presented in terms of scripture, directly related to daily realities in rural Morelos where the wealthy were taught to give alms, and the poor learned humility and reliance on the charitable while they waited for a better life in another world.[16] Not surprisingly, García Pimentel considered spiritual guidance on the haciendas "as important as the material aspect" and told his son how he viewed his estate dependents:

> I the same as my father, see in them men redeemable
> by Jesus Christ no more and no less than myself. It is
> not necessary to consider the workers like oxen or
> horses, but as they are, Christians put under our juris-
> diction and protection, and whose souls we should
> look after, because when you give much, you can ask
> for much.[17]

Hacendados consciously viewed their haciendas as institutions of socialization. The paternalism of the García Pimentel family centered around disseminating their version of morality and education as a way of molding the hearts and minds of their workers, fostering acceptance of the status quo, and insuring general acquiescence in the countryside.

The mix of paternalism and repression employed by both the government and landlords did not eliminate unrest. Governor Preciado faced social disturbances that he blamed on "el caracter de los indios." The governor complained that social tensions never ceased because the campesinos "want a general and complete division of the land." He became frustrated at the constant conflict and disruptions in his state. When a dispute emerged in a timber-rich area in 1890, between the pueblo of Santa María Ahuacatitlan, home of future Zapatista general Genovevo de la O, and the neighboring hacendado of Temixco, Governor Preciado sought to resolve the situation and set an example at the same time. He wrote President Díaz and said that he planned to intervene and declare Ahuactitlan's lands nationalized. Díaz told him to restrain himself, or his actions would enrage the pueblo citizenry, something Morelos did not need any more of. The president then told Preciado not to make the state shoulder an unnecessary burden. Based on his years of experience, Díaz rhetorically asked the overzealous governor why the state should run all the risks and generate hostility in the pueblos when it could use other methods instead. Díaz calmly instructed the frustrated Preciado, "You can lower your social responsibility through the survey companies: that is to say, why do the dirty work when someone else can do it for you."[18] Díaz instructed the heavy-handed governor in the subtleties of how to achieve a desired outcome without alienating public sentiment. He recommended delegating the confiscation of pueblo land to private interests like the surveying and timber companies, thereby deflecting criticism that would have otherwise been directed at the political leadership. When it came to the country people of Morelos, Díaz's sage recommendation to the governor was, "Do not agitate them."[19]

Despite his difficulties, Governor Preciado felt confident enough by 1891 to tell Díaz that "the inhabitants of the state, bellicose by nature and accustomed to anarchy, are slow to take up the advancement of material and intellectual progress, but the fact is that the causes that were the origin of so many evils do not exist now; every day the public confidence grows more and more because the vices of the past have been substituted with respect for the law and the love of work." There was some truth in the governor's words. It was probably not the "love of work" that increased public confidence and respect for the law, but the *availability* of work certainly mattered, especially in light of dwindling alternatives for village agriculture. Many otherwise independent cultivators who retained some land, but not enough to sustain their families, relied on finding hacienda work to make ends meet. Other opportunities were scarce, as explained by future Zapatista Señor Andrés Ávila of Atatluhacan, who said that people who lacked land had to go to the haciendas and ask for work because they could not find it anywhere else. With such limited alternatives outside of the haciendas, the availability of work on the estates was crucial for maintaining social stability.[20]

The Politics of Progress

Although the haciendas provided important employment alternatives, their expansion onto both village and public lands continued to fuel discontent, as did changing patterns of water use. Alejandro Arena, the owner of the haciendas Zacatepec and San Nicolás Obispo, near Jojutla, received permission in the summer of 1897 to use five thousand liters of water per second from the Río Verde, as well as the right to build a dam to irrigate the hacienda Temilpa from a powerful underground spring that creates an oasis at Las Estacas and feeds the beautiful stream that flows from it. Five years later, Manuel Alarcón, the former head of the Morelos *rurales*, took the reins as Díaz's choice for governor of the state. He soon became a hacendado himself, raising sugarcane on the newly irrigated fields of Temilpa.[21]

The Díaz administration allowed numerous concessions like the one granted Arena. A few examples illustrate a larger pattern. Ignacio de la Torre y Mier, Díaz's son-in-law, received permission in 1900 to use thirty-five hundred liters of water per second from the Cuautla River to irrigate his sugarcane fields at the hacienda Tenextepango. He also obtained the right to expropriate lands needed for aqueducts, canals, station houses, and accessories, with indemnification for the previous owners. His contract stated that any "national property in his path, he could occupy and use."[22] If property disputes arose, de la Torre y Mier and the other claimant were supposed to appear before a local judge who would decide the case within three days. The arrangement was justified as an act for the "public good," but it served private gain.

Meanwhile, at the hacienda San Gabriel de las Palmas, the Amor brothers installed a new irrigation system that carried water 900 meters at 175 liters a second, which allowed the hacienda to raise cane on 125 additional acres that formerly depended on rain (see Figure 12). Alarcón offered a trickle-down theory that disingenuously argued that the arrangements being made benefited everyone in Morelos because sugar production would go up, and with it tax revenue that would help all citizens of the state. The justification proved absurd in the extreme. When sugar production really began to take off around 1905, the governor proposed a tax reduction on the sugar haciendas, including the one he owned.[23] Business and government collusion was rampant under Díaz, and hacendados controlled politics in Morelos.[24]

Figure 12. Irrigation canal cutting through cane fields, nineteenth century. Note workers dressed in the traditional white cotton of the Morelos campesinos.

Hacendados dominated rural society, but their rule did not go unchallenged. For example, the vecinos of Yuatepec filed a claim in 1904 against the Escandón family that owned the hacienda Atlihuayán. They said that the proprietors and the administrator, Don Juan Alarcón, enjoyed special influence and power. According to the vecinos, the owners of Atlihayan received favorable treatment in the courts because one of them, Pablo Escandón, served as a personal assistant to President Díaz while the hacienda's administrator, Juan Alarcón, was the brother of the governor of Morelos. The vecinos of Yautepec complained when Juan Alarcón encouraged some of the hacienda's resident workers to confiscate more than four hundred head of Yautepec's cattle. The vecinos protested the theft, and when local authorities did nothing, they turned to the federal government. They requested that federal courts intervene to check the abuse of the local authorities, including the *juez de primera instancia* and the *jefe político* of Yuatepec, who had sided with Alarcón and Escandón. The vecinos specifically wanted to know why the laws did not seem to protect them. They felt doubly vexed when, after taking their cattle, the Escandóns then demanded they pay to get the animals back.[25]

Yautepec hired a lawyer named Jovito Serrano to represent them. Serrano offered a history of the case and noted that in previous years "the acts of which my clients are the victims would have been cause for an armed conflict or uprising because of the indignation they caused in the poor indígenas." Although he presented the possibility of rebellion in terms of history, Serrano was inferring that a future rebellion was both possible and justifiable. He asked Díaz to have the federal courts step in because the district court in Morelos was abusing its authority in a dangerous way.[26] The story was a familiar one to rural working people in Morelos, and similar episodes played themselves out across the state. For example, twenty cases reached the Supreme Court complaining of local abuses by the lower courts in Morelos for the year 1906–7. The transgressions included two practices common to dictatorships: arresting people without charging them, and illegally conscripting men into the army. An additional complaint was made against the arbitrary revoking of pueblo huertas. Foreshadowing future discontent, the citizens of Morelos directed more complaints at licenciado Rafael Ramos Alarcón, the juez de primera instancia in the heavy sugar-producing district of Cuautla, than they did against any other state official. The Cuautla Valley was the largest sugar-producing part of the state, and the epicenter of the Zapatista uprising.[27]

Back in Yautepec, people felt victimized by the Escandóns, betrayed by local representatives, and mocked by the courts. Although important in its own right, the case transcended the particulars of the incident and offered insight into the villagers' world. Their petition noted that in earlier times

> when a humble resident of a pueblo committed some
> infraction contrary to the law, he was apprehended,
> punished, and sometimes sent into military service,
> and if the act was grave, if it constituted a serious
> crime, he was thrown in jail to face severe penalties,
> and if he announced himself against the prevailing
> order and rose up in arms he would get the death
> penalty, so it stood that all the weight of the law fell
> against the indígenas.... Why then is equal rigor not
> observed for *all* delinquencies, even when not committed by indígenas, if the law has been broken are we not
> in a popular democracy which holds equal rights under
> the law supreme?[28]

The vecinos of Yuatepec wanted answers to the same basic questions asked by those at Apatlaco thirty years earlier, but updated to match contemporary circumstances and the Díaz regime's claims to democratic representation.

The Yautepec claimants reflected part of an evolving campesino worldview that saw extreme social inequalities exacerbated by repeated local abuses and nepotism, and supported by institutional injustices and corruption. The case also indicated campesino incorporation of Liberal dogma as expressed by the desire for popular democracy and for equal treatment under the law. Contrary to some portrayals, the Mexican peasantry in general, and campesinos in Morelos in particular, did not present an inert, fundamentally conservative, backward-looking, or reactionary social vision. They demanded the fulfillment of the Liberal promise, amended to accommodate the continued existence of communal control of resources and locally based self-rule.[29]

During his first fifteen years as president, Díaz faced the same sorts of disturbances that had made Morelos notorious. Although sometimes credited with bringing much needed political stability that transformed an anarchic Mexico and allowed for economic growth, Díaz does not deserve that credit. The civil wars had ended, the Conservatives had already been defeated and disgraced, and the country had made a peaceful constitutional transition to civilian rule from Juárez to Lerdo before Díaz seized power. What Díaz did succeed in doing was to make effective use of state control in order to eliminate opportunities for localized popular actions to blend with larger political and ideological alternatives like they had in earlier moments of elite crisis, foreign invasion, and civil war. The resulting pacification of Morelos was achieved by the early 1890s and lasted from then until the eve of the revolution with only minor disturbances along the way.

The years from 1890–1910 saw unprecedented increases in sugar production, made possible by land and water expropriations from the pueblos that were supported by all levels of government policy and the courts. Thus the main question becomes: Why was there relative social tranquility during the twenty years when one would expect the opposite? The answer begins with the fact that peace in Morelos was partially imposed and partially resulted from the sugar industry's ability to absorb the people it displaced.[30]

As the former head of the rurales, Governor Alarcón was a stern figure, experienced in law enforcement, and willing to use violence to impose stability on the state. No one knows how many times he used the infamous *ley fuga* (shooting someone for attempted escape) when he served as commander of the rural police, but he used it with

Antonio Francisco, an aged Tepalcingo village official who took a boundary dispute to the courts against land expropriations by the García Pimentel family. A band of rurales commanded by Alarcón found Antonio Francisco and took him to the outskirts of his pueblo in 1886, where Alarcón is said to have told the old man, "Well, you're going to stay right there as a boundary marker," and shot him dead. Not surprisingly, Tepalcingo became a hotbed of Zapatista activity during the revolution and, as punishment, government troops burned it to the ground in 1913.[31]

Despite, or maybe because of, Alarcón's ruthlessness, Díaz made him governor, and he proved politically astute. It is unlikely, though, that many in Tepalcingo mourned Alarcón when he died on the eve of the revolution. The elections held to replace him uncovered the social stress created by the policies he had enforced as Díaz's surrogate. Although much has been made of the transition to a new governor, regardless of the very real differences in personality, family wealth, urban refinement, and the paths they took to the office, very little ideological difference separated Alarcón from his successor, Pablo Escandón. Díaz handpicked both, both were hacendados, and, most importantly, both dedicated themselves to maintaining the social inequality that plagued Morelos.[32]

The Limits of Hacendado Hegemony

The hacendados finally succeeded in dominating Morelos during the Porfiriato, but planter power only reached so far. They could control events in their state and influence them in Mexico City, but the international market was a different story. Sugar production in Morelos responded to steady and growing market opportunities because of the mechanization of the productive process, improvements in water works, expansion onto village lands, and the advent of the railroad. The hacendados pursued all those things, but they did their job too well. They displaced the Morelos peasantry, turned it into a large wage-labor force, flooded the Mexican sugar market, and then failed in international trade. That combination created the conditions for the Zapatista revolution.

The fundamental problem was that by 1900, Mexican sugar production exceeded domestic demand. The only way to maintain prices and also keep the mills operating at full capacity was to export the surplus sugar.[33] The idea had been discussed before, but as production rose and threatened to drive prices down, it became a necessity. Refined sugar had been in demand for export back in 1884 and had sustained good prices. *El Cronista de Morelos* reported in 1886 that the newspaper *El Partido Liberal* thought Morelos needed to export sugar or the industry would eventually collapse under its own weight. The *El Cronista* editors disagreed at the time, but the debate revealed that producers were looking ahead, anticipating future problems, and thinking of ways to maintain profits.[34]

Export possibilities contributed to expanding production. The *Boletín de la Sociedad Agrícola* published an article in 1903 that said, "To give an idea of the great importance that the cultivation of sugar-cane has for Mexico, we need to take note of a few facts about the consumption of various classes of sugar in the English and American markets" and pointed out that the British consumed about sixty million pesos worth of sugar, most of it coming from outside their colonies.[35] The *Boletín* concluded that the problem in Mexico was that "it was not possible for sugar merchants to sell all the sugar within the country, so they shipped some of it to foreign markets in order to sustain the high domestic price that they fixed for their merchandise."[36] At the time, Mexico produced about one hundred million kilos of sugar but consumed only eighty million. Mexican sugar producers needed to secure a slice of the foreign market for themselves. The other approach was to speculate on, and hoard, sugar in an effort to create scarcity and reduce domestic oversupply.

Various groups tried to solve the situation by forming cartels to manipulate the domestic market. One of these groups, the Negociación Azucarera, counted large sugar producers Ignacio de la Torre and three other major Morelos hacendados as members. The strategy was to buy sugar, corner the market, and maintain consumer prices at home. The cartel tested its plan in 1903 when it purchased a little more than seventy-nine thousand kilos of sugar at twelve million pesos, but then only managed to sell twelve thousand kilos for two million pesos. Their efforts to corner refined sugar in Mexico and then limit its availability were unsuccessful.[37] The group blamed the failure of their price-gouging scheme on independent hacendados who broke their promises and sold more sugar than they said they would. The losses forced the Negociación Azucarera to dissolve in 1904.[38] It was soon replaced by a more inclusive trust called the Unión Azucarera Mexicana, which attracted a wider range of producers and continued the same strategies, formulating a plan to have each producer manufacture a percentage of their sugar for export to Europe. That effort failed too.

Failure abroad posed serious problems at home. The domestic market was the most important for Morelos producers, and the

Sociedad Agrícola warned that "sugar cannot continue to accumulate in the country without causing a tremendous crisis, favorable for the consumers and fatal for the Trust and for the producers." But, stating the obvious, the article said, "There is a way to impede the accumulation, and that is to export the sugar."[39] Mexican merchants began selling excess sugar overseas at seven cents a kilo when it was selling at home for twenty-two cents.[40] Foreign competition within Mexico posed little problem because Díaz levied a high protective tariff of fifteen cents per kilo from 1877 to 1904, allowing the hacendados to reap the benefits of artificially high prices.[41]

Other sugar-producing countries retaliated against the combination of Mexican protectionism, on the one hand, and Mexican dumping at below cost, on the other. They met at the important Brussels sugar convention of 1903 and voted to impose special duties on Mexican sugar.[42] Mexico responded to the pressure and radically reduced its import tariffs to only one dollar and twenty-five cents per one hundred kilos. That drove the price of sugar down in Mexico, leading to the dreaded combination of oversupply and falling prices. Despite government intervention five years later, prices never really returned to their pre-Brussels levels for any length of time. Meanwhile, despite various efforts, exporting Mexican sugar remained difficult.

Major sugar producers in Morelos, though, like Luis García Pimentel, still held hopes for expanding into foreign markets. When his sons asked for his opinion on the matter in 1904, he responded: "With respect to the extremely interesting branch of exportation, I already have news of the project to export to the United States and Canada...and the hacendados should pursue it energetically."[43] García Pimentel's and other growers' hopes were dashed when the country found itself in dire economic straits due, in part, to circumstances beyond Mexican control. When U.S. financial markets collapsed in 1907, a large number of banks failed, American demand for imports dropped off, and Mexico, which sent about 75 percent of its exports to its northern neighbor, began to feel the effects of the U.S. recession. For example, freight on the Interoceanic Railroad fell from 901,804 tons in 1907–8 to 822,010 tons a year later.[44] At the same time, the value of silver, Mexico's single-largest export earner, dropped 19 percent. The country slid into a depression.[45]

Morelos fit the national pattern. Sugar production continued to soar, but exports collapsed, falling from thirty-eight thousand tons in 1904–5 to only four thousand tons in 1908–9. The next year, sugar production in Morelos dropped for the first time in over a decade.[46] Not an ounce of sugar left Veracruz, the busiest port on the Gulf of Mexico, for either the United States or the United Kingdom in 1909.[47] The already saturated domestic market was the only recourse, but it was a classic case of overproduction and underconsumption, marked by declining prices from 1903–9. Perhaps giving up on foreign markets as a solution, the Mexican government again attempted to protect the domestic market and doubled the import duty on sugar, raising it to two dollars and fifty cents per one hundred kilos in 1908. That allowed domestic prices to temporarily recover from the pounding they had been taking since 1903, but they spiked for only a few months and then fell back, stumbling along at less than 80 percent of their pre-Brussels prices until the revolution broke out. Writing during the tumultuous year of 1910, the editors of the *Boletín de la Sociedad Agrícola* warned that "Mexico . . . is producing more sugar than it can consume."[48]

With Mexican sugar exports already battered, surging Cuban production destroyed the possibility of Mexican competition. U.S. intervention in the Cuban war for independence led to the Spanish-American War of 1898, and the imposition of the Platt Amendment of 1901. That opened the door for the extension of an American political presence in Cuba, which facilitated American economic intervention and helped U.S. corporations producing sugar in Cuba gain preferential access to the American market. A good example of the effort being put forth by U.S. investors was the creation of the Cuban American Sugar Company of New York. Founded in 1906 as a holding company, it controlled more than three hundred thousand acres in Cuba by 1909, with sixty-six thousand of them cultivated in cane, and it owned six factories capable of producing 145,000 tons of sugar; an awesome figure for only one company and a number that surpassed Morelos's total output.[49] That sort of commitment from U.S. investment capital overwhelmed the Morelos sugar barons. Booming Cuban production provided sixty-six million of the sixty-eight million dollars worth of sugar the United States imported in 1909. That year Cuba produced 1,750,000 tons of sugar, the U.S. consumed 2,540,539 tons of it, while Morelos produced less than 54,000 tons.[50] So, although sugar production in Morelos went up dramatically in the decade following the Spanish-America War, Cuba's output completely dwarfed it. Making matters worse, total world production doubled in ten years. Beaten badly on the world market, Morelos's sugar hacendados faced real problems at home.

Along with the hacendados' economic travails, a political crisis loomed. When Manuel Alarcón died, Díaz called an election to name his replacement. The ensuing political struggle revealed the deep social fissures in the region and provided a vehicle for the expression of widespread discontent seething under the surface of Porfirian "peace."

Reform or Revolution?

Díaz and the larger Morelos establishment chose Pablo Escandón, personal aide to President Díaz and part of the wealthy and powerful family that owned the hacienda Atlihuayán, as Alarcón's successor for governor. Dissident Morelenses backed the engineer Patricio Leyva, son of the first governor of Morelos. Manuel Araoz, owner of the haciendas Treinta Pesos and Acamilpa, led the official commission to find a suitable candidate, but Araoz also served as the vice president of Díaz's Reelectionist Party. Leyva found his initial support among middle-class people like shopkeepers, teachers, small-scale farmers, and journalists. Members of that group probably posted the anonymous *"hojas sueltas"* (radical editorials) that appeared on Cuernavaca street corners denouncing the government. Progressive lawyers who represented the villages in their disputes with the hacendados also supported the Leyva campaign. Some apparently hoped the election would be a legitimate electoral contest after Díaz indicated he would be happy to accept whoever the Morelos voters chose. Several pro-Leyva political "clubs" emerged in the cities of Cuernavaca and Cuautla, including El Club Democratico Liberal Morelos, the club Sebastian Lerdo de Tejada, the club Melchor Ocampo, and the ladies group Josefa Ortiz de Dominguez, which had five hundred signatures.[51]

Like many others of their group across Mexico, the Morelos middle class sought greater political democratization and was dissatisfied with the stagnant nature of Mexican politics at the time. What most of them lacked, though, was the radical alternative political vision of rural labor. When the Morelos campesino population became involved in the election, they transformed it from just another formality along the way to a basically Díaz-appointed position masquerading as an election, into a legitimate campaign that provided the first real opportunity in a generation for the public expression of repressed worker and peasant aspirations. The election offered a public forum where they demonstrated their disgust at prevailing conditions. The initial bourgeois political challenge to dictatorship represented by Leyva in Morelos, and Madero on the national stage, unexpectedly turned into a call for deep social change when Mexican campesinos began to offer an alternative vision for their society, and those in Morelos actually tried to implement it.

Perhaps the best way to appreciate what the rural landscape was like for campesinos in late Porfirian Morelos, and what they were trying to change, is to look at it through the eyes of some of the rural working people who fought in the revolution. Born in 1893, Pedro Placencia, grew up in Villa de Ayala where he and his father raised bananas on a small piece of his grandfather's land. According to Señor Placencia, almost all the other families of Ayala lacked farm land, and only had small gardens around their houses. As a result, they were forced to seek work on the neighboring haciendas to survive. Señor Placencia remembered that on the haciendas "there were a variety of jobs. They weren't the same all year around. During the harvest some went out and cut the cane, others worked the ox teams and scattered and covered the cane seeds." The Placencia's home in Ayala neighbored Emiliano Zapata's hometown of Anenecuilco. The Zapata family raised some cattle and had a little corral, but they too lacked their own crop land and had to rent an unirrigated plot from the hacienda Hospital. The Zapatas probably paid from three to five cargas of corn for each tarea they rented, since that was the going rate in the area.[52]

Many men from the neighboring pueblos worked on the nearby haciendas Tenextepango and Hospital, where they earned two or three reales a day. Women worked on the haciendas too, but not in the fields. Señor Placencia recalled that hacienda cane fields totally surrounded Ayala and Cuautla, to the point that "the only land that wasn't the haciendas was where the town itself stood." When he was young, Pedro Placencia usually found work cutting cane during the zafra. Workers received housing, although the dwellings were "pure trash," according to Señor Margarito Pimentel Mata of Moyotepec, who also worked at Tenextepango. Peónes of the haciendas had permanent work and therefore some material security, but they had limited freedom. According to Serafín Placencia, who also lived in Ayala like Pedro did, if a hacienda peon refused to work, the police would come and take him to jail. The government also imposed a hated universal head tax, and the rural police picked up anybody who failed to pay it.[53]

Born in Puebla in 1888, Manuel Sosa Pavon arrived in Cuautla around 1900. He found his first work chasing birds from rice fields when he was about twelve. As he grew up, Manuel found that people in Morelos were generally passive and complacent, but not content. When he was not working he played with some other boys near the Zapata's house. He knew Emiliano Zapata, but Zapata was around twenty at the time and about to become the head of the household because his older brother Eufemio had started his own family and moved out. Although they had to rent land from neighboring hacendados, the Zapatas had their own house and were better off than the "*acasillados*" living in "*jacales*" on the haciendas, who were obliged to work and could not leave without permission. Señor Sosa Pavon said that a dependent peon's labor obligations in Morelos were understood and that when the value of a hacienda was calculated, the people of the "real" were factored into the equation like the oxen and the rest of the estate's assets. The presence of "contractors that took people off to Quintana Roo" intimidated those who might have challenged the prevailing status quo during the Porfiriato. Many people were afraid to step out of line because of the threat of punishments that included jail, impressment into the army, forced labor on a road gang, or exile to some far away plantation work camp.[54]

On January 19, 1909, having no way of knowing exactly where their actions would lead them, a group of twenty-eight men, including the elderly Carmen Quintero, former community leader of Apatlaco, and thirty-year-old Emiliano Zapata, followed the lead of Anenecuilco's local schoolteacher and the owner of a small store, Pablo Torres Burgos. The group took the bold step of challenging Díaz by putting their names on a petition in support of Patricio Leyva for governor of Morelos. As the election campaign unfolded, it became obvious that Leyva enjoyed greater popularity in the rural towns than Escandón did. His political opponents reacted by accusing him of inciting the masses through irresponsible appeals to their age-old desires for the redistribution of land and water.[55]

Escandón's supporters were right; the rural populace in general supported Leyva. The pro-Díaz and Escandón ruling class attributed that support not to grassroots dissatisfaction with hacendado rule, but to an effective propaganda campaign run by outside agitators. Accepting that argument allowed them to deny the political consciousness of peasants and rural workers. Those groups, largely illiterate, have sometimes been portrayed as having such limited experiences and localocentric concerns that they are either unaware, uninterested, or unable to engage in state-level or national political discourse. The same argument surfaced in previous episodes when Morelos's rural population took action that coincided with events at the national level. The history of the region, the 1909 gubenatorial election, and the revolution itself, contradict that aristocratic view. The lack of a written record composed by the rural population that might reveal their thoughts and feeling presents obstacles to those interested in their level of political awareness, but the record of events, including the public tumult that accompanied and followed the election, answers the basic question. Many campesinos had a clear enough idea of what was at stake to become involved in the election for the governor in a public way that changed the nature of the political debate in Morelos. Locally prominent men like Zapata and Torres Burgos, and others who were virtually anonymous, such as the hacienda peon Prospero García Aguirre, supported the political challenge to the dictatorship, and as Leyva toured the sugar-producing areas, he began drawing large and lively crowds.

The reports reaching Díaz from longtime lieutenant governor Luis Flores in mid-January told him that audiences for Leyva's speeches had turned into unruly throngs in several towns. Flores informed Díaz that the rural population in Morelos felt Escandón's candidacy was inspired by "gachupínes," and that the Leyva campaign's propaganda was sowing anger among the "workers and popular classes" against the candidate put forward by "los señores hacendados and the more comfortable people of this city and surrounding districts." Flores said that the masses apparently believed Escandón's interests ran contrary to those of the pueblos. Díaz instructed Flores to keep him informed. Flores reported back a few days later that Leyva was campaigning around Ayala and Anenecuilco and drawing large raucous crowds where people were yelling out "*muchos vivas*" for Leyva and shouting out "*algunos mueras* [death to] *al* Señor Escandón." Leyva himself understood some campesino desires, but he had not lived their lives; he lacked their rage and disapproved of the "*mueras*." Once the political situation exploded and the revolution broke out, his role as a campesino advocate faded to the point that Zapata eventually refused to negotiate with him.[56]

Flores ordered the arrest of several people who, guilty or not, subsequently admitted to shouting the mueras. Then, in either an incredible miscalculation, or in just a typical effort by a local authority to downplay popular discontent for which he may have been held partly responsible, Flores remained focused on outside agitators, instead of the prevailing social situation, for the volatile political environment. He did, however, tell Díaz that Leyva's promises of land and water for the pueblos were eroding public respect for the authorities. Meanwhile, Leyva's campaign aroused people in Cuautla, Jojutla, and Tlalquitenango, and Flores requested special vigilance from the jefes políticos of those towns. Flores expressed misgivings about the reliability of the jefe político of Jojutla and sent people of "confidence" to monitor the situation there. He also told the president he was "very worried about Cuautla which presents difficulties." With some relief, he reported that news from Yautepec (whose ayuntamiento had been at the service of the Escandóns for some time), Jonacatepec, and Tetecala was favorable.[57] But he had been right about Cuautla. The day after he voiced his concerns to Díaz, a stone-throwing anti-Escandón riot broke out. Leyva looked like the popular choice in rural Morelos, but Díaz still ruled Mexico. Escandón won the election and assumed the governorship, but things had changed.

Villagers across Morelos found hope in Leyva's talk of restoring the land to its rightful owners. The election allowed them to express years of anger and frustration, exacerbated by economic uncertainty brought on by the Porfirian approach to development. The social implications of the Díaz approach appeared in a letter the people of Cuachichinola, in Tetecala, wrote to President Díaz. In it they told him that the owners of the haciendas Santa Ana and San Gabriel had gradually, over the years, field by field, reduced the pueblo's land to the point that only the haciendas' sugarcane grew where they had once planted their crops. One by one, they named the fields that had been usurped, when and how, and then told how they had recently planted a field to which they held title, and that the hacendado had let them. They soon discovered, though, that he had only been waiting until the young ears of corn sprouted to turn his cattle loose in their milpas to trample the crop. The vecinos of Cuachichinola captured the feelings of many campesinos in the Morelos lowlands when they painstakingly listed the wrongs that had been done them, asked for help, and swore that "these lands are ours before the eyes of God and Justice."[58]

The real problems in Morelos were not going to be solved through electoral politics alone and had little to do with who was governor, whether Pablo Escandón, Manuel Alarcón, or Patricio Leyva. Campesino concerns included the burning issue of land with resentment over how they were treated at work, in the courts, by the political system, and the feeling that they remained second-class citizens in their own country. For example, future Zapatista coronel Carmen Aldana of Tepalcingo repeated the charge that others made and said that when he worked at the hacienda Tenango the notoriously abusive administrator, Fernando Segovia, "the Radish," had threatened to brand the workers. José Lora Mirasol of Jonacatepec recalled that when he was at the hacienda Santa Clara, they worked six days a week, "from sunup to sundown, and they told us the time was coming soon

Figure 13. Typical rural scene, nineteenth century.

when they would brand us just like the cattle on the haciendas, that's what brought on the revolution, not Zapata." Agapito Pariente worked at the haciendas Tenextepango and Chinameca, where life was "hard" and where the administrator hit some people, "the slow ones." The problem in Morelos, then, was a social one, rooted in the unequal nature of agrarian society, exacerbated by the heightened land and water expropriations of the Porfiriato, and laid bare by declining sugar markets and growing unemployment (see Figure 13).[59]

Many campesinos continued to live in their pueblos during the Porfiriato, but had to rent land from the hacendados to raise crops and graze livestock, and then stood in lines hoping for work during the zafra. They usually found jobs, but in 1909, frosts hit Mexico's Mesa Central in late September, resulting in the devastation of crops and forcing the government to seek large imports of basic foods from abroad, as the price of corn shot up in "an alarming manner."[60] The frosts reached into central Mexico, down to the Capitol. Lying further south and at lower elevations, the warmer sugar-producing parts of Morelos escaped most of the direct damage. The indirect effect, though, was the transfer of crops out of state to feed places to the north, which created local shortages and drove up prices at exactly the moment when work suddenly became less available. Hacienda work was seasonal in Morelos, and because of the region's specialized economy, there were few alternatives for employment. Compounding matters, hacienda expansion had seriously eroded campesino self-sufficiency, leaving many people vulnerable and dependent on the hacendados for land, grazing and water rights, and work. The conversation between hacienda worker Plácido Amacende Pérez and interviewer Laura Espejel in 1974 offered the following image:

> LE: Were there times when you had no work?
> PA: Yes.
> LE: So, did you have to move to other places?
> PA: Well, one that had his own little cart would go sell a
> small load of fire wood, he would go cut it and then sell
> it in Joncatepec, and that's how we got by.... I should
> mention again that there were no jobs, no work... you
> could almost say that the last time there was work was
> in 1900, when the train came down in La Cuera.[61]

Limited options, localized unemployment, and land loss characterized rural conditions in Morelos. The situation represented one example of the hidden social costs of Mexico's chosen path to modernity.

When the Mexican economy contracted in 1908–9, sugar production in Morelos dropped for the first time in years, from 52,230,155 kilos to 48,547,600 kilos in 1909–10. The planters responded by laying off rural workers, and they inadvertently drove their highly polarized society to the brink of rebellion. Unable to find legitimate political representation and unable to find justice in the law, many rural people—poor, underfed, disenfranchised, and already living on the margins—suddenly found themselves not only landless but also unemployed. The combination galvanized long-standing resistance to the sugar estates and provided the catalyst for the outbreak of the Zapatista revolution.

Chapter Nine

THE ZAPATISTA
REVOLUTION

When Francisco Madero, son of a wealthy hacendado of the state of Coahuila, formed the Anti-Reelectionist Party to challenge Díaz's seemingly never-ending reelection, he attracted the attention of people in Morelos. Middle-class urbanites who had supported Patricio Leyva for governor, as well as parts of rural society, including otherwise unknown hacienda peons like Prospero García of the San José Vista Hermosa estate and schoolteachers such as Pablo Torres Burgos of Anenecuilco, eventually gravitated toward Madero. When Díaz recognized that Madero posed a realistic threat, he jailed him until after the presidential elections. Once released, Madero fled to Texas, and on November 20, 1910, he called for a national revolt to overthrow Díaz.

Down in Morelos, the pueblo of Anenecuilco had just elected Emiliano Zapata as their leader and entered into a serious land dispute over access to crucial farm land with the Alonso family who owned the neighboring hacienda Hospital. After having to cut through a fence of bureaucratic red tape, and then being repeatedly rebuffed by the hacendado and state officials, Zapata led his fellow vecinos in an armed occupation of the disputed ground, and they began to farm it with their rifles ready. Surprisingly, and probably because of unrest in other parts of the country, a pueblo delegation sent to explain the situation to President Díaz won recognition of their rights to the land.[1]

Despite that success, some people from Anenecuilco and Villa de Ayala began to meet at the home of local teacher Pablo Torres Burgos to discuss their circumstances and a vague statement in Article 3 of Madero's famous Plan de San Luis Potosi that would return "immorally acquired" land to the "original owners." Meanwhile, rural unrest reminiscent of earlier periods of elite factionalism surfaced elsewhere in Morelos, as well as in Guerrero, Puebla, Oaxaca, Veracruz, Sonora, and Chihuahua. Seeking to improve matters in their own area, Zapata, Torres Burgos, and Rafael Merino met at the annual Lenten Fair in Cuautla on March 10, 1911, and decided to join the Madero rebellion. The next night, in Villa de Ayala, they overpowered the village police and called a local assembly where Torres Burgos read the Plan de San Luis to the townspeople gathered on the plaza. Torres Burgos, Zapata, and about sixty men from Anenecuilco and one hundred seventy from Ayala, openly joined the Madero rebellion against Díaz and headed to the nearby pueblos, haciendas, and ranchos to find recruits.[2]

With Torres Burgos as nominal leader, their first major military effort was to take the nearby commercial hub of Jojutla. The *federales* and rurales sent to defend the town abandoned the scene, allowing the rebels to ride in uncontested. Despite Torres Burgos's orders, the men with him looted part of the town, which discouraged the idealistic teacher. He resigned his post and started walking back to Villa de Ayala with his two sons. The next day though, they ran into federal police who shot and killed all three of them. With Torres Burgos dead, Zapata was elected the "Supreme Chief of the Revolutionary Movement of the South."[3]

People in rural Morelos had ample reason to rebel. Zapata quickly recruited a people's army from the pueblos and haciendas in the Cuautla sugar valley. Carmen Aldana, for example, was tilling some pueblo land in Tepalcingo and working part-time at the hacienda Tenango. Señor Aldana explained how he experienced the early days of the Madero revolution:

> LE: Now, you had heard of Francisco I. Madero?
> CA: Of course.
> LE: What did you hear, what were they saying around here?

CA: Well, first, that Francisco I. Madero was saying that
Porfirio Díaz wanted to reelect himself as president,
that son of a bitch Porfirio Díaz had added thirty years
to his term and wanted to re-elect himself again....
Then Madero rose up...then we rose up. The hacienda-
dos had already taken away Zapata's lands, and here we
were, screwed, that's why many people rose up. Right
here I recruited 650 men, I still have the old list.

Once it started, the revolution swept up thousands, including José
Lora Mirasol. One day he was carrying bags of sugar from the *casa de
calderas* at the García Pimentel's hacienda Santa Clara, when someone
came running up saying that rebels were there. When José and other
workers went to see what was happening, they saw about five hundred
armed men sacking the tienda de raya. José, whose brother was in the
crowd, lacked a weapon but joined the revolution on the spot. Zapata
was there and had José and everyone else who wanted to join him sign
a book. Then they killed the notoriously abusive administrator, Don
Celso, who some jornaleros wanted to burn alive, and rode off. Many
of the new recruits followed on foot, some carrying shotguns, some
only machetes. When the crowd arrived at the main house of the
neighboring hacienda Tenango, they killed Fernando Segovia, the
despised administrator there. Many of Tenango's workers left and
joined the revolution at that point. The scene replayed itself as Zapata
rode through the Cuautla Valley, the ranks of his army swelling (see
Figure 14). Carmen Aldana helped explain the formation of this people's army. He and other vecinos of Tepalcingo joined "those from
Casasano and Cocoyoc," and after that, he said, "we were all com-
rades." During the ensuing years of struggle, Señor Aldana attained
the rank of coronel.[4]

According to Señor Pedro Placencia of Villa de Ayala, when
Madero rebelled, Torres Burgos, Zapata, and others active in the effort
to elect Patricio Leyva for governor, started meeting at night in the
hills nearby. When they launched the revolution in Morelos, the
Mexican army responded by moving in to conscript people. Men had
to choose one side or the other, or hide in the hills. Some took their
families and left Morelos altogether. Señor Placencia joined the
Zapatistas. He saw his first action on a raid for horses and guns at
the hacienda Chinameca. He and fellow insurgent Prospero García
Aguirre provided a firsthand account of who became Zapatistas. Their
stories paint a broader image than the common perception of them

Figure 14. Group of Zapatistas early in the revolution.

as humble villagers and communalist peasants. Instead, they reveal that large numbers of dependent hacienda workers abandoned the great estates and joined the revolution.[5]

Prospero García Aguirre was a dependent peon living in a ranchería settlement on the hacienda San José Vista Hermosa when the ragtag Zapatista army arrived. When Laura Espejel asked him what "the dependent hacienda peónes that lived on the estates" did when the Zapatistas showed up, he responded, "The peónes left and became soldiers."

> LE: All of them?
> PG: Almost all of them, the captain of the plough teams
> at the hacienda San José was Pancho Peneda, he left to
> become a soldier; Zapata made him a coronel, and
> then they recruited more people . . . and almost every-
> one among the workers left.

Pedro Placencia, who came from the same town that Zapata rebelled in, joined the revolution early and watched it spread across the countryside as it drew in people from both the pueblos and haciendas:

> LE: And when you arrived at the haciendas did the
> resident peónes join you, or did they not?
> PP: No, all those that were from the hacienda left to
> join the revolution.
> LE: None stayed and kept working on the hacienda?
> PP: Well, some did.[6]

Serafín Placencia was in Ayala when Torres Burgos and Zapata rebelled. He said that people who joined Torres Burgos and Zapata at that point, like he himself did, really had no choice but to continue with the revolution after that, because they were then marked men whom the government would have killed like they did Torres Burgos. The Zapatistas, though, were all volunteers, not conscripts. Many hacienda residents joined the revolution, but the Zapatistas did not force them to enlist. In fact, some who hoped to avoid trouble continued working on the estates. Most Zapatistas came from the pueblos or walked out of the hacienda cane fields, and new recruits constantly arrived to join the fight. Having been there from the beginning, Serafín Placencia witnessed the ragged recruits join the "army" taking shape.

> LE: Out of the resident workers that lived on the
> hacienda, did any join you?
> SP: Yes, they lived poorly, so yes, of course they joined
> the revolution.[7]

The Zapatistas recruited people throughout the sugar-producing areas of the state, including peónes acasillados from ranchería settlements, like Prospero García, or men from what was left of the communal pueblos, like the Placencias.

While Zapata gained a following around Cuautla, troops in northern Mexico serving Madero, but under the direct command of Pasqual Orozco and Francisco (Pancho) Villa, defeated Díaz's soldiers and took Ciudad Juárez on the Texas border on May 21, 1911. On May 25, Díaz resigned and sailed into exile in France. The immediate political goal of ousting the longtime dictator was realized. The real revolution, though, was just beginning.[8]

Zapata rose up in the name of Madero, but he was really operating independently. His rebellion had recruited about three thousand men who laid siege to and took Cuautla in bloody fighting on May 19. After occupying the city, he sent instructions to village elders and other pueblo leaders in the area to reclaim lands the plantations had usurped from them. Groups of villagers carrying machetes and guns began to appear on the fringes of the estates to reclaim their old ejidos. It marked the beginning of a grassroots agrarian reform in Morelos that lasted throughout the revolution.[9]

The independent redistribution of private property being carried out by the Zapatistas lacked the support of Madero and incurred the hostility of the interim president Francisco Leon de la Barra. De la Barra had served as Mexican foreign secretary under Díaz, and he had no interest in seeing an agrarian revolution take shape. Under the terms of the Treaty of Ciudad Juárez, under which Madero and Díaz negotiated the dictator's resignation, de la Barra was supposed to hold office until a formal election was held. It was widely assumed that the election would install Madero as president of Mexico. Meanwhile, though, not only was there a high-ranking official of the old regime serving as president, but also the Treaty of Ciudad Juárez allowed the reappointment of the old Porfirian state officials all across the country. That included governors like Pablo Escandón and corrupt municipal presidents of towns such as Cuautla and Ayala. That was clearly not the "revolution" the Zapatistas had in mind.

The dictator was gone, though, and Madero arrived in a jubilant Mexico City on June 7. He met with Zapata and thanked him for his service to the revolution, promised him action on the agrarian question, offered him a post as the head of the Morelos federal police, and asked him to dismiss his troops (see Figure 15). Zapata grudgingly complied, and the demobilization took place outside Cuernavaca, where Zapatistas turned over approximately thirty-five hundred weapons. Disbanding his troops did not diminish their militancy though. As had happened before in Morelos, during the revolution of Ayutla and after the U.S. and French invasions of the mid-nineteenth century, demobilized campesino veterans pressed their local claims within the context of the larger national upheaval. They occupied their old communal landholdings and asked the new government to reward them for their part in the revolution and to live up to the agrarian promises in the Plan de San Luis. Emboldened by their victory, the vecinos of Cuachichinola, who had unsuccessfully petitioned Díaz to restore their lands "like a good father," now published an attack in a Mexico City newspaper against "tyrannical bosses who have made of Morelos one vast sugar factory." So-called bandit activity also broke out in various parts of the state, as campesinos continued to occupy disputed lands. No national authority endorsed the occupations, and the hacendados protested vigorously.[10]

Figure 15. Emiliano Zapata (right) and Francisco Madero (left).

The national political situation remained extremely murky because federal troops had never been summarily defeated, and revolutionary leaders with various local agendas were operating in the name of Madero, even though he wished some of them, like Zapata, would stop. With no federal action or signs of support for agrarian reform coming out of Mexico City, a dispute that broke out in Puebla between revolutionary and federal troops, combined with rumored assassination plots against Madero, served as a pretext for Zapata to call up his men again. Those circumstances provided a cover, but the most likely reason for his action was that he knew that the agrarian reforms he and his followers were hoping for would find no place in the political resolutions to come, unless armed advocates pushed forward with conviction.

As interim president, de la Barra ordered Zapata to disband his men, or be considered an outlaw by the government. Madero attempted to negotiate the impasse, but he failed, partly due to the duplicity of de la Barra, who wished to see the revolution end with as little social change as possible, and partly because Madero, himself, did not support autonomous action on the part of campesino revolutionaries. The planters and old Porfirians considered the Morelos rebels bandits and criminals, while most Maderistas considered them crude and uncultured followers at best, not makers of political agendas. Madero allowed de la Barra to send federal brigadier general Victoriano Huerta into Morelos with an infantry battalion to disarm Zapata and his men. Villagers in the timber-rich mountains north of Cuernavaca around Santa María, who had risen up with local leader Genovevo de la O to protect public access to their woods against government concessions to American-owned timber companies, harassed Huerta's column. In response, de la Barra ordered Zapata's arrest.

Zapata's army had not yet reconstituted itself, and Huerta's men pursued Zapata deep into Puebla. Commanding only a handful of men at the time, Zapata barely escaped Morelos with his life. At one point he was surprised at the hacienda Chinameca and narrowly evaded an arrest party by running through the hacienda's cane fields. He fled toward Puebla, a hunted man riding alone on a donkey through the mountains. He managed to reconnoiter with some of his troops, though, and slipped back into Morelos by the time Madero took office as president on November 6, 1911. Madero, instead of taking action to restore pueblo lands, again demanded that Zapata disarm and surrender immediately.

Fed up with the lack of action on the restoration of pueblo lands, Zapata replied with the now famous Plan de Ayala of November 25, 1911.[11] In the preamble, Zapata argued that "the so-called Chief of the Liberating Revolution of Mexico, Don Francisco I. Madero, through lack of integrity and the highest weakness ... left standing most of the governing powers and corrupted elements of oppression which are not the representation of National Sovereignty." He added that "Madero has tried with the brute force of bayonets to shut up and to drown in blood the pueblos who ask . . . from him the fulfillment of the promises of the revolution."

Articles 6 and 7 of the plan represented its main social planks. Article 6 stated that "the fields, timber, and water which the landlords, *científicos*, or bosses have usurped, the pueblos or citizens who have the titles corresponding to those properties will immediately enter into possession of that real estate of which they have been despoiled . . . and the usurpers who consider themselves with a right to them will deduce it before the special tribunals which will be established on the triumph of the revolution." The proviso that the pueblos would occupy and make use of disputed lands, and that the hacendados would have to petition a revolutionary tribunal for it, completely reversed the procedures that existed before. That alone would have been a radical change, but the seventh article went even further: "In virtue of the fact that the lands, timber, and water are monopolized in a few hands . . . there will be expropriated the third part of those monopolies from the powerful proprietors of them, with prior indemnification, in order that the pueblos and citizens of Mexico may obtain ejidos, colonies, and foundations for pueblos, or fields for sowing or laboring."

The Zapatista Plan, while not totally confiscatory because it offered payment, was important because it called for a significant division of landed wealth in Mexico and the creation of greater opportunity through broadened access to the nation's natural resources. It also offered a clear statement of principles about what they were fighting for. The Zapatistas did not threaten the idea of private property. They allowed for the continuation of small holdings and haciendas too. The haciendas would simply be reduced in size by one-third, unless a large landholder resisted the proposed land reform. In that case, they would be labeled enemies of the revolution and would have their lands nationalized in their totality.

The Plan de Ayala leveled an eviscerating critique at Madero and the existing agrarian social structure in late 1911, but its meaning transcended both the region and the historical moment. It became an enduring statement of principles that reached beyond the borders of Morelos because it struck at the heart of the historic injustices and inequalities across the nation. Writing from Cuencame, Durango, in 1914, the revolutionary general and agrarian radical Calixto Contreras called Zapata a brother of the cause and expressed his support for his beliefs in liberty and land for which both had initiated and carried out "this bloody fight which we will carry to the end."[12] Zapata became a national hero because he fought for the most down-trodden segment of Mexican society, was the most prominent revolutionary figure who never compromised, and because he stood his ground against overwhelming odds "until victory or death." The Plan de Ayala made sense to the rank-and-file Zapatistas and articulated what many must have felt. Coronel Carmen Aldana's understanding of the plan, "That we were going to take back the lands from the government, from the hacendado," cut to the essential meaning that the fifteen-point document held for most insurgents.

Madero responded to Zapata's plan by sending Brigadier General Juvencio Robles into the state to capture or kill Zapata and to carry out a scorched-earth campaign against the people and pueblos of Morelos. Like the authorities had done years before at Apatlaco, Robles went after the families of the rebels, especially the women, taking Zapata's mother-in-law, sister, and two sisters-in-law from Villa de Ayala to Cuernavaca, where they were thrown in jail. And like official actions of the past against the plateados, entire villages of "*pacificos*" that supported the Zapatistas were burned to the ground, and thousands of men were conscripted into the federal army, as Robles tried to reconcentrate the population and deprive the rebels of their base. Robles also ordered the torching of ranchería settlements on the hacienda Tenango, according to José Epitia Ruiz, who lived in one. Robles's troops even burned major towns like Tepalcingo, making people run for the hills and live in caves. As part of his plan to terrorize the population into acquiescence, Robles ordered his troops to slaughter cattle, conscript men into his army, and shoot suspected rebels by the dozens throughout the Cuautla region.[13]

The Zapatista revolution weakened, but continued, even as Robles laid waste to the countryside, forcing people to flee for their lives. Some hacendados protested the heavy-handed tactics, arguing that instead of eliminating Zapatistas, they created them. Well-intentioned Maderistas in Morelos turned away from the open repression and attempted to address the root of the social problem in order to end the insurrection. Madero formed a commission to investigate the underlying causes of unrest in Morelos. The commission circulated a questionnaire amongst the hacendados, asking them if they thought an agrarian problem existed in the state, and to enumerate what other factors might be contributing to the upheaval in the region. The government made no concomitant effort, however, to ascertain the feelings of pueblo leaders or hacienda workers in the countryside.[14]

With the revolution exploding all around them, their stores being ransacked, their administrators killed, their lands occupied, and their workers streaming off the estates ready for war, the hacendados blindly absolved themselves of all responsibility for the social conflict. Several joined to craft a response to the government's ten-question document, in which they painted this picture:

> The owners of the sugar estates have always provided
> their workers the greatest advantages, and, as is well
> known, the wages in this region are higher than in any
> other part of the country. All the haciendas maintain
> schools that are in good condition; they pay for doctors
> and medicines for the sick and their families; they
> support those that have been disabled by their work
> and provide pensions to widows and orphans of men
> that have served with loyalty and honor.

The hacendados attacked the idea circulating in some quarters that the only way to bring peace to Morelos was to give the vecinos of the pueblos land. The hacendados disagreed, insisting that "the truth of the matter is that what has brought the landowners so much suffering is that over the years ambitious agitators have planted bad seeds in the minds of the simple country people of this area, who, due to their absolute lack of aptitude, are unable to understand the real intentions of these instigators." The hacendados argued that two groups existed in Morelos: one was made up of "those men, who, with the pretext of the revolution of 1910, rose up in arms in the middle of March of 1911, in Villa de Ayala," and then went to all the surrounding towns and let people out of jail, creating panic. The other group was "the rural masses at large who have continued in their agricultural labors and have been labeled 'Zapatistas pacificas.'"

The hacendados believed that any effort to establish peace should only begin once "the hordes that have escaped all rules of law and decency, both public and private are brought to order." They thought the problem in Morelos had "been deemed agrarian without any reason, when it really has no other character than that of pure anarchy." The hacendados insisted that any discussion of returning lands to the pueblos of Morelos in an attempt to abate the conflict would be a very bad idea and should be considered only if law and order were reestablished first. Otherwise, people would think that rebellion was an acceptable, effective vehicle for change.

Meanwhile, though, campesino rebels were learning the opposite lesson; that rebellion was indeed the only effective vehicle for change in rural Mexico. The hacendados promised that "once the principles of authority and the respect of other people's rights are restored, the landholders of the state of Morelos will study with the utmost attention, the conflicts that might arise with towns immediately bordering the estates, and will do everything in their power to improve the material conditions of the campesinos, and above all, elevate their morality."

The hacendados, even when forced into a situation that required them to compromise, retained their feudalistic mentality and intended to make themselves the arbiters of the agrarian disputes, not the federal government. Their response demonstrated that even at such a critical juncture they sought to continue their antiquated social relations and to be the primary rulers in the countryside. Their statements suggest the retarding influence they had on Mexican social development and a broader based, participatory civil society. It also indicates quite clearly that the impetus for social change, in this case agrarian reform, came from below. The evidence suggests that if left to their own devices, the hacendados would have imposed the most backward seignorial relations on society that they could have.[15]

Not satisfied with that joint statement, though, Juan Pagaza, who owned the important haciendas Zacatepec and San Nicolas, felt obliged to offer his own on May 29, 1912. His position reflects one widely held by his peers and offers a window into the mentality of Morelos's dominant class. Juan Pagaza believed that the trouble stemmed from

> the vicious and highly immoral customs of the vast
> majority of the people of this state... the unrest that
> has existed since the revolution of 1910, owes a great
> deal to the politicians who with total treachery and
> seeking only their personal advancement, have main-
> tained a latent spirit of antagonism between ignorant,
> perverse people and honorable people, made up of the
> middle class and the hacendados, and finally, the pro-
> pagandists that abound in Morelos find their favorite
> way of making a living in the incessant exploitation of
> the neighboring pueblos, flattering them by attributing
> rights to them that they never had and sustaining their
> ambition to take lands that are not theirs, particularly
> those that belong to the haciendas. *In light of this, the*

unrest in the state of Morelos, in no way represents an agrarian problem.

With respect to alleged long-standing local abuses, consistently cited by the Zapatista insurgents as deeply insulting, dehumanizing, and as major causes of their anger, Pagaza continued, "The workers in the fields have been treated well everywhere... and those considered victims have invariably known to appeal to the authorities, where they have found support and justice."[16]

When asked about the critical issue of the land, and whether haciendas had systematically despoiled pueblos of their patrimonies, Pagaza responded, "I know of no hacienda that has absorbed any pueblo in the state of Morelos; but I do know that some vecinos of the pueblos bordering the haciendas have sold parcels at the highest prices, and in most cases residents of the pueblos have bought lots from their neighbors and then sold them to the haciendas at fantastic prices, alienating the land from the pueblos."

The last part of Señor Pagaza's statement was partly true, as a result of the Ley Lerdo, hacendados had been able to buy up former pueblo lands bit by bit. That explains the Zapatista condition that lands restored to the pueblos, whether communally or individually, could not be sold so they would not be lost again. Despite the pattern of land turnover, Pagaza insisted that "an infinity of small property owners exist in the state who cultivate rice, corn, oranges, bananas, and other tropical fruits, and a great number of cattle herders pasture their animals on the lands of the haciendas." He concluded his commentary on the working people of the state by saying that "only delinquents and the corrupt can complain about situations that they themselves have created."

Pagaza's assessment did not reflect some narrowly held position. Rather, it resembled those of his fellow hacendados, including Luis García Pimentel, who also sent his individual responses to the Madero inquiry. According to García Pimentel, there were two main causes of the "anarchy and unrest" in Morelos. The first was that "among those who have risen in arms, are a large number of criminals who were set free... by the rebels at the beginning of the Madero revolution." The second cause for unrest was that among the rebels and "peaceful Zapatistas," there existed "a crude idea of agrarian socialism. There is no reason for it, because in Morelos the haciendas are smaller than in the rest of the Republic, and property is more divided. This idea of socialism has its origin in the preaching of ignorant and ambitious

agitators that have promoted candidates for state government." García Pimentel complained that incendiary propaganda grew with the Maderista revolution and claimed that propagandists and agitators were deceiving the ignorant people of the pueblos "with absurd and unrealizable promises, igniting class and racial hatreds that no longer have any reason to exist."

Although Pagaza, García Pimentel, and other hacendados saw nothing wrong with the inequalities of rural Morelos, thousands of campesinos did, and they were willing to kill and be killed to change them. The Morelos revolution was forcing the hacendados to consider social changes, but accustomed to having their way, they struck a rigid, superior, and uncompromising posture and failed to accommodate any campesino demands. Today, those demands appear quite measured compared to some other revolutionary movements that exploded across the globe, but to the hacendados of early twentieth-century Mexico, they were radical indeed.

The Zapatistas were poorly armed, as José Lora Mirasol found when he left the hacienda Santa Clara and joined the revolution (see Figure 16). Señor Mirasol recalled how some fighters carried no gun;

Figure 16.
Zapatistas. Note their
clothing, sandals, and
weapons. The men in
suits in background
are journalists
covering the war.

some only had short-range pistols or one-shot Mausers. The only time they obtained decent weapons was when they took them from the federal army after an ambush (see Figure 17). They also lacked ammunition for the guns they did have. As a result, men without guns or bullets cut sacks into small squares and filled them with metal shards or small rocks mixed with some gun powder, then they stuck a fuse on it and went out and fought the opposing army with slingshots. Most bands of Zapatistas traveled without medics, treated their own wounds, and when shot, had to look for doctors in the cities.[17]

The men who joined Zapata fought without pay and without uniforms. They fought "in pants and shirt" of coarse cotton, they went without regular meals, and usually had to supply their own mounts and weapons. Cavalry major Félix Vásquez Jiménez said they often relied on younger boys from the pueblos to bring them food when large numbers of enemy troops were around and they were forced to hide up in the hills. Initially, the Zapatistas could usually get meat because they slaughtered cattle, but they were always searching for tortillas, and sometimes had to go into the pueblos and beg for them. But Robles began to slaughter cattle en masse, leaving behind their

Figure 17. Federal army in Morelos. Compare their weaponry with that of the Zapatistas.

rotting carcasses, in an effort to starve the rebels and force them to wander back into the towns and surrender.

Throughout the revolution, the Zapatistas relied on the good will and support of the pueblos for food, for intelligence about enemy maneuvers, and as a place to blend in and conceal their identity as rebels. Many Zapatistas wore images of the Virgen de Guadalupe on their sombreros and sandals on their feet. Señor Vásquez Jiménez said that the Zapatistas did not sack towns, but did confiscate things like cloth from merchants without paying. The pueblos supported them because they believed in the same things. Vásquez Jiménez said that he himself was fighting "for land, for water, for the hills." But because they were poorly armed and always low on ammunition, the Zapatistas found themselves at a huge disadvantage that severely limited their ability to fight in major engagements, or to press advantages when they had them. The disparity in equipment and ammunition was beyond extreme, especially after 1915, when the Zapatistas often lacked real bullets and fired "wooden balls" while they were being shot at with bullets fired from modern weapons.

Doctor Juan Olivera López of Mexico City volunteered for the White Cross and tended to Zapatista fighters in 1914. He believed that

Figure 18. Zapatista cavalry.

rank-and-file Zapatistas knew what they were fighting for. Dr. Olivera independently reinforced the statements made by most Zapatista combatants who said that they did not kill or terrorize peaceful people when they entered towns, and that Zapata issued specific orders to treat the pueblos with respect. Those who abused pueblo residents were severely punished, and Zapata even had some, such as Felipe Neri, killed for their excesses.[18] It was a war though, and a bitter one. The Zapatistas executed enemies in the towns and blew up trains carrying soldiers and supplies, even when they knew those trains also carried civilian passengers. As a result, certain elements of the national press portrayed them as bandits and terrorists.[19]

Dr. Olivera recalled that a good number of women moved with the Zapatistas, usually cooking and washing, but some also fought. One woman, Coronela Rosa Bobadilla, served in the cavalry and commanded a group of men. She joined the revolution because of the death in battle of her husband, Pedro Casas, and she always traveled with her oldest son at her side when on campaign. Señora Bobadilla survived the revolution and returned to private life in Cuernavaca when the fighting ended. She was by no means the only female fighter; indeed, according to Señor Andrés Ávila, *soldaderas* were there from the start, having fought alongside him in the first siege of Cuautla. Nearly every Zapatista knew at least one female combatant.

Robles's failure to crush the insurrection prompted the Madero government to search for a mediated solution. The large number of men, women, and boys who remained in arms after the overthrow of Díaz and the supposed victory of the revolution, combined with Zapata's refusal to compromise on the land question, left Madero no other choice. It is unlikely that such an effort would have been made had it not been for the sheer tenacity of the popular uprising, and that open repression of the most extreme kind failed to subdue it. But, even at that juncture in 1912, some hope probably still remained for a negotiated settlement. After the withdrawal of Robles, the Comisión Agaria Ejecutiva, studying the situation and the hacendado responses, concluded, "Because of the special way that revolutions have always affected the state of Morelos, the commission has taken a serious look at the causes that have created this special situation, and has arrived at the conclusion that *there does exist an agrarian problem.*"[20]

That declaration came over the strenuous objections of the hacendados. The commission then examined the causes of unrest and recommended that the government devote

> their efforts to the education of the pueblos; and to the growth and protection of individualism amongst their inhabitants... removing all economic and administrative obstacles to the accumulation of small properties which have [until now] greatly favored the formation of large properties due to the slow and steady accumulation that large holdings have made of smaller ones... developing within the pueblos the hatred of private property and the feeling that they lack the protection necessary to become small property holders.

The commission then issued a strong indictment of the intransigence of the hacendados that was reminiscent of Juan Álvarez's reproach a half century before.

> The large landowners of the state of Morelos should recognize the difficult situation the state is in and view it with a more open mind; more liberal and more patriotic, than that of pure business concerns [that are] purely personalistic and profoundly egotistical, and if they take this point of view they will not vacillate in sacrificing whatever is necessary of the interests and

> prerogatives that they previously enjoyed.... [If not] the
> ill will in the countryside will not go away, and it is the
> government's responsibility to do something about it.

The government's suggestion echoed those of both Manuel Arizcorreta in the late 1840s and Juan Álvarez a decade later. The Madero government's solution was radical in relation, though, because it actually suggested that the hacendados return some of the land to the pueblos. At the same time, the government was still trying to impose the Liberal elite's vision of small-scale land ownership on a population with a history of communalism.

By then, however, Zapata had become so distrustful and alienated because of his previous experiences with Maderistas that he would only enter into negotiations with the government on his own terms. He made that clear in a letter to General Genovevo de la O and Pedro Celestino on March 17, 1912. The issue was Zapatista support of a pueblo's effort to regain its lands, where Zapata told them not to negotiate with the government under any circumstances because "everything the government offers is a lie, they never come through . . . you all take possession of the lands yourselves in accordance with the titles and maps of the pueblo, and in case the government does not recognize it, you settle it with weapons in hand."[21]

Ultimately, the Madero government's efforts to mediate the Morelos uprising were rendered moot when Madero was overthrown by a reactionary military coup. The coup was facilitated by the U.S. ambassador who was representing an American administration that hoped to protect American property and investments and believed that General Victoriano Huerta could impose stability where Madero had failed. The coup brought Huerta to power and resulted in Madero's murder on February 22, 1913. Huerta dumped the more conciliatory, intelligent approach Madero had finally arrived at, reverting instead to brute force in an effort to crush the Zapatistas once and for all. He sent Robles back in to carry on as ruthlessly as before, and the Zapatistas continued to fight as tenaciously as ever. When asked if the Zapatistas had intensified their struggle at that point because of the treacherous murder of Madero, Coronel Aldana replied "Enough about Madero, what bullshit, we fought to get the land for the people" (see Figure 18).[22]

Regardless of his antipathy for Madero, Zapata and the Morelos insurgents fought against the usurper Huerta, as did the larger revolutionary forces of the North. Despite superficial expressions of concern about dictatorship on the part of the Woodrow Wilson administration, these cannot be taken seriously given the U.S. government's role in the overthrow of Madero. Instead, Huerta's inability to pacify the country caused Wilson's administration to turn its back on him. Mexico's relentless civilian rebels then defeated the federal army, driving Huerta from Mexico in 1914. But there was little time to enjoy the victory. The northern revolution split in late 1914 between the more conservative "Constitutionalist" faction headed by the former Porfirian governor of Coahuila, Venustiano Carranza, and the popular "Conventionalist" forces of Pancho Villa.[23]

Carranza, like Madero, had a limited view of the goals of the revolution. He conceived of them in mainly political, not social terms, and his vision definitely did not include the dividing up of the private property of great estates amongst communal pueblos. Despite his nationalism, and efforts to protect the country's national resources, Carranza was not a revolutionary looking forward to a new, more egalitarian, Mexico. Instead he looked backward to the restoration of the Constitution of 1857. As president of the republic in 1918, Carranza claimed, "I never was a revolutionary, nor am I, nor will I ever be, I am a fervent Constitutionalist, and I pride myself upon having reestablished the constitutional order. Everything has been done."[24]

The Zapatistas felt little had been done, other than what they had done themselves. Zapata sided with Villa against Carranza because the Villistas recognized the principles of the Plan de Ayala.[25] He rejected Carranza as a personalist and patrician who did not have the best interest of the pueblos at heart. The two factions represented very different elements of Mexican society and had different ideas about how to restructure it. As a result, once the civilian revolutionaries defeated Díaz and then Huerta, they turned on each other in a massive struggle over the ultimate meaning of the revolution and the future of Mexico.[26]

What Was Won and What Wasn't

The Zapatistas and Villistas enjoyed some initial successes, including the capture of Mexico City in December 1914, but their hold on power was fleeting. Álvaro Obregón, Carranza's best general, aided by weapons funneled from the United States through Veracruz, smashed the Villistas in the biggest battles of the revolution in 1915. Villa's forces were seriously hamstrung because of a U.S. arms embargo that dried up access to weapons from across the border, and they never recovered from their beatings in these major battles. That left the Zapatistas to carry on their struggle, poorly armed, without sufficient ammunition, greatly outnumbered, and alone.[27]

In the meantime, with the Carrancistas preoccupied with Villa, the Zapatistas had tried to realize their vision of a more just society in Morelos. During 1914 and 1915 the pueblos carried out a significant locally driven agrarian reform that restored public access to water and woods and divided hacienda and other lands amongst the pueblos. The land divisions were made according to the recommendations of village elders, who based decisions on collective memory and on the ancient maps and titles marking the boundaries of their fundos legales and ejidos that they had preserved for generations or had found on their trips to the national archives. Across the state, pueblos began to reclaim land the hacendados had acquired.

Sympathetic students from the National School of Agriculture in Mexico City arrived in Morelos and carried out the land surveys according to the decisions of the pueblos. When disputes arose between settlements, Zapatista headquarters mediated them. Zapata sent a directive out of his offices at Tlaltizapán, saying that the "repartition of lands will be carried out in conformity with the customs and usages of each pueblo . . . that is, if a certain pueblo wants the communal system, so it will be executed, and if another pueblo wants the division of land in order to admit small property, so it will be done." When asked if Zapata was able to carry out any kind of land reform during the revolution, and for whom, Serafín Placencia replied, "Well, for everyone."[28] Everywhere, autonomous pueblos, each responsible for their own local self-government, began making decisions on the allocation of the state's natural resources, creating what historian Adolfo Gilly called "the Morelos commune."[29]

During the period in which the Zapatistas controlled Morelos, the agrarian reforms emanated from within the communities themselves. That made them fundamentally different from other land-reform programs that came before or after. Other models posited some outside authority, like the federal government, as supreme decision maker and dispenser of justice. While it lasted, the Morelos revolution shattered that. Pueblos acted without waiting for some designated authority to grant them permission to occupy land that they believed legitimately belonged to them. The Zapatista model also included a progressive plan to take proceeds from sales of properties confiscated from hacendados and other "enemies of the Revolution," and create agricultural credit banks to assist the ejidos. The ejidos were supposed to operate like producers' cooperatives.[30]

Morelos's great revolutionary experiment, though, was not allowed to develop. Struggling to win adherents to his side, Carranza issued his famous agrarian law of January 6, 1915. It was a pale version of the Zapatista program already underway and a transparent effort to offer a reasonable looking alternative to undercut the threat of radical Zapatismo. The Zapatistas had already authorized campesinos to seize the initiative and distribute the land, based on their own judgments and those of their neighbors. The seizures would be subject to government review and formalization later, once the revolution was won. Carranza's law, by contrast, forced the pueblos to ask the government for land first, and then the government would consider their appeal and either grant it to them or not. The two approaches differed tremendously. One represented a direct effort to empower the populace and initiate extensive reform immediately, from the bottom up. The other was a grudging bureaucratic response to the first that would administer change from the top down, as had been the case in Mexico from the Spanish Crown to the Díaz dictatorship.

After his armies defeated the Villistas, Carranza took over the presidency and attempted to assert federal control and crush the independent Zapatistas. The Carrancistas used a two- pronged approach. First, they tried to appease Mexico's agitated rural populace with the famous Article 27 of the Constitution of 1917, which codified the general land-reform proposals of 1915. The second prong was an all-out war launched by the new "revolutionary" government against the Morelos rebels. It turned out to be as vicious as any in the revolution. Thousands of people died and thousands more became homeless refugees. Señora Leonor Alfaro lived through it. When Carranza's army arrived in Villa de Ayala, the Carrancistas burned a good part of Ayala, soldiers chased the women, and many, including Señora Alfaro, ran and hid in the hills and caves again, sometimes staying for months at a time. They grew thin and weak, reduced to living off of scavenged fruit. Despite their own conditions, when they could, the citizens of Ayala helped roving Zapatista bands with food, because many of the bedraggled men shooting wooden bullets out of one-shot Mausers were friends and relatives from the pueblos and surrounding hacienda hamlets.[31]

From 1916 to 1919, life was hard in Morelos. Many people fled and many were killed. Pedro Placencia left Morelos and went to Mexico City from 1916 to 1919. Government troops ravaged the state, broke down and sold off the major sugar-milling machinery, destroyed crops and slaughtered cattle to demoralize the pueblos, and left villages charred and deserted. In the midst of the general devastation, coyotes wandered in from the hills and canyons and roamed the streets of Cuernavaca, while the population of Morelos shrank by 40 percent. Under the circumstances, some Zapatistas switched sides and joined the Carrancistas, who were paying a peso a day. Others, like Serafín Placencia, stayed and fought. Some who stayed were women, like the well-known Señora Bobadilla, as well as Esperanza Chavarria, who was shot in the leg, and "La Guera Amalia," a coronel respected by her men for killing numerous government soldiers.[32]

The widespread rural support the Zapatistas enjoyed in Morelos made the war there especially brutal for sympathetic noncombatants, or "Zapatistas pacificos," especially after the Villistas were beaten. Villa's defeat left the Zapatistas isolated, without money or access to weapons or ammunition and no longer able to fight any large battles as a result. They broke up into small bands, were always on the run, depended on guerilla tactics, and were frustrated by their inability to launch any serious offensives. Although they had proven impossible to defeat for almost a decade, the Zapatistas could not adequately protect the civilian population that supported them, or prevent government troops from punishing the people in the pueblos. That situation began to cost them support.

Discerning who the Zapatistas were not, tells a lot about who they were and why they continued to fight. They were not mercenaries, they were not conscripts, they were not professional soldiers, they did not fight because they had to, and they did not fight for the money. Formal proclamations of the leadership offer an idea of what higher values they were fighting for, but they take on greater meaning when combined with statements of rank-and-file Zapatista veterans, who emphasize that they fought because they believed in their cause and felt it was just. For a campesino-turned-revolutionary, it was a grueling struggle full of suffering and death that offered little glory or reward. When asked if he received pay for fighting alongside Zapata, Serafín Placencia replied: "No, where the fuck from? We fought from our hearts...everyone was always dirty and ragged." The year 1918 marked the beginning of the end of the revolution in Morelos, but the ideals supporting the cause did not vanish with military losses.

The Zapatista revolution was rooted in the desire for agrarian reform, but it encompassed more than that. Manuel Sosa Pavon, who worked on the railroad and became a train engineer and Zapatista general, said that he was not fighting for land, had never had any, and did not want any. When asked why he joined the Zapatistas then, if the

215

Figure 19. Zapatistas carrying the banner of the Virgen de Guadalupe.

main goal of Zapatismo was agrarianism, General Sosa Pavon responded that many Zapatistas fought for the *principles* of Zapatismo, not because they were peasants, for example, "to say that Gildardo Magaña...was simply an agrarian; that is, a worker of the land, he wasn't. You have Otilio Montaño, he was a professor, why did he join with Zapata? Antonio Díaz Soto y Gama, an intimate friend of mine, I have letters from him, he was a lawyer. And railroad workers, there were many that followed and came with me." Thus, although agrarian reform lay at the heart of Zapatismo, many saw it as a struggle for greater social justice in general. That is why it attracted railroad workers, students, schoolteachers, doctors, intellectuals, and others seeking a thorough transformation of society (see Figure 19).[33]

Large numbers of people living in the pueblos were landless, and large numbers of Zapatistas were workers. They may have been workers in the fields, or industrial workers in the mills, but many were wage-earning rural laborers, not part of a landed peasantry. That is why in his "Call to the People" in August 1918, Zapata labeled Carranza a reactionary, saying that

> instead of satisfying national aspirations by resolving
> the agrarian and worker problem by distributing land
> or dividing the large estates...he has restored their
> numerous country estates to the hacendados....

> The revolution distributes land to the peasants and
> endeavors to improve the conditions of the city work-
> ers. No one fails to recognize this great truth. In the
> region occupied by the revolution, haciendas and lati-
> fundia do not exist because General Headquarters has
> carried out their division in favor of the needy.[34]

Not only did pueblo citizens receive lands, but so did the "needy" workers living on the estates with no claim to any land, communal or otherwise. That crucial fact demonstrated quite obviously that the Zapatista revolution was not reactionary, backward looking, or static. It did not simply try to redress grievances and protect or reclaim lost lands. Instead, materially, it demanded a completely new division of the nation's landed wealth from capital to labor. Culturally and polit-ically, it offered a different approach to balancing the conflicting needs of society than that which had been pursued previously. That includ-ed new ideas about how private property rights, the rights of the indi-vidual, the rights of the community, and the obligations between the government and the governed were to be negotiated.

Victory in Death?

It has been argued that the Mexican revolution lacked logic, or clear-ly understood goals, that it sucked people in through sheer inertia and attracted those who hoped to prosper personally but lacked any real idea of the larger significance of what they were doing and what it meant to the nation. That view seems to be a conclusion drawn after the fact, not from the actual historical moment. It probably comes from the ultimate defeat of the most radical elements of the revolu-tion, and from comparisons to other upheavals in places such as Russia, Cuba, and China, where tighter and more well-developed ide-ologies triumphed and more thorough-going social changes were car-ried out. But it is a mistake to judge the intentions and convictions of those who were actually fighting and dying in the Mexican struggle in 1915 by the results three generations later.[35]

Most Zapatistas had a good understanding of what they were fighting for, and those who joined as grown men knew what they were doing, in a local sense, from the start. Perhaps those who entered as boys of fifteen or sixteen did so with a limited understanding of the underlying reasons for the war. But the same can be said of most young soldiers in most wars, most places, both then and now. Some men joined the Zapatistas because they thought it better to die on their own soil than be conscripted by the federal army and be buried amongst strangers in the North. The larger significance of this is that the localist perspective in Morelos eventually expanded into a national one as the revolution dragged on. The Zapatista leadership thought of their struggle in national terms, sought international recognition from the Wilson administration and elsewhere, and negotiated with, or fought, every major contender for national office.

As early as 1914, Zapata wrote Woodrow Wilson, appealing to ideals of equality and hoping to persuade him of the justice of the Zapatista cause. He explained that the hacendados in Mexico had taken all the land, forcing the average Mexican in the countryside to work in miserable conditions. He said that many of the hacendados "because they are Spaniards, or sons of Spaniards, consider themselves with the right to act as if they were in the time of Hernán Cortés; as if they were still the masters and conquerors, and the 'peónes' simply slaves, subject to the brutal laws of conquest." Zapata made it plain that his ideas were not confined to the situation in Morelos, and that he was carrying on regardless of the impact his letter had on the American president, "You can be sure that there will be no peace in Mexico until the Plan de Ayala is elevated to the rank of law or constitutional precept, and recognized everywhere."[36]

By the middle of 1919, Carranza's government had carried out no significant land reform, was eroding pueblo autonomy by appointing municipal presidents by executive fiat, and was reversing the Morelos experiment of 1914–15 by allowing the hacendados to repossess lands Zapata and affiliated military leaders had let the pueblo citizenry and hacienda workers distribute in the areas under their control. Meanwhile, seriously low on ammunition, and with his forces dwindling from ongoing surrenders by exhausted supporters who had been at war for almost a decade and yearned for peace, Zapata became increasingly desperate. Allowing himself to become overly hopeful, he was deceived by a Carrancista officer who offered to switch sides and join Zapata with about six hundred men and all the weapons and ammunition at his disposal. Zapata went to a meeting at the hacienda Chinameca on April 10, 1919. He and his escort of ten men rode through the main gates to the sounds of a bugle call and the sight of hundreds of federal troops formed in ranks as if to salute him. Instead, the assembled soldiers fired from point-blank range. The hail of bullets knocked Zapata off his horse before he could even draw his weapon. He was probably dead by the time he hit the ground.[37]

Celebrating Zapata's death, and protected by Carranza's army, the hacendados and their agents that had begun to trickle back into the state started to reassert their land claims with more confidence. Meanwhile, the southern rebels fell into temporary disarray as they tried to settle on a new leader. Small bands of Zapatistas surrendered throughout the year. Some continued to hold out, when, in mid-April 1920, the ambitious Álvaro Obregón Salido rebelled against Carranza. Obregón served under Carranza, but he bolted because Carranza intended to avoid a legitimate presidential election and was instead going to try and maintain his influence by naming his own successor. Obregón, however, had expected to win the scheduled election before Carranza interfered. The Zapatistas, weakened and obviously unable to win their war on their own, and feeling no one could be any worse than Carranza, finally threw their lot in with Obregón.

Obregón had taken refuge in the southwestern state of Guerrero, but he was from Sonora and his rebellion gained wide support in the North. When it became obvious that the rebellion was spreading, Carranza fled Mexico City for Veracruz on May 7, 1920, but was betrayed and shot before he made it. Obregón recognized the need to address campesino aspirations and workers' demands that had fueled the revolution in the first place. Even though he intended on subordinating them to government control, his flexible stance contrasted with Carranza's more openly repressive one. Obregón entered Mexico City from Morelos, accompanied by prominent Zapatistas like Genovevo de la O and their men. Some of the intellectual leaders like Gildardo Magaña and Antonio Díaz Soto y Gama, became incorporated into the new government as well. Fighters from Zapata's old "Liberating Army of the South" were absorbed into the federal army as the new "Division of the South," with de La O becoming a division general. More importantly, though, Obregón's government immediately began to recognize vital aspects of the agrarian reform that the pueblos had initiated and that the Zapatistas had been fighting for during the entire decade. Almost incredibly, the massive government-sanctioned redistribution of land from the hacendados to the villagers and workers began. It looked like the Zapatistas had somehow snatched victory out of defeat.[38]

To the utter disbelief of the hacendados, the old lords of the land, the agrarian reform that took place exceeded the initial demands of the Plan de Ayala. It is debatable as to whether Obregón acted because he shared the convictions of the agrarian rebels of Morelos, or if he acted in a Machiavellian way to gain political support and mollify a particularly volatile region that had been inflamed for ten years. But, considering the extent of the land reform in Morelos, compared to his record in the rest of the country, it was probably the latter. Whatever his motive, the change in land ownership in Morelos from 1909 to 1925 was astounding.[39]

Pedro Placencia, Zapatista veteran from Villa de Ayala, offered insight into the immediate postwar attitude in Morelos following the overthrow of Carranza, when he said that most people only came to accept Obregón as a legitimate ruler because he divided the land. When asked who initiated the agrarian reform in Morelos, Prospero García Aguirre, Zapatista general and former dependent peon on the hacienda Vista Hermosa, reminded his interviewers that the Zapatistas had already divided the land during the revolution. He acknowledged, however, that it was crucial that the federal government officially recognized and legalized the pueblo initiated reforms. After making his point regarding who instigated the change, General García said Obregón was responsible for legalizing the reforms because "if not, there would have been no peace."

In the end, it did not matter what kind of government claimed to rule Mexico, revolutionary or reactionary; if they did not agree to redistribute hacienda lands to the pueblos, Zapata fought them all. And when Zapata was killed, others continued the struggle. It was locally conceived at first, but spread geographically, evolved politically, and although unable to triumph militarily, helped push the country beyond the limited political reforms of Madero's rebellion.

The long social history of Morelos demonstrates that the agrarian reform in Mexico was thrust on a recalcitrant state by popular pressure from below. The Morelos revolutionaries forced the country's entrenched elites to accommodate a social alternative that they despised and resisted with all their powers. Against their will, elites were forced to accept a major division of wealth and greater equality, in what was an extremely unequal society. Beyond that, the ideals driving Zapatismo worked their way into the national consciousness for the rest of the century and helped redefine the rights of rural Mexicans and the responsibilities of their government. Mexico became one of the few places in the world where a government actually had an obligation to provide land to its rural citizenry.

Despite their successes, the inequalities that the Zapatistas fought against did not go away. Mexico remains a highly unequal society, and the problems and demands of many peasants and rural workers still resonate with those who fought alongside Zapata. That is why they continue to invoke his name in their struggles. The government, wise to the symbolic power of Zapata's name and image, has attempted to appropriate him and claim, like Carranza did, that "everything has been done."

Conclusion

In many ways the sugar industry in Morelos symbolized the Porfirian era's model of rapid growth and dependent development. It upset traditional patterns of work and life and replaced them with an unstable alternative that relied on imported technology, foreign investment, and far-away markets. Although a portion of the rural population resisted that from the outset, public anger associated with hacendado attacks on communal land tenure was largely overcome so long as the sugar industry offered employment and relatively high wages to the dispossessed. When foreign markets dried up after 1908, though, and the negative aspects of the system outweighed the benefits, pueblo villagers and hacienda workers rejected it violently, condemned it morally, demanded the restitution of old rights, claimed new ones, and waged a war that thrust their version of justice into the national dialogue for the rest of the century.

The Morelos revolutionaries demanded two basic things. The first was a fundamental redistribution of land and wealth and the political inclusion of a long-oppressed and violently excluded rural populace. The second was presented as a cultural challenge that emphasized cooperation. They imagined a network of semiautonomous cooperative communities with shared obligations and group access to resources, instead of the ideology of individualism promoted by the country's rulers who based their social model on competition and the pursuit of personal interests. A combination of influences shaped the ideas of Morelos rebels, including Mexico City intellectuals, a popular interpretation of nineteenth-century Liberalism, and anarchist theory including the writings of Ricardo Florés Magón and the Partido Liberal Mexicano. The rural populace in Morelos was exposed to all those influences, as the hacendados repeatedly complained. They then adapted them, picking and choosing the parts that served their needs.[1]

The agrarian ideology coming out of Morelos evolved over time, moving from a focus on purely local concerns to encompass a regional, and ultimately, national perspective. The U.S. and French invasions of Mexico, and the repeated collapse of state authority during the mid-nineteenth century allowed grassroots aspirations to surface more readily, especially when elite-led factions vying for national control sought to recruit the popular classes by appealing to their wants. Rural communities with disparate ethnic backgrounds and local peculiarities then began to overcome their provincial outlooks and joined together to challenge the social structure in Morelos. From there, villagers and rural workers began to try and influence the national government because it represented both a major source of their problem, and its solution.

Meanwhile, hacendados in Morelos responded to social instability by organizing their own private forces. Some even turned to the troops of invading foreign armies for protection from an insurgent rural citizenry. Workers and peasants resisted the loss of their communal lands in the courts, protested against noncash wages, staged work stoppages, burned hacienda sugarcane fields, and destroyed water works. Some responded to the pressures being exerted on them through social banditry and theft. The combination of those activities caused hacendados, politicians, and businessmen to label the rural populace an impediment to national progress.

That accusation blended with the fact that Spaniards, creoles, and many educated and urban Mexicans had consistently evoked racist images of Mexico's indigenous population since the conquest, portraying them as uncivilized, ignorant, backward, and violent. During the nineteenth century they extended those characterizations to the rural masses in general, adding that they were torpid and stubborn. Peasants and workers defended themselves by asserting certain elements of elite-initiated Liberal ideals concerning freedom and equality drawn from enlightened thinking and the desire for social advancement. They used the available language to condemn the owners of the great estates for their feudalistic and backward behavior. That behavior included violating the wage system and limiting workers' freedom of choice through scrip monies instead of cash, demanding compulsory labor services, using corporal punishment, and maintaining private jails where people were held without trial. Focusing on those antimodern practices allowed pueblos and workers to portray the landed-elite as a retrograde group operating their personal fiefdoms outside of civil authority and retarding Mexico's social evolution. They then asked the government to do its job, deliver on the promise of personal freedom, and protect all citizens through the equal application of the law. Their exposure of corporal punishment and other forms of hacendado abuse inverted the long-standing racist representations by portraying the Spaniards, or "whites," as the ones who were backward, barbaric, and brutal.

Meanwhile, Mexican resistance to foreign external threats, especially the French invasion, heightened national consciousness. Mexican resistance gave the country vivid symbols of nationalism and independence, such as the Cinco de Mayo. The situation in Morelos, however, was mixed. While some hacendados welcomed the imperial invaders as protectors, some villagers also seized the opportunity to petition Maximilian's government, hoping to take advantage of his promises to protect their lands and reverse the privatization of rural holdings sanctioned by the Ley Lerdo of 1856. Although an increasing consciousness of nationhood and citizenship began to take shape among the rural populace at the time, as evidenced by popular resistance against the empire, the "imagined community" at the national level still ran second to the immediate needs of the real communities in which they lived.[2]

When Porfirio Díaz took power, land transfers and organized pueblo resistance were already underway. The Porfiriato stands out, though, because it accelerated the process and brought railroads, mechanization, the telegraph, greater markets, and the increased alienation of the peasantry, and especially, because it created a large rural proletariat. During that period, local action merged with other national movements. The election campaign for a new governor in Morelos in 1909 allowed the previously excluded rural working class to become involved. They quickly stretched the boundaries of the political dialogue until it included them. After their candidate lost a rigged election, Zapata and his fellow farmers from Anenecuilco carried out land occupations that echoed previous pueblo actions under Manuel Arellano and others. Zapata's movement grew, however, because it coincided with Francisco Madero's rebellion in the North.

A strong social continuity existed in rural Morelos during the period covered in this study. In 1864, Carmen Quintero had led the villagers of Apatlaco in the defense of their community against a powerful hacendado who wanted to deprive them of water and drive them off the land. The hacendado hired an armed gang to terrorize the town and burn down Quintero's house, and the shacks where more than one hundred of his neighbors lived. Forty-five years later, having been driven from Apatlaco, Quintero was an old man sitting on the board of elders in neighboring Anenecuilco. The pueblo was in a serious struggle to defend itself against another hacendado who wanted their land. Quintero and the other elders presiding over the proceedings watched the thirty-year-old Emiliano Zapata become council president, as the struggle the old man had known his whole life was taken up by the next generation.

Epilogue

This book has sought to make five main points. First, the changes in the Morelos countryside began before the Porfiriato, during the 1840s, which is important because during the intervening years the social responses to those changes evolved from local protests and social banditry, to national consciousness and revolution. Second, the transformation of the countryside displaced a large number of peasant villagers from the land, creating a rural working class. That meant that hacienda workers played a much more significant part in the revolution than has been previously acknowledged. Third, and most importantly for understanding what happened in Morelos in a broader perspective, the revolution came at a point when the sugar industry was in crisis, suffering from overproduction and deflated prices. Hacienda expansion and the capitalist transformation of the countryside created the preconditions for the uprising in Morelos, and the situation there fit a larger pattern of rebellion sparked by economic instability and a recession of national scope.

Although there were important regional variations, the agrarian reform in Mexico came in response to intense popular pressure surging from the bottom up. The fourth main point, therefore, is that the agrarian reform took place because of the persuasive way in which the Zapatistas articulated their vision to the nation, and the sheer tenacity with which they pursued it. Fifth, and most important today, local values emanating from revolutionary Morelos became accepted on the national level as just and fair by a large portion of the Mexican public. As a result, they have influenced government policy for most of the twentieth century and continue to affect popular expectations regarding the obligations of the Mexican government to its rural citizenry.[3]

CONCLUSION

Today, the image of Emiliano Zapata remains the most powerful symbol of the revolution and of the larger struggle to defend the land and a way of life that "modernizers" since the mid-nineteenth century have deemed anachronistic. In 1992, Mexican president Carlos Salinas de Gortari "amended" the hard-won Article 27 of the constitution, bringing an end to land distribution and establishing procedures for the voluntary privatization of existing ejido lands. Salinas and his successor, Ernesto Zedillo Ponce de León (1994–2000) pursued a neoliberal agenda that was more extensive, yet reminiscent of Porfirian practices. They sought to modernize Mexico and make it a first-world nation by expanding agrobusiness, recruiting large infusions of foreign investment, privatizing state-owned industries, and fostering a rural-to-urban demographic transformation. The low wages of Mexican workers and government control of the labor movement were intended to attract foreign manufacturers and create jobs. Privatizing communal landholdings and dividing the ejidos into small individual plots that could be bought and sold was designed to encourage individual mobility, in a manner much like the architects of the Ley Lerdo envisioned more than a century before. Like their nineteenth-century predecessors, these leaders promoted a philosophy equating personal freedom and modernity with individualism and industry in the cities, and with private property and wage labor in the countryside. They hoped those values would supplant the collective decision-making rights of corporate communities. Their actions represented a major shift in the policies of the postrevolutionary state and signaled an end to the government's constitutional obligation to redistribute land in response to petitions from landless peasants and agricultural workers.

The ejido privatization program has been justified by the low productivity of Mexico's agricultural sector. Given the history and cultural significance of collective land use in the country, however, the value of the ejido cannot be measured in economic terms alone. The reforms, although welcomed by some ejiditarios, including some in Morelos, have met stiff resistance in the southern state of Chiapas, where regional elites successfully evaded meaningful land reform after the revolution. Most of the existing arable land there is already claimed by large ranching operations or coffee plantations, and the largely Maya peasant population has expanded beyond the capability of their existing lands to sustain them. As a result, some people clear trees and move deeper into the jungle, while others have launched incursions onto privately claimed land. The frequency of land occupations increased during the 1980s and 1990s. In fact, those actions have effectively stalled the federal government's efforts to end land reform in Chiapas. Instead, the state government has been forced to buy large amounts of land and parcel it out to invading peasants.

On January 1, 1994, the day the North American free Trade Agreement (NAFTA) was to take effect, a largely Mayan Indian rebel force calling itself the Zapatista Army of National Liberation (EZLN) launched an armed rebellion in Chiapas. They intended to bring attention to the plight of the rural poor and to Mexico's native people, who they feel have been abandoned by the government. At the time of this writing, they are still in rebellion and are demanding that the government reinstate Article 27 and provide land, work, schools, electricity, health care, and a functioning democracy to the people of rural Chiapas and the nation. Although Salinas shamelessly used the memory of Zapata to legitimate the end of land reform, which was completely contrary to what the leader of the agrarian revolution fought and died for, Zapata's real legacy belongs to those who continue to invoke his name in their ongoing struggles.

What the result will be in Chiapas remains unclear. Since the uprising, the national government has begun to pay more attention to social services in what was a previously neglected backwater. Those efforts are mixed with repression, though, and are designed to reduce support for the Zapatistas, not to address the fundamental inequalities that turned people into Zapatistas in the first place. The future privatization of collective land across the rest of the Mexican countryside outside of Chiapas appears certain. It will probably benefit a minority of people, while the vast majority will be driven from the land and into the slums of the cities, or, given the incapacity of the Mexican industrial and service sectors to absorb them, into the United States. Like Emiliano Zapata and the Morelos revolutionaries, today's Zapatistas seek the amelioration of local conditions, but they recognize that local issues cannot be adequately addressed without challenging national politics. Zapata's legacy lives on in rural Mexico because the injustices he fought against, and the public consciousness he helped arouse, persist.[4]

Appendix

The following table shows all the communities in Morelos that appealed for land grants after the revolution, from 1925–27, what they received, and from whom and where. This kind of data offers one tangible way of measuring the change wrought by the revolution in Morelos. It should also be useful for comparative studies of other regions and how they experienced the agrarian reform.

The years used here were chosen because they came during the presidency of Plutarco Elias Calles, who is not remembered for his generosity in bestowing land to the peasantry; therefore, this data does not represent an aberration carried out by a president adamant about agrarian reform. Also, many of these claims originated in 1920 and 1921 and had worked their way through the system, allowing a view of the process and results.

The cases show that a variety of communities, not just pueblos, petitioned for and received land, including rancherías, congregaciones, and even some, like that in case number 46, simply labeled "lugar." Equally important, the data demonstrates what happened to the once-dominant hacendados, who saw their estates divided up and the land and water they had used redistributed not just to neighboring pueblos but also to previously landless resident peons, as well as unofficial settlements.

The change in power and influence from pre- to postrevolutionary Mexico can also be seen by the names of communities, many with long histories of land loss and legal defeats, which won land from those same hacienda owners who had defeated them in the past. Item number 37, for example, documents the forced distribution of the lands of the hacienda Temilpa, previously the property of Governor Manuel Alarcon, while number 19 shows the similar fate of the hacienda Xochimancas, property of the family of former governor Pablo Escandón. Those outcomes were unheard of before the revolution.

The data also indicate the problematic nature of the agrarian reform. Some medium-sized landowners, such as the case in document number 60, lost their land too. They complained bitterly to the government that those results were unjust and not in the spirit of the agrarian reform. The demographic changes wrought by the revolution also come out, as in case number 65, where an entire community was depopulated.

Lastly, and perhaps most importantly at this point in the evolving history of the agrarian reform, the documents show how the federal government and the office of the president of Mexico took control of the program and transformed a locally inspired pueblo and worker- initiated redistribution effort begun by the Zapatistas, into a state-run, top-down operation. That process placed the federal government and the president at the center of the reforms, thus making the highest offices the final arbiters and the granters of favors, as opposed to merely legitimating prior actions carried out by citizens on the local level. It is significant that many communities sought "*restitución*," which required that they prove prior entitlement and demonstrate that they had been despoiled of their holdings since the passing of the Ley Lerdo in 1856. Almost all communities, however, received "*dotación*" instead. That meant they lacked titles, or could not establish how and when they were despoiled of the land. As a result, dotación meant that the government was simply *granting* them land, not recognizing their long-standing rights to it. Some unofficial localities, like congregaciones, were glad to receive land and legal recognition in that manner, but it was a far less desirable outcome for established pueblos that believed they held legitimate title.

Despite its problems, the agrarian reform provides an important element in explaining the long-standing support for the governing Partido Revolucionario Institucional (PRI), on the part of many rural Mexicans during much of the twentieth century. That support has often been portrayed as simply a case of co-optation, patronage, coercion, or even as nonexistent. There is some truth to those charges, especially after 1940; nevertheless, the agrarian reform did provide some legitimacy for the government in the eyes of a large segment of the rural populace. The PRI's popularity waned, however, as the agrarian reforms faded. The PRI then plummeted after President Carlos Salinas ended the reform, although there were, of course, many other reasons for its decline.

PROPERTY ADJUSTMENTS

CASE NO.	NAME OF CLAIMANT	POP.	HEADS	REQUEST	PREVIOUS SIZE	AMOUNT RECEIVED	LAND AND OWNER EXPROPRIATED
01	Pueblo Panchimalco	452	122	Restitución	14 hs	Dotación 547 hs 225 riego 247 temporal 75 pastos	Hcda San Nicolás Obispo, Juan Pagaza
02	Congregación de Tecomalco	105	31	Dotación	Had no land, totally surrounded by hcda Tenextepango	Dotación 310 hs	Hcda Tenextepango, Ignacio de la Torre y Mier
03	Buena Vista del Monte			Dotación	No boundary	None. Area depopulated and community disappeared	
04	Congregación de Chipitlan	123	45	Dotación		Dotación 370 hs temporal no irrigated lands exist	Hcda Temixco, Concepción T. G. de Fernandez
05	Pueblo de San Antonio			Dotación		Dotación 315 hs	Hcda Temixco 295 hs Rancho Atzingo 20 hs
06	Congregación Ixcatepec de Tepepa	503	144		Barrio of Cuautla had 70 hs urban space; 282 riego, 780 temporal	752 hs of all types	Hcda Cuahuixtla, Manuel Araoz
07	Pueblo de Ocuituco			Restitución of water/Dotación of land		Water restitution denied; told to seek dotación. Receives 1,769 hs temporal through dotación	Hcda Santa Clara, Luis García Pimentel
08	Pueblo Los Elotes		15	Dotación		300 hs	Hcda Calderon, widow of Vicente Alonso
09	Pueblo San Juan Texcalpan	135	55	Restitución/ Dotación	892 hs	Restitución/dotación denied	None Ruling is pueblo has enough land

PROPERTY ADJUSTMENTS

CASE NO.	NAME OF CLAIMANT	POP.	HEADS	REQUEST	PREVIOUS SIZE	AMOUNT RECEIVED	LAND AND OWNER EXPROPRIATED
10	Ranchería Atlacomulco	148	77	Dotación	was part of hcda Atlacomulco	Dotación 201 hs	Hcda Atlacomulco, Estate of Delfín Sanchez
11	Pueblo Tejalpa	250	70	Dotación		Dotación 200 hs	
12	Poblado Juitepec		161	Restitución	472 hs	Dotación 308 hs	50 hs from Atlacomulco, Delfín Sanchez 258 from San Gaspar y Chiconcuac, Delfín Sanchez
13	Pueblo de Huatecalco		88	Restitución		Dotación 116 hs riego 228 hs temporal 264 hs cerril	Hcda Acamilpa, Manuel Araoz
14	Villa Tlaltizapan	753	167	Restitución		Dotación 1,226 hs	Hcda Temilpa, Manuel Alarcon's widow
15	Ranchería Ixtilico		81	Dotación	38,679 hs	Dotación 1,308 hs	Hcda Tenango, García Pimentel
16	congregación Huitchila		73	Dotación		860 hs	Hcda Tenextepango, Ignacio de la Torre y Mier
17	Pueblo Jaloxtoc	390	95			760 hs 38 de riego 55 de temporal	
18	Pueblo de Amilcingo		206	Dotación de tierras/ Restitución de aguas		Dotación 1,713 hs 97 hs de riego 102 de temporal primera 850 de temporal segunda 664 de cerril y monte	Hcda Santa Clara, García Pimentel

232

PROPERTY ADJUSTMENTS

CASE NO.	NAME OF CLAIMANT	POP.	HEADS	REQUEST	PREVIOUS SIZE	AMOUNT RECEIVED	LAND AND OWNER EXPROPRIATED
19	Pueblo Ticuman			Restitución/ Dotación	50 hs urban space 2,040 hs total	Dotación 58 hs riego 158 temporal rest is cerriles	Hcda Xochimancas, Antonio Escandón
20	Pueblo de Texcala	276	88	Dotación		Dotación 440 hs	65 hs from Atlcomulco 375 hs from succession de Sr. Adrian Carrillo
21	Pueblo Bonifacio García	104	30	Dotación	1,104 hs comunales de cerriles	Dotación 156 hs 24 de riego	Hcda Temilpa, Alarcon's widow
22	Pueblo Zacualpan Amilpas	###	286	Dotación	857 hs	Dotación 567 hs plus 132 hs de terrenos ejidales	Hcda Santa Clara, Luis García Pimentel
23	Pueblo Chalcatzingo	283	101	Restitución	30 hs urban space 130 hs of old fundo legal	Dotación 901 hs 51 riego 648 temporal 202 de cerril	Hcda Santa Clara, García Pimentel
24	Pueblo Jantetelco		273	Restitución	98 hs de riego	Dotación 1,813 hs 19 hs first-class land 1,566 second class 329 third class	
25	Pueblo San Pedro Tlalmimilulpan			Restitución		Dotación 457 hs	260 of monte Apapasco from hcda Santa Catalina Cuilotepec 197 hs from hcda Santa Clara, García Pimentel

PROPERTY ADJUSTMENTS

CASE NO.	NAME OF CLAIMANT	POP.	HEADS	REQUEST	PREVIOUS SIZE	AMOUNT RECEIVED	LAND AND OWNER EXPROPRIATED
26	Ciudad Jonacatepec		537	Restitución		Dotación 2,925 hs 140 de riego (fix, lost data)	Hcdas Santa Clara and Tenango, García Pimentel
27	Villa de Xochitepec		288	Dotación		Dotación 1,330 hs 246 temporal 725 de riego 360 de cerril	Hcdas El Puente and Chiconcuac, Delfín Sanchez
28	Poblado Pueblo Nuevo		64	Restitución		Restitución denied Receives 225 hs through Dotación 159 de riego rest is temporal	Hcda Acamilpa, Manuel Araoz
29	Pueblo San Francisco Oxocaltepec	357	78	Restitución		Dotación 277 hs	Rancho Talatlaco
30	Ranchería Nexpa	167	44	Dotación		Dotación 792 hs	Hcda Calderon and Chinameca, Vicente Alonso's widow
31	Congregación Acamilpa		89	Dotación		Dotación 402 hs 160 de riego the rest temporal plus 240 litros de agua a second source: 'el salto'	Hcda Acamilpa, Manuel Araoz
32	Pueblo de Atotonilco	517	155	Dotación		Dotación 1,393 hs 74 de riego 70 litros of water per second	Hcdas Santa Clara and Tenango, García Pimentel

PROPERTY ADJUSTMENTS

CASE NO.	NAME OF CLAIMANT	POP.	HEADS	REQUEST	PREVIOUS SIZE	AMOUNT RECEIVED	LAND AND OWNER EXPROPRIATED
33	Pueblo Amayuca		406	Restitución		Dotación 2,039 hs 203 de riego (lost data)	Hcda Santa Clara, García Pimentel
34	Pueblo San Gabriel Amacuitlapilco	123		Dotación	167 hs	816 hs	Hcda Santa Clara, García Pimentel
35	Congregación Tlayca	305	96	Dotación		Dotación 1,152 hs 576 temporal 576 cerril	Hcda Santa Clara, García Pimentel
36	Pueblo Itzamatlan	183	71	Restitución/ Dotación		Dotación 271 hs riego and temporal	Hcdas San Carlos and Oacalco, Estate of Tomás de la Torre
37	Congregación de Temilpa	100	38	Dotación	3.5 hs de zona [?]	Dotación 66 hs de riego 132 litros of water a second	Hcda Temilpa, Alarcon's widow
38	Pueblo Tlacotepec	824	254	Restitución		Dotación 2,754 hs 152 riego 1,090 temporal 1,512 cerriles	Hcda Santa Clara, García Pimentel
39	Pueblo San Miguel Huajintlan			Restitución		Dotación 2,407 hs 2,949,373 cubic meters of water a year	Hcda San Gabriel, Emmanuel Amor

PROPERTY ADJUSTMENTS

CASE NO.	NAME OF CLAIMANT	POP.	HEADS	REQUEST	PREVIOUS SIZE	AMOUNT RECEIVED	LAND AND OWNER EXPROPRIATED
40	Congregación Chosco		49	Dotación	10 hs urban area	Dotación 568 hs 102 de riego 93 temporal 373 cerriles	
41	Pueblo de Tehuixtla		158	Restitución		Dotación 1,075 hs temporal, cerril, and riego	Hcdas San Gabriel and San José Vista Hermosa, E. Amor
42	Pueblo Tepaltzingo		864	Restitución		Dotación 7,965 hs temporal and cerril	Hcda Tenango, García Pimentel Hcda Tenextepango, Ignacio de la Torre
43	Congregación El Estudiante		23	Dotación		Dotación 552 hs	Hcdas San Gabriel and San José Vista Hermosa, E. Amor
44	Lugar Telixtac	594	200	Recognition as Pueblo		Dotación 38,679 hs temporal and pastoral	Hcda Tenango, García Pimentel
45	Ranchería Cuaxitlan		74	Restitución		Dotación 1,395 hs	Hcda Calderon, Vicente Alonso's widow
46	Lugar Calderon	166	49	Dotación		266 hs riego, temporal, cerril	Hcda Calderon, Alonso's widow
47	Congregación Santa Catarina		27	Restitución		Dotación 336 hs riego temporal and cerril	Hcda Oacolco, Francisco Velez, and terrenos nacionales
48	Congregación de Santa Rita	120	46	Dotación		552 hs	Hcda Chinameca, Alonso's widow
49	Pueblo Santa María Alpuyeca	820	247	Dotación		1,237 hs de temporal y de cerriles	Hcdas El Puente San José Vista Hermosa

PROPERTY ADJUSTMENTS

CASE NO.	NAME OF CLAIMANT	POP.	HEADS	REQUEST	PREVIOUS SIZE	AMOUNT RECEIVED	LAND AND OWNER EXPROPRIATED
50	Congregación San Miguel Tlaltelolco	151	51	Restitución		Dotación 456 hs	San Diego Huixtla o Tepantongo
51	Pueblo Tepetlixpita	89	32	Dotación		Dotación 208 hs	San Diego Huixtla
52	Pueblo Atlatlahuacan		361	Restitución	3,159 hs	Dotación 1,847 hs	Hcdas San Diego Huixtla and San Carlos, Tomás de la Torre Hcda Cuahuixtla, Manuel Araoz and others
53	Pueblo San Miguel Ixtilico	654	203	Restitución		Dotación 2,482 hs	Hcda San Carlos, Tomás de la Torre Hcda Cuahuixtla, Manuel Araoz Hcda Casasano, Velez de Goribar Hcda Santa Clara, García Pimentel Hcda San Diego Huixtla Hcda Xalea
54	Pueblo Totolapan	790	286	Restitución		Dotación 2,127 hs	San Diego Huixtla and Hcda Buenavista, Benito Arenas's widow
55	Congregación de San Rafael Zaragosa		53		2,981 hs	205 hs de riego	Hcda Chinameca, Vicente Alonso
56	Congregación San Ignacio	249	80	Dotación		Dotación 490 hs	Hcda Tenango, García Pimentel
57	Villa de Yecapixtla		584	Dotación		Dotación 2,845 hs	Hcda Cuahuixtla, Manuel Araoz and Jalapa
58	Pueblo Zahuatlan		92	Dotación		Dotación 736 hs	Hcda Cuahuixtla, Manuel Araoz
59	Congregación Coccyotla		109	Dotación		741 hs de riego, temporal, ceril	

PROPERTY ADJUSTMENTS

CASE NO.	NAME OF CLAIMANT	POP.	HEADS	REQUEST	PREVIOUS SIZE	AMOUNT RECEIVED	LAND AND OWNER EXPROPRIATED
60	Pueblo de Huesca			Dotación		Dotación 234 hs total	Hcda Cuahuixtla, Manuel Araoz Rancho Tezontitlan Potrero el Pochote
61	Congregación Chavarria		109	Restitución		Dotación 1,066 hs	Hcda San Diego Actopan, Emmanuel Amor
62	Pueblo de Tilzapotla		269	Dotación		Dotación 5,918 hs	Hcda San Gabriel, E. Amor
63	Pueblo Mexquemeca	212	52	Dotación		Dotación 472 hs	Hcda Cuahuixtla, Manuel Araoz
64	Pueblo Xochitlan	612	188	Restitución		Dotación 506 hs	Finca Adrian Carrillo and hcda Atlacomulco, Delfín Sanchez
65	Pueblo San Agustín Tetlama	170	59	Dotación		496 hs	Hcda Temixco, Concepción T. G. de Fernandez
66	Congregación San Gaspar	137	48	Dotación		Dotación 241 hs	San Gaspar anexa a San Vizente, Delfín Sanchez
67	Pueblo de Asunción Ahuatlan	72	37	Dotación		230 hs	Finca Cuatepec
68	Pueblo Cuentepec	718	225	Restitución	58 hs urban zone	Dotación 4,957 hs	Hcda Temixco, Concepción T. G. de Fernandez, and terrenos nacionales
69	Pueblo San Sebastian		19			Dotación 57 hs	Hcda San Carlos, Tomás de la Torre
70	Pueblo San Agustín Amatlipac		28			Dotación 61.5 hs de riego	Hcda San Carlos, Tomás de la Torre
71	Villa de Oaxtepec	147	77	Restitución	2,147 hs	Dotación 249 hs riego y temporal	Hcda San Carlos, Tomás de la Torre

PROPERTY ADJUSTMENTS

CASE NO.	NAME OF CLAIMANT	POP.	HEADS	REQUEST	PREVIOUS SIZE	AMOUNT RECEIVED	LAND AND OWNER EXPROPRIATED
72	Pueblo de San José de los Laureles	168	59	Dotación	45 hs communal land	Dotación 87 hs riego	Hcda San Carlos, Tomás de la Torre
73	Pueblo Xochzalco	73	39	Dotación	63 hs	Dotación 564 hs cerril, monte, temporal	Hcda Santa Clara, García Pimentel
74	Villa de Axochiapan		708	Dotación	100 hs urban zone 1,112 de temporal	Dotación 3,540 hs	Hcda Tenango, García Pimentel
75	Poblado San Andrés Cuautempan	197	63			Dotación 204 hs	Hcda San Diego Huixtla Hcda San Carlos, Tomás de la Torre
76	Pueblo de Atlacahualoya			Dotación	51 hs urban zone 1,050 ejido land	Dotación 1,056 hs	Hcda Tenango, García Pimentel
77	Congregación Tlayayo	173	64		urban zone 9 hs	448 hs	
78	Pueblo San José Quebrantadero	869	253	Dotación		2,024 hs	Hcda Tenango, García Pimentel
79	Poblado San Francisco Zacualpan		294	Restitución		Dotación 1,202 hs	Hcda San Vizente, Delfín Sanchez Hcda Temixco, Concepción T. G. de Fernandez

Glossary

Measurements

Arroba	11 kilos
Caballeria	250 acres
Carga	181.63 liters
Cuartilla	.25 arroba
Fanega	1.5 bushels
Fanega de sebradura	about 9 acres
Hectare	2.47 acres
Tarea	.75 acre
Vara	33 inches

Labor Terms

Gañan	laborer, dayworker, contract worker
Jornalero	worker, day worker
Laborio	resident laborer, peon
Labrador	peasant farmer, campesino

Notes

Introduction

1. See R. Anderson, *Outcasts in their Own Land*. For a history of urban and working-class life during the revolution, see Lear, *Workers, Neighbors*. For an interesting comparative thesis treating the role workers in export-driven enterprises play in shaping their national histories, see Bergquist, *Labor in Latin America*.

2. For more on northern Mexico, see Meyers, *Forge of Progress*; Nugent, *Spent Cartridges*; R. E. Ruíz, *People of Sonora*; and R. E. Ruíz, *Great Rebellion*. See also Tinker-Salas, *Under the Shadow*; Wasserman, *Capitalists, Caciques*; Walker, "Homegrown Revolution"; Walker, "Villista Legacy."

3. The term *campesino* is a general expression that usually applies to peasants, rural wage laborers, hacienda peons, and people who are some combination of those things. I use the term campesino to refer to a person who is part peasant and part wage worker, as most were in the period studied here. The term peasant is used less often, but denotes an individual, family, or community that has independent access to land sufficient to provide most, or all, of their subsistence needs.

4. For discussions of Mexican Liberalism, see Hale, *Mexican Liberalism*; Reyes Heroles, *Liberalismo mexicano*. For analyses of "popular" Liberalism, see Mallon, *Peasant and Nation*; as well as Thomson, with LaFrance, *Patriotism, Politics*.

5. Skocpol's thesis linking defeat in foreign war to elite instability and state crisis that can allow for successful peasant mobilizations is useful in this context. Although elite instability can come from a number of sources besides foreign war, including economic stagnation, these elements played a part in the agrarian unrest that characterized Morelos at different times in the nineteenth century. See Skocpol, *States and Social Revolutions*; and Moore, *Social Origins of Dictatorship and Democracy*.

6. Wolf, for example, has argued that the real revolutionaries are the capitalists that come in and upset traditional economies. See Wolf, *Peasant Wars of the*

Twentieth Century.

7. Some significant works on the revolution and the nineteenth century in Morelos are Ávila Espinosa, *Orígenes del zapatismo*; Brunk, *Emiliano Zapata!*; Melville, *Crecimiento y rebelión*; de la Peña, *Legacy of Promises*; Rueda Smithers, *Paraíso de la caña*; Sotelo Inclán, *Raíz y razón*; Warman, *"We Come to Object"*; and Womack, *Zapata*. Some very good studies of Morelos have concluded that land transfer was largely complete before the Porfiriato, and that it was carried out during the Liberal reforms of the mid-nineteenth century. While there was indeed an increase in land transfer following the Liberal reforms of the mid-1850s, pueblos consistently challenged the change underway and sometimes successfully resisted it because of the elite turmoil and the added chaos caused by the French occupation that marked the period. The stability achieved during the early Porfiriato allowed the successful completion of land transfer, and then hacendados set their sights on other resources, especially water. See, for example, Crespo, *Hacienda azucarera*, 7–36; Melville, *Crecimiento y rebelión*.

8. Tutino persuasively advances these ideas for understanding agrarian unrest in *Insurrection to Revolution*.

9. See Scott, *Weapons of the Weak*, for his discussions on everyday forms of peasant resistance and contested hegemony, which have influenced many subsequent works. Also see Scott, *Moral Economy*; and Moore, *Injustice*, which stresses the moral outrage disadvantaged groups must feel for rebellion to occur even when great inequality prevails. Scott's thesis that peasants view the world through a moral lens is useful in analyzing agrarian unrest in Morelos during the period under consideration. Indeed, the morality, justice, or fairness of changes were a constant preoccupation of campesino grievances in the nineteenth century. See also Victor Turner's *Ritual Process*.

10. Sotelo Inclán, *Raíz y razón*, discusses this contest between individualism and communalism in rural Morelos that dates from the colonial period. He places the blame at the feet of the Spaniards who altered social structures and introduced new enticements, which he argues fostered individualism and eroded the integrity of the community. For a more general discussion and historical overview, see Carrasco, "People's of Central Mexico." The historical literature on Europe deals with this extensively; two of the best works are Hobsbawm and Rude, *Captain Swing*; and Ladurie, *Peasants of Languedoc*. Popkin, *Rational Peasant*, offers a critique of the moral-economy approach and challenges it as overly romanticized. He argues that peasants see themselves as individuals first and put themselves before the community. The individualist versus communalist tendencies in the Morelos countryside are addressed more fully in this text.

11. The ethnic variation in Morelos has often been largely ignored, leaving an impression of a more homogenous countryside than actually existed. The scholar who most closely examines the ethnic makeup of rural lowland Morelos is von Mentz in *Pueblos de indios*.

12. Geertz, *Interpretation of Cultures*, defines culture as "a historically transmitted pattern of meanings embodied in symbols, a system of inherited conceptions expressed in symbolic forms by means of which men communicate, perpetuate, and develop their knowledge about and attitudes toward life."

13. C. E. Martin remarked, in *Rural Society*, that the political turmoil of the nineteenth century disrupted record keeping, making it difficult to reconstruct rural history for that time period.

14. For more on the history of the Mexican revolution, see Gilly, *Mexican Revolution*; Hart, *Revolutionary Mexico*; Katz, *Secret War*; Knight, *Mexican*

Revolution; R. E. Ruíz, *Great Rebellion*; and Womack, *Zapata*. For a wide-ranging analysis of rural revolt in Mexico and its evolution over time, see Tutino, *Insurrection to Revolution*.

Chapter One

1. For more on the topography of Morelos, see Riley, *Fernando Cortés*; and Lewis, *Life in a Mexican Village*. Technically, the Valley of Mexico is a basin, since it has no natural outlet, but it is generally referred to as a valley anyway.
2. Domenéch's *Guía general descriptiva*, describes the area of Las Amilpas as one that includes the Cuautla, Yautepec, and Jojutla valleys, the latter being entirely in the tierra caliente. See also Riley, *Fernando Cortés*, 2, 3.
3. De la Peña, *Legacy of Promises*, 18.
4. Lewis, *Life in a Mexican Village*, 86; Riley, *Fernando Cortés*, 41–42. See also Cline, *Libro de tributos*.
5. See Riley, *Fernando Cortés*, 50–56, 75, for sugar exported out of Veracruz coming from the hacienda Tlaltenango and for the product also going to Acapulco.
6. See Gerhard, *Historical Geography*, for demographics in Morelos. Scholars debate the figures for the demographic collapse, especially preconquest estimates, but one thing is agreed: a lot of people died in a short period of time, and it is clear from contemporary chroniclers on the scene that epidemic diseases radically reduced the native population, as did war, slavery, overwork, and abuse. For a very good overview of the demography debate, including the work of Sherburne F. Cook and Woodrow Borah, H. F. Dobyns, A. L. Kroeber, and Cook and Lesley B. Simpson, see Whitmore, *Disease and Death*.
7. The indigenous population rebounded after 1680. See C. E. Martin, *Rural Society*, for a discussion of the granting of mercedes. Also see Hernández Chávez, *Propiedad comunal*, 18.
8. See Haskett, *Indigenous Rulers*, for insight into politics and society at the time.
9. Jesús Sotelo Inclán discusses these issues in Anenecuilco in *Raíz y razón*, 38, as do Chapters 6 and 7 of this work. For the case of Atlacholoaya and Xochitepec, see AGN, Hospital de Jesús, leg. 38, exp. 600, 1685.
10. AGN, Hospital de Jesús, leg. 439, exp. 1, 1643, helps illustrate the impact of death on land tenure.
11. For case of Huitzilac see AGN, Hospital de Jesús, leg. 28, vol. 49, exp. 1. For Atlacholoaya, see exp. 2. The documents in the Hospital de Jesús offer a good history of changing patterns of land tenure during the colonial era, complete with maps, census data, and inventories.
12. It is not the objective of this chapter to document how the haciendas took root and expanded in the colonial era, but for a very good, detailed discussion of the various ways haciendas acquired land and came into being, see C. E. Martin, *Rural Society*, esp. 16–20; also see Hernández Chávez, *Propiedad comunal*, and Hernández Chávez, *Anenecuilco*. See also von Wobeser, *La formación de la hacienda*; and von Mentz, *Pueblos de indios*; Sharrer Tamm, *Azúcar y trabajo*; and Barrett, *Sugar Hacienda*; and for a more general discussion, see Chevalier, *Formación*, which also discusses the process of private land acquisition in Morelos.
13. For more on the fundo legal, see Mendieta y Nuñez, *Problema agrario*. One vara measured thirty-three inches.
14. Haskett, *Indigenous Rulers*, discusses efforts to maintain local independence in the face of growing Spanish authority during the early colonial era in Cuernavaca; and Sotelo Inclán, *Raíz y razón*, offers a good history of the role of the fundo legal as seen through the struggles of Anenecuilco.
15. This interpretation is based on an analysis of court records regarding land

disputes between haciendas and villages and between villages and their own citizens and is discussed in the later chapters of this text. It has previously influenced many scholars of Morelos, including Sotelo Inclán; Díaz Soto y Gama, *Revolución del sur*; Womack, *Zapata*; Warman, *"We Come to Object"*; and de la Peña, *Legacy of Promises*.

16. See Brady, "Emergence of a Negro Class," 6–35; and Palmer, *Negro Slavery*; and Palmer, *Slaves of the White God*. Also see Carroll, *Blacks in Colonial Veracruz*; and Crespo et al., *Historia del azúcar*, including chart on 1:614.

17. See Barrett, *Sugar Hacienda*, for a good discussion of the division of labor on an early Morelos sugar hacienda. For more on the African American experience in Mexico, see Aguirre Beltrán, *Población negra*; and von Mentz, *Pueblos de indios*, for an ethnographic history of Morelos's sugar-producing zones. The encomienda was a system by which the Spanish Crown offered the right of usufruct over a certain land area as well as access to the labor and tribute of its inhabitants to a conquistador or other meritorious citizen. The recipient, or *encomendero*, was supposed to offer them protection and religious instruction in return. In practice, though, the system was extremely exploitative and rife with abuse.

18. See Sandoval, *Bibliografía general*.

19. Palmer, "Negro Slavery," 146.

20. Ibid., esp. 161. The quote from Phillip II is cited in Aguirre Beltrán, *Regiones del refugio*, 189. Initially, a mestizo was a mix between a person of Spanish descent and a native Mexican, but the idea behind mestizaje transcends that limited definition and includes the general melding of all the different people in Mexico.

21. Ibid., 163.

22. See Aguirre Beltrán, *Regiones de refugio*; and Palmer, "Negro Slavery," for discussions of cimarron, or maroon societies and the experiences and resistance of slaves more generally.

23. For an excellent discussion of the period, see von Mentz, *Pueblos de indios*. For more on the evolution of local religion, saints, and images in rural Mexico, see Taylor, *Magistrates of the Sacred*, esp. ch. 11. The book offers a comprehensive discussion of issues revolving around the interaction of the church and rural populace in Mexico. For more on "el Cristo Negro de San Gaspar," see the essay with that title in *Crónica morelense*. Jiutepec has been basically absorbed by greater Cuernavaca.

24. The quotations on the population of the Cuautla Valley and on zambos come from Gerhard, *Historical Geography*, 93, 97. Borah and Cook discuss the trickiness of calculating indigenous population totals in their ground-breaking study, *Population of Central Mexico*, esp. 38, n. 44. The other pitfall in population statistics is that ethnic mixing brought African and Indian families together confounding statistical efforts to estimate their numbers while depending on data derived from counting tributaries. This is to say nothing of how social determinants of race affected the numbers.

25. For data on eighteenth-century Mapastlán, see Salinas, *Bosquejo histórico*, 19. For more general demographic information, see Gerhard, *Historical Geography*. The archive and book of Jesús Sotelo Inclán contain nineteenth-century disputes of Aneneculico and Ayala with neighboring haciendas with commentaries on the ethnic categorizations of the witnesses. See Sotelo Inclán, *Raíz y razón*, and the archive of Aneneculico. A copy of that archive is held at the AGN and provides the bulk of the material upon which Sotelo Inclán based his history.

26. Crespo et al., *Historia del azúcar*, discusses the prices of sugar, as do C. E. Martin, *Rural Society*, and Chevalier, *Land and Society*.

27.   See von Wobeser, *San Carlos Borromeo*, 69–80; and Hernandez Chávez, *Propiedad Comunal*, 81–114, on the origins of the haciendas in Morelos.

Chapter Two

1.   James wrote the classic history of the Haitian revolution, *Black Jacobins*. Tutino, *Insurrection to Revolution*, develops the idea of symbiosis between haciendas and villages where villagers provide labor and the hacienda provides work and alternative income. He analyzes the forces that changed it and explores the social ramifications during the independence struggle, the nineteenth century, and the revolution. C. E. Martin discusses the effects of the Bourbon reforms and the growing role of commercial agriculture in supplying the urban market in late-colonial Morelos, in *Rural Society*, ch. 5. Of course, other places better situated to exploit the export market benefited more from the collapse of Saint Dominigue than interior parts of Mexico did. See, for example, Schwartz, *Sugar Plantations*, which shows that even Northeast Brazil experienced a revival as a result.

2.   For the original research of this and other episodes, see Gruzinski, *Man-gods*, esp. 70–80, for a discussion of Antonio Pérez and the use of religious interpretation to resist the imposition of outside authority.

3.   Ibid.

4.   For a good discussion of the ethnic and cultural significance of corn in Nahua diet and society, see Sandstrom, *Corn Is our Blood*.

5.   Quoted in Gruzinski, *Man-gods*, 160.

6.   Ibid., 161.

7.   For more on the meaning and significance of the municipio libre, as well as popular Liberalism and the corrido, see Heau's excellent article, "Tradición autonomista." The AGN, Inquisición, tomo 1356, vol. 3, fojas 25–29, has the case of the Cuahuixtla worker, and tomo 1358 has the one from Jilotepec, Mexico State.

8.   See Gruzinski, *Man-gods*, 161, for the late-colonial era; see the collection of interviews of former Zapatistas by Chiu, "Peónes y campesinos," for the revolution. Other interviews with Zapatista veterans as well as people from the region who lived through, but did not participate in the revolution, are discussed in Chapters 7 and 8 of this work and can be found at the *Program de Historia Oral*, INAH archive. For those interested in these documents, Rueda Smithers has incorporated and interpreted some of them in his works, including "Oposición y subversión" and *Paraíso de la caña*. Brunk, *Emiliano Zapata!*, used some of these interviews for a slightly later time period in his history of the Zapatista revolution.

9.   Of the various types of colonial land concessions, the fundo legal provided space for the homes and inhabitants of a community, while the ejido provided land for pasture and public use, and the *tierras de comun repartamiento* allowed parcels for individual usufruct, although as part of the collective village patrimony. Propios were common lands meant to provide for the expenses of the pueblo that were often rented out to generate income. The fundamental text on this is Mendieta y Nuñez, *Problema agrario*. By calling communal lands fundos legales, I am conflating the uses because the fundo survived the longest, and because by the mid-nineteenth century people were using the word in a general way that encompassed these distinctions. For more on this topic, see M. Bazant, "Desamortización."

10.   Archivo Jesús Sotelo Inclán, the document originally came from AGN, Tierras, vol. 2052, exp. 1; it is document number 5.5 in the Inclán papers. The

archive is made up of a variety of papers relating to Anenecuilco and gathered by Sotelo Inclán in his research for his comprehensive and indispensable *Raíz y razón*. Much of it comes from the document group Tierras at the AGN. It is difficult to demonstrate in an acre-by-acre fashion the spread of the haciendas over time, but the documents from Tierras for the colonial period, and those from a variety of sources for the nineteenth and twentieth centuries allow historians to re-create the contours, and most importantly for this study, the social implications of the process, if not the systematic graphing of it. A good initial resource for the cases in Tierras pertaining to Morelos is the *Católogo documental tierras de Morelos* (AGN, 2000).

11. See Chapter 4 below for a more in-depth discussion of the impact of the Liberal reforms.

12. Sugarcane cultivation required good irrigated land. Pueblos were frequently left with very little of that and usually relied on fields of *temporal* (those watered only by seasonal rainfall) for the necessities of life. An invaluable source for understanding elite perspective and historical interpretation is the survey sent by the Madero government to hacendados in Morelos. One response from the hacendado Juan Pagaza explains the pattern of growing cane and offers practical reasons based on climate and efficiency for why small independent cane growing never took hold in Morelos. His explanation, though, leads one to consider the fact that hacendados controlled the mills and simply refused to mill a campesino's cane in order to deny that source of income and keep the campesino in the position of hacienda worker and subsistence tiller. See the questionnaire sent by the Madero government under the auspices of Patricio Leyva to the hacendados of Morelos asking for their assessment of the causes of the revolution in their state. A copy of the survey is at the INAH archive in Tlalpan, the originals came from the AGN, Secretaría de Gobernación, Asuntos Varios, Islas Marías, Estados 1911–1914, exp. 298.

13. AJSI; this episode comes from the original at the AGN, in Tierras, vol. 2052, exp. 1. For a more developed discussion of local identities and the concept of the identity of village and church and other forms of remembering, including legal testimony, see Van Young's "Paisaje de ensueño."

14. For a history of Anenecuilco based on archival evidence that also indicates how that pueblo's experience represented larger patterns in Morelos, see Hernández Chávez, *Anenecuilco*.

15. The interpretation of pueblos as closed corporate communities popularized a generation ago by Eric Wolf, has influenced the work of many historians and anthropologists. While much of the characterization is true, some scholars have tended to romanticize village cohesiveness, isolationism, and communalism as villagers strike a defensive posture against an exploitative and aggressive outside world. Taking the same basic idea of a closed community but offering a portrayal of a burdensome and unwanted communalism, while stressing internal village repression and hierarchy, Popkin, *Rational Peasant*, argues that Vietnamese villagers eagerly threw off the constraints of communal, self-sufficient land tenure and therefore responded in a rational way to outside market opportunities. Although many of his points about the confining nature of small village life are well taken, he ignores how peasants may have taken advantage of new opportunities while, at the same time, attempting to retain the best aspects of their inherited community organization. Instead he concentrates on the peasantry's imposed isolation and deprivation and argues that peasants see market capitalism, the erosion of community cohesiveness, and the entrance into dependent market production as producers of a single cash crop as some sort of liberation. Any kind

of rigid characterization one way or the other fails to capture the reality and essence of these human communities in flux.

16. Salinas offers a sampling of land disputes from the sixteenth to nineteenth centuries from across the state that takes fifteen pages just to list in his *Bosquejo histórico*, ch. 5.

17. This is a meager sampling of a much wider story and the best way of understanding this process is, of course, to see the evidence. For a preliminary sampling of the Ramo de Tierras at the AGN, previously mentioned, see the *Católogo documental tierras de Morelos*. It lists 1,010 cases with a brief description of each dispute. For two very good works based on local studies of this larger pattern in the colonial era, see Sotelo Inclán's classic *Raíz y razón*; and Hernández Chavez, *Anenecuilco*.

18. See von Mentz, *Pueblos de indios*, 80, for these figures. Her detailed ethnographic work offers important information about the sugar-producing areas of the state and allows for a better understanding of the structural changes and cultural developments in the area.

19. For more on the size, operation, and labor organization on these haciendas, see Barrett, *Sugar Hacienda*, which has an excellent appendix that demonstrates the place of origin and number of slaves at hacienda Atlacomulco and the change from slave labor to other forms. See also Sharrer Tamm, *Azúcar y trabajo*; as well as C. E. Martin, *Rural Society*; and Crespo et al., *Historia del azúcar*. For the size and ownership of the haciendas on the eve of the revolution, see Crespo and Vega Villanueva, *Tierra y propiedad*, which is a compilation of raw data based on the Manifestaciones de Haciendas, Estancias y Fábricas, done for a reevaluation of taxes in 1909. For what happened to these haciendas after the revolution, see the Appendix to this book.

20. See Skocpol, *States and Social Revolutions*. Her discussion of the resulting destabilization of political control associated with the diminished repressive power of the state is useful here, and although this circumstance differs from those she describes, the implications of the state's demise are similar.

21. Alamán, *Documentos diversos*, 4:266; and García Cantú, *Utópias mexicanas*. There are several excellent studies on independence, for more on the popular aspects of the struggle, see Hamill, *Hidalgo Revolt*; Hamnett, *Roots*; and Hamnett, "Economic and Social Dimension." For an in-depth analysis of the social origins and local and national meanings of the independence movement, see Van Young, *Other Rebellion*. See Van Young, "Agrarian Rebellion," for a discussion of the "localocentric" view of most Indian rebels the very different agendas they had from the creole directorate of the independence effort. For a broad analysis of the social bases of independence and rebellion in general, see Tutino, *Insurrection to Revolution*.

22. For more on this episode, see C. E. Martin, *Rural Society*, 194–95; and Tutino, *Insurrection to Revolution*, 140–51, for an analysis of the social causes of the independence struggle in the area. For good standard texts that cover this period, especially the role of José María Morelos and the battle for Cuautla, see Salinas, *Historias y paisajes*; and Mazari, *Bosquejo histórico*. Some landowners such as Francisco Ayala sympathized with the independence effort.

23. Not all historians share this view of independence. For an important interpretation of the independence movement that concentrates more on urban sectors and educated elites and refocuses the discussion on social elements critical to the realization of independence, other than the rural masses, see Rodríguez, *Origins*.

24. The term *gachupín* literally meant a person from Spain, but was still applied to large landowning creoles and to well-off shopkeepers in the nineteenth

and early twentieth centuries. José María Bocanegra discusses the stripping of Spaniards of government jobs, exiling them to Spain, and other forms of official and popular hostility toward Spaniards in Mexico following independence; see his *Memória*, esp. 337–38. Also see Sims, *Expulsion*.

25. C. E. Martin, *Rural Society*, 196, describes the troubles of some landowners as the less efficient faded after independence. Her work on Morelos coincides with that of Chowning, who found a new group of ambitious landowners in Michoacán that replaced inefficient or highly indebted producers there as well; see Chowning, *Wealth and Power*.

26. For exports in 1807–14, see Huerta, *Empresarios*, 110, 121; and for comments on the domestic market, see von Mentz, *Pueblos de indios*, 79.

27. Based on her research in notarial archives, Huerta's *Empresarios* provides the names of newcomers, the haciendas they acquired, where they came from, and the political connections they developed. See also Crespo et al., *Historia de azúcar*, 1:ch. 2, and vol. 2, both based on contributions by some of the leading scholars on the Mexican sugar industry and the history of Morelos. See also Warman, *"We Come to Object,"* chs. 1 and 2; as well Landazuri Benitez and Vázquez Mantecón, *Azúcar y estado*; and Síndico, "Azúcar y burguesía," 15,16, for more on sugar prices and markets.

28. Huerta, *Empresarios*, 118–20, relays how Icazbalceta survived the anti-Spanish furor. For raw data on that hacienda, see AJTS, doc. 113; Síndico, "Modernization"; and also Síndico, "Azúcar y burguesía."

29. AJTS, doc. 65 contains hacienda account books with production figures, wages for a variety of labor, and data on the distribution of sugar for the hacienda Tenango.

30. The social meaning people attached to the wage scale will be developed more fully throughout the text, including Chapter 3, which considers the violence at the hacienda Chiconcuac in the Cuernavaca Valley in 1856 in its larger context. See also Chapter 6 for an analysis of issues brought out in the court case of Apatlaco versus the hacienda Cuahuixtla in the mid-1860s. Taken together with the causes and patterns of banditry discussed in Chapter 7, and the interviews with Zapatista veterans that conclude the text, they provide a sense of how material conditions were interpreted by those experiencing them.

31. This description of labor activity is based on labor cycles from the AJTS for Tenango and Acamilpa and is supported by the work of Síndico and Warman. Balance sheets for expenditures and sales exist at the AJTS for several haciendas, including Tenango and Acamilpa, in the mid-nineteenth century. In 1847, Nicolás Icazbalceta owned Tenango and San Ignacio and had about 490,000 pesos in debt, while his landholdings were valued at about 700,000 pesos and his yearly income from sugar and rum production alone totaled between 40,000 and 70,000 pesos. AJTS, doc. 113.

32. See Gramsci, *Selections*, ch. "Notes on Italian History."

33. For comparative insight into these processes and the creation of a protoindustrial countryside on the eve of rebellion in Russia, see Edelman, *Proletarian Peasants*. For a good example from a different region of Mexico, see Meyers, *Forge of Progress*.

34. Helguera, López, and Ramirez estimate in "Tenango, de real a pueblo" (in *Campesinos de la tierra*) that the hacienda used only 2,237 of its 68,181 hectares to raise sugarcane. The rest was divided up between pastures, forests, mountains, and fields watered by seasonal rains. The surface area of this hacienda used to raise sugarcane was lower than the overall average, though, because the hacienda was larger than any other and drier than most.

35. AGN, Exposiciones extranjeras, Estado de Morelos, caja 51, exp. 11.

The documents here contain data on production and land use by acre gathered by the Secretaría de Fomento in 1899 in preparation for participation and display of Mexican sugar in the Exposición de Paris de 1900. For Mexico's official portrayals of itself internationally at these expositions, see Tenorio-Trillo, *Mexico at the World's Fairs*.

36. Hernández Chávez, *Propiedad comunal*, 119, discusses how Tenango affected its neighbors. This is a general descriptive outline; more evidence will be introduced in the course of the work. For those interested in primary sources on these themes, consult the Archivo de la Reforma Agraria; the Comisión Nacional Agraria, Resoluciones Presidenciales (AGN); and the Junta Protectora, which offer the best places to start. Chapter 8 below offers an in-depth treatment of the case of Apatlaco, which illustrates a larger pattern. Since I am interested in understanding the interplay of economy, society, and culture in order to understand the social origins of Zapatismo, most of the references I make to hacienda expansion come in relation to the social conflict it generated, although one could obviously explore it in a different way.

Chapter Three

1. See communications between Nicholas Trist, U.S. commissioner to Mexico, to James Buchanan, U.S. secretary of state, and of Winfield Scott, general in chief of the U.S. army in Mexico, written to Trist from Scott's headquarters in Jalapa, Veracruz, in May 1847, in the *Diplomatic Correspondence of the United States, Inter-American Affairs*. The italics are Scott's; the underlined portion is mine. Scott's letter also said, "You are right, in doubting, whether there be a government, even de facto in this Republic. General Santa Anna, the nominal president, has been, until within a day or two, in the neighborhood of Orizaba, organizing bands of rancheros, bandits or guerillas, to cut off stragglers of this army, and, probably, the very train, all important to us, which you propose to accompany into the interior." See also Saka, "We Are Citizens!"

2. For a good analysis of the role of taxes and their association with centralism, and the way campesinos responded to increases of them in the case of Guerrero in the early 1840s, see Guardino, "Barbarism or Republican Law?" esp. 200–201, as well as his discussion of the impact of landlord efforts to collect rents around Chilapa and the response that elicited, 198. Also see Guardino, *Peasants, Politics*, where these themes are developed more fully.

3. The expression *gente decente* translated as "civilized people," which meant Spaniards and creoles, and included urbane mestizos. See Alamán, *Documentos diversos*, 4:466; and Barrett, *Sugar Hacienda*, 38.

4. Alamán, *Documentos diversos*, 4:470–71.

5. See Saka, "We Are Citizens!" on resistance to the Americans; Hernández Chávez, "Tradición republicana," 55–57; as well as Thomson, "Bulwarks of Patriotic Liberalism." See also Mallon, *Defense of Community*, for an important discussion with comparative implications on the meaning and sources of state formation and nationalism in the Peruvian highlands, a theme which she has developed for mid-nineteenth-century Mexico as well in *Peasant and Nation*. See also Brading, *Origins*, on nationalism often being a response to foreign threats, be they military or cultural.

6. Zavala, *Viaje*, 371, quoted in Brading, *Origins*, 73.

7. For three excellent discussions of Mexican political and economic thought at the time, see Hale, *Mexican Liberalism*; Reyes Heroles, *Liberalismo mexicano*; and for a slightly later period see Perry, "Modelo liberal."

8. For a view on the differences between North American and Mexican realities

as seen through the eyes of Padre Servando Teresa de Mier, see Brading, *Origins*, 63.

9. Mora, *Obras sueltas*, 385; italics are mine.

10. See Potash, *Banco de Avío de México*, 180–84. Alamán's ideas for national development were somewhat like Alexander Hamilton's regarding the pursuit of protective tariffs to foster industry.

11. See Mora, *Obras sueltas*, for attitudes on Indians; and also Lira, *Espejo de discordias*, 79, and 82 for the above quotes. Brading, *Origins*, talks of indígenismo emanating from elites, but that talk was mainly related to dead Indians and to an idealized reconstructed past. It did not deal in any real sense with the indigenous or mestizo campesinos alive at the time who were beginning to assert themselves politically.

12. See Hale, *Mexican Liberalism*, esp. chs. 1 and 7; and Mallon's pioneering article, "Peasants and State Formation."

13. See the "Respuesta de los propietarios de los disritos de Cuernavaca y Morelos"; and also see Álvarez, "Manifiesto del ciudadano Juan Álvarez."

14. See Reina, *Rebeliones campesinas*, 157, for evidence of this; and Alamán, *Documentos diversos*, 4:442, for the quote.

15. Quoted in von Mentz, *Pueblos en el siglo XIX*; see also González Navarro, *Anatomía*, 163–64, on hacendado views of socialism and the development of commerce and industry; and Rueda Smithers, *Paraíso de la caña*, for more on this time period and the efforts of Villaseñor.

16. For the varied activities of other clergy than these well-known figures, see Taylor, *Magistrates of the Sacred*.

17. See González Navarro, *Anatomía*, 33; and Reina, *Luchas populares*, 77, although neither source indicates exactly which towns were involved. See also Powell, "Priest and Peasant," which enumerates a multitude of grievances against abusive and exploitative priests and vicars. Sometimes clergy were seen as benefactors, and other times as agents of repression. Both existed in Morelos as seen by this example of Rojo, on the one hand, and by the experiences of a foreign visitor named Pal Rosty and his account of a rural priest fleeing to the safety of Cuernavaca to escape an angry lynch mob, and some later Zapatista interviews condemning local priests as agents of the hacendados, on the other.

18. Reina, *Rebeliones campesinas*.

19. See Díaz Soto y Gama, *Revolución del sur*; and also Reina, *Rebeliones campesinas*, both of which report this and other episodes of agrarian rebellion.

20. Cited in Hernández Chávez, *Propiedad comunal*, 133. See also González Navarro, *Anatomía*; and Rueda Smithers, *Paraíso de la caña*. The repartamiento was a forced-labor system where men from various towns were compelled to work on a rotational basis for a Spaniard granted access to their labor. In theory, they were supposed to paid, but they were routinely overworked and abused.

21. For more on the Yucatán see, Rugeley, *Yucatán's Maya Peasantry*; and Reed, *Caste War*.

22. Quoted in Hernández Chávez, *Propiedad comunal*, 133.

23. Although organized resistance was embryonic, it encompassed and exceeded the everyday forms of low-level resistance identified by Scott and subsequently elaborated on by others. For a provocative interpretation of "everyday" resistance and nonviolent, counterhegemonic activity, see Scott, *Weapons of the Weak*; and Scott, *Domination*.

24. The concepts developed by Scott in *Moral Economy* are useful in this context and help explain how ideas of justice and fairness are shaped and go beyond base material conditions.

25. See Knight, "Weapons and Arches," which discusses the value of looking at the Mexican revolution through a wide lens that sees it as an important phase "in a longer process of social, political, economic and cultural change."

26. Quoted in Hernández Chávez, *Propiedad comunal*, 137; italics are mine.

27. *El Monitor Republicano*, June 24, 1849, no. 1503, Hemeroteca Nacional. See Reina, *Rebeliones campesinas*, 162–63, for the national guard quote.

28. González Navarro, *Anatomía*, 161.

29. For an excellent discussion of the second half of the nineteenth century in Morelos, see Rueda Smithers, *Paraíso de la caña*, esp. 63–95, where he offers an analysis of Ramírez in both the context of the struggle over land in Morelos and in relation to the ideas being developed about how to govern and develop the nation.

30. See Katz, "Rural Rebellions after 1810," for a general overview and analysis; for the colonial period, see Taylor, *Drinking, Homicide*. See also Hart, *Anarchism*, for the influence of anarchists Plotino Rhodakanaty and Francisco Zalacosta on the rebellion of local Chalco campesino Julio Chávez López and his actions against the estates. See the case of José Maneul Arellano from Tetecala, Morelos, discussed here and by Reina, González Navarro, and Mallon elsewhere. Outsiders and the formally educated, especially lawyers, played an obvious role in the handling, presentation, and representation of pueblos in legal disputes, where their language, experiences, and knowledge of larger contemporary political events no doubt affected the terminology and tone legal appeals took. That influenced the written record and must be kept in mind when interpreting those documents.

31. For a broad-ranging analysis of the outbreak of revolution and its relation to the lessened repressive powers of the state as a result of defeat in foreign war, see Skocpol, *States and Social Revolutions*.

32. Hernández Chávez, *Propiedad comunal*, 135.

33. For a well-documented discussion of the convergence of local agrarian issues with national politics, see Thomson, with LaFrance, *Patriotism, Politics*, esp. chs. 5–10, the last of which offers an assessment of the benefits some local participants gained in Puebla. For more on Chávez López, see Hart, *Anarchism*. Also see Mallon's discussion of the influence of local intellectuals in *Peasant and Nation*.

34. Villaseñor, in von Mentz, *Pueblos en el siglo XIX*, 17.

35. Hernández Chávez offers this quote from Villaseñor's much-cited *Memória política y estadistica de la prefectura de Cuernavaca, presentada al superior gobierno del estado libre y soberano de México, 1850*, in *Propiedad comunal*.

36. See Rueda Smithers, *Paraíso de la caña*, 90, who cites Ramírez's *Obras completas*.

37. González Navarro, *Anatomía*, 64, cites an anonymous letter, which, when taken in conjunction with other hacendado statements and actions, like those Rueda Smithers cites from *Respuestas de algunos propietarios de fincas rusticas* (1849), from *El Siglo XIX*, and the later *respuesta* to Juan Álvarez, and Manuel Mendoza Cortina's statements in the mid-1860s, and the hacendado survey from 1912 from the AGN, Secretaría de Gobernación, Asuntos Varios, Islas Marías, Estados 1911–14, that represented hacendado mentalities over time.

38. González Navarro, *Anatomía*, 167.

39. Johnson, *Mexican Revolution of Ayutla*, 27.

40. Reina, *Rebeliones campesinas*, 167.

41. See *Santa Anna y Juan Álvarez, frente a frente*. For a close treatment of peasant politics in Guerrerro and Álvarez's role in them, see Guardino, "Barbarism or Republican Law?"; and Guardino, *Peasants, Politics*, esp. ch. 5.

42. For an excellent discussion of the social origins and previous actions of Álvarez's Guerrero troops, see Reina, *Rebeliones campesinas*, where she devotes an entire section to movements in Guerrero. See also Guardino's discussion of revolts during the revolution of Ayutla, *Peasants, Politics*, ch. 6.

43. One of the most obvious examples of this advocacy was his previously cited manifesto. See also Muñoz y Perez, "General Don Juan Álvarez," which, although it is a hagiography of Álvarez, contains useful documents and data, and see Reina, *Rebeliones campesinas*.

44. See Cockcroft, *Intellectual Precursors*.

45. See Reyes Heroles, *Liberalismo mexicano*; and Hale, *Mexican Liberalism*.

46. This attitude can be seen from the writings of Lorenzo de Zavala to those of Ignacio Ramírez and Ponciano Arriaga. For Arriaga's quote, see Márquez and Abella, *Ponciano Arriaga*.

47. Powell, "Liberales" discusses some of these issues, as does Hernández Chávez, *Propiedad comunal*.

48. Leonard, *Baroque Times*, provides a feel for the element of recreation in small towns; de la Peña, *Legacy of Promises*, explains the development of regional social bonds and the role of fiestas and trade.

49. Writing in France in 1848, José María Luis Mora argued that indigenous agrarian rebels had to be suppressed; see Hale, *Mexican Liberalism*, 239.

50. The national guard in Morelos was somewhat enigmatic, with armed agrarian rebels emerging from their ranks and wealthy hacendados contributing funds and weaponry. José Manuel Arellano was a lieutenant colonel in the national guard under Álvarez while hacendados Angel Pérez Palacios, Antonio Gutiérrez, and the engineer Domingo Díez were financial contributors to the national guard. For a fine-grained analysis of the national guard in Puebla, which explores more fully issues mentioned here, see Thomson, with LaFrance, *Patriotism, Politics*. For the incident regarding Negrete, see Hart, "Miguel Negrete."

51. See Reina, *Rebeliones campesinas*, 32, 175–76; Mallon, "Peasants and State Formation," 23.

52. Villaseñor, in von Mentz, *Pueblos en el siglo XIX*, 9. See also Reina, *Rebeliones campesinas*, 33, 170; Mallon, "Peasants and State Formation," 23.

53. Reina, *Rebeliones campesinas*, 35, 170; Mallon, "Peasants and State Formation," 23, 24.

54. AGN, Gobernación, Tranquilidad Pública, sect. 1A, box, 460, exp. 8, Apr. 24, 1857, reports this murder and reveals that assaults against Spaniards and hacienda managers and long-term estate employees were not generally seen as isolated incidents at the time but were portrayed as symptomatic of a climate of social antagonism. They generated concern among local elites that went beyond the issues of each particular episode and made the authorities speak of "la conspiración ...contra los espanoles en Cuautla de Morelos."

55. For the details of this well-known episode, see Salinas, *Historias y paisajes*, 41; Reina, *Rebeliones campesinas*.

56. Salinas, *Historias y paisajes*, 42.

57. Mallon, "Peasants and State Formation."

58. Salinas, *Historias y paisajes*, 91.

59. Reina, *Rebeliones campesinas*, 172.

60. Condumex Archive, documents collection, fondo del siglo xix, doc. dccclviii, Feb. 1857. This commission was in addition to those forces formed earlier and operated more in conjunction with governmental authorities. The private forces formed and funded by the hacendados a few years before had been deemed insufficient to insure security at this point.

61. Brading's discussion of nationalism is associated with foreign competition

and is useful, but mainly speaks from the perspective of the creole elite. Here, though, it appears to have impacted the lower classes as well and played a part in their formation of a national consciousness and what they expected of their country's leaders. See Brading, *Origins*.

62. Coatsworth, "Patterns of Rural Rebellion," argues that the Mexican peasantry was taking the initiative during much of the mid-nineteenth century to recapture lands and prerogatives deemed usurped, and in so doing were the aggressors in many of the conflicts of the day. This was true, and they were demanding not only *old* rights, but *new* ones that included labor relations and political representation, not through votes, but through legislation that protected or pushed their agendas vis-à-vis rival ones. After the late 1840s, if governments failed to address these issues they lost their legitimacy in the eyes of many rural Morelenses. Those feelings reached their apogee during the Zapatista revolution, but came from this period when various segments of society were struggling for influence over the trajectory of Mexican national development and its ideological paradigm.

Chapter Four

1. "Recollections of an American Journal." The author would like to thank Professor William Beezley for providing a copy of this manuscript and background on Pal Rosty.

2. For other descriptions of Morelos, see Doménech, *Guía general descriptiva*; Robelo, *Revistas descriptivas*; Mazari, *Historias y paisajes*. Morelos was part of the state of Mexico and became an independent state in 1869.

3. "Recollections of an American Journal."

4. MRP, BLAC, doc. 6320, Mar. 18, 1857, reported a "new incident among those which abound in the district of Tetecala," and also the destruction of the boundary markers at hacienda San Gabriel.

5. MRP, BLAC, doc. 6235, Mar. 2, 1857, is a letter from Secretary of State Urquidi to Riva Palacio and mentions the concerns of A. Villaseñor in Cuernavaca.

6. MRP, BLAC, doc. 6128, reveals the common preoccupations of Morelos's hacienda administrators with order and hierarchy. Not only was it important to them that there was a proper place for everyone, but it was essential that everyone understood what their place was.

7. For a discussion of how these public parades and other popular events could be used to deliver social messages and vivid manifestations of resistance through mockery or unflattering portrayals of social elites, see Leonard, *Baroque Times*; Beezley, *Judas*; and Beezley, English Martin, and French, *Rituals of Rule*.

8. MRP, BLAC, doc. 6238, is a letter from hacendado Joaquín García Icazbalceta to the governor.

9. See Gimenez, *Así cantaban*, 245. Of course, it has a more lyrical quality in Spanish than it does in this translation.

10. Womack, *Zapata*.

11. MRP, BLAC, doc. 6253, Mar. 5, 1857, is a personal letter from Vicente to his father.

12. MRP, BLAC, doc. 6303, Mar. 14, 1857, is a letter from Álvarez.

13. See AGN, Bienes Nacionalizados, esp. caja 365, exp. 88/69; and caja 369, exp. 64/38, which offer lists for the bienes nacionalizados in Morelos for 1866 and 1873 respectively and provide a sense of the scale of the measure. See cajas 365–75, for a wide assortment of claims and counterclaims by pueblo vecinos, outsiders from the larger towns, and hacendados. Many cases arose from the nationalization of private property mortgaged by the

church, which forced hacendados to refinance, or come up with 15 percent down payments.

14. MRP, BLAC, doc. 6235, Mar. 2, 1857, is the previously mentioned letter from the Mexican secretary of state. The assertion that most villagers opposed them is substantiated by the huge corpus of legal cases, disputes, appeals, and letters of concern like the ones cited here and by the well-documented example of Anenecuilco.

15. MRP, BLAC, doc. 6320, contains the record of the second episode mentioned here as reported by Joaquín Noriega to Riva Palacio, the first is from González Navarro, *Anatomía*.

16. MRP, BLAC, doc. 6598, May 25, 1857, reports an insurrection in Cuautla District and asks the governor for troops to protect Spaniards.

17. MRP, BLAC, doc. 6621, June 2, 1857, reports bandits and "pronunciados" in Jonacatepec.

18. MRP, BLAC, doc. 6680, June 21, 1857, also reports bandits threatening the haciendas, including the references to Tenango and Tenextepango.

19. MRP, BLAC, doc. 6809, Aug. 12, 1857, reports increased banditry and murder near Jonacatepec, done by organized bands with recognized leaders, which indicated they were not just spontaneous outbursts.

20. MRP, BLAC, doc. 6815, Aug. 13, 1857, letter from Comonfort about bandit activity and offering forces to deal with it.

21. MRP, BLAC, doc. 6843, Aug. 20, 1857, reports public sympathy for bandits in Jonacatepec and hatred of Spaniards in the area.

22. Ibid. Also, for an analysis and discussion of the literature on banditry as social protest, see Joseph's article "On the Trail," which tracks studies of banditry from Hobsbawm's original contribution of *Primitive Rebels* and then *Bandits*, to revisionist interpretations that diminish the social aspect of "social bandits." For another treatment of the subject and a well-developed Mexican example, see Vanderwood, *Disorder and Progress*. For a brief, but interesting discussion on the topic that suggests using a criminological definition of banditry and studying banditry as a form of crime in relation to structures of social control instead of studying it as a form of resistance to structures of domination, see Birkbeck, "Latin American Banditry."

23. See MRP, BLAC, docs. 6303, 6329, 6235, 6843, for examples. One of the citations here regarding people going to Mexico City in search of land titles is for Chalco, but the same thing was going on in Morelos, as evidenced by the municipal archive of Anenecuilco, carpeta 4, which documents the personal donation of between three to fifteen pesos by forty-eight people of Anenecuilco to finance the "busca de los titulos primordiales de las tierras del pueblo" and the eventual mustering of four hundred pesos to do it. Three to fifteen pesos was a lot of money for most vecinos, and this amount might show a couple of things, including the differences of wealth within the community, but it might also demonstrate an important level of solidarity as those with more money joined their poorer neighbors instead of trying to denounce land themselves. These contributions were still significantly less than purchasing the land under the rules of the Lerdo law. Also see Mallon's discussion of Tepoztlán in *Peasant and Nation*. Sotelo Inclán, *Raíz y razón*, discusses the cases of other towns around Cuautla and how they defended their lands as well.

24. See the Junta Protectora at the AGN for an extensive array of land claims from across central Mexico submitted in the wake of the Ley Lerdo. Also see Hernández Chávez, *Propiedad communal*, 141, and her appendix; and for a list of pueblos with a brief synopsis of the disputes they were involved in, see Mazari, *Bosquejo histórico*. For more on the heavily documented case of

Anenecuilco, see the Archive of Anenecuilco donated by Jesús Sotelo Inclán to the AGN. Sotelo Inclán's book *Raíz y razón*, also mentions other towns, such as Ahuehuepán and Olintepec. For a treatment of these issues in eastern Morelos, see Warman, *"We Come to Object."*

25. The case of Apatlaco discussed in Chapter 8, below, provides a good example of this.

26. Although the Ley Lerdo has been a topic of heated debate since its implementation, Reyes Heroles pointed out that "it is practically impossible to measure the direct effect of the Law of Disamortization on property," in *Liberalismo mexicano*, 3:633. Crespo, who has carefully studied the issue in Morelos, believes that reaching a definitive conclusion regarding the effect of disamortization on communal landholding requires studies that are able to match the empirical data of those that have measured the effects on ecclesiastical properties done by J. Bazant, *Bienes de la iglesia*; and Knowlton, *Bienes del clero*. That has not been done yet, and given the dispersion of data, may not be possible. As a result, we can only use the evidence available from specific incidents and look at associated social conflicts over land and water to piece the picture together. For more on the matter, see Crespo, "Pueblos de Morelos." See also Molina Enriquez, *Grandes problemas nacionales*; and Silva Herzog, *Agrarismo mexicano*.

27. AGN, Secretaría de Gobernación, Asuntos Varios, Islas Marías, Estados 1911–1914, exp. 298, June 6, 1912.

28. AGN, Secretaría de Gobernación, Asunto Varios, Islas Marías, Estados 1911–1914, exp. 298.

29. For data on land ownership, see Crespo, "Pueblos de Morelos," 72.

30. The papers held under the general heading "Gobernación, Bienes Nacionalizados" contain cases in which local residents denounced lands and property, and the pueblo or town went to court over it, claiming the property in question to be communally held. These cases demonstrate the rift that Sotelo Inclán discusses in his book. They contain, however, a far greater number of cases of outsiders denouncing lands in another community. See, for example, caja 367, docs. 10/105 and 10/107–110, for cases in which individuals from Cuautla denounced cofradía and other lands in Yautepec. See also JPCM, vol. 4, exp. 15, which deals with the towns of Xochitepec, Cuentepec, Ahuehuezingo, and others, and discusses how the vecinos of those places complained of the "abusos, vejaciones y malos tratos de que son victimas por parte de los hacendados colindantes," and shows the pressures facing the villages and their fundos legales at the time. For a good discussion of the issues revolving around the Reform laws, supported by a detailed case study, see Purnell, "With All Due Respect"; also see Purnell, *Popular Movements*, esp. ch. 2, which shows how the Lerdo law played out differently in different places.

31. JPCM, vol. 1, exp. 21. Although these cases were brought forward during the time of the Intervention, the disputes originated with the denuncios of the Ley Lerdo.

32. See Reyes Heroles, *Liberalismo mexicano*; and Mejia Fernandez, *Politica agraria*, for a discussion of Álvarez and Arriaga, as well as popular rebellion and campesino programs. See Hernández Chávez for a list of lands denounced in Morelos, which are few before 1870 and hard to document because almost all appear as the lands of former cofradias. The place where I found the most evidence of its attempted application was the Junta Protectora, AGN. See also Mazari, *Bosquejo histórico*.

33. AGN, BN, caja 369 88/37. The quoted parts of the document read, "de que nos tenemos notícia los poseían con igual carácter" and "Para los indígena

Mexicanos como lo somos." Also, JPCM, vol. 4, exp. 12, and vol. 5, exp. 16.

34. MRP, BLAC, doc. 6833; and see Mallon, *Peasant and Nation*; and Thomson, with LaFrance, *Patriotism, Politics*, for an examination of pueblo options, attitudes, and impact on the Wars of the Reforma and the struggle between Conservatives and Liberals.

35. RP, BLAC, doc. 039, Oct. 1, 1857.

36. Mallon treats this episode in *Peasant and Nation*, 140–41. Some historians have convincingly argued that campesinos were attracted to the Liberals and federalism because these allowed for greater municipal autonomy in working out local issues revolving around land and water disputes. Centralists, or Conservatives, generally tended to support larger municipalities and their creole or mestizo leaders, with predictably negative results at the community level. Mallon argues, "Thus peasants in Guerrero and Morelos...could agree on the need to fight for a decentralized polity in which municipalities could work through these new issues in a relatively autonomous fashion." In the abstract, that was true. Pueblos did want local autonomy and, at times, fought for it. At other times, however, the generalization does not fit. Liberals, as the federalists in Mexico, supported the blanket national legislation that most directly attacked community landholdings and, by decentralizing power, left the implementation to local, low-level, often corrupt officials who were in league with, friends of, or in some instances, actually *were* the hacendados themselves. As a result, ethnically indigenous barrios of larger towns suffered, as did unincorporated hamlets such as Apatlaco (see discussion in Chapter 8, below), which had to seek authority from outside their immediate locale, and at the national level, for intervention against an abusive administrator and his magistrate friend.

37. See Hernández Chávez, *Propiedad communal*, 147; for two differing ways of interpreting village life in Tepoztlán, see Redfield, *Tepoztlán*; Lewis, *Life in a Mexican Village*.

38. See von Mentz, *Pueblos de indios*.

39. MRP, BLAC, doc. 7016, from José B. Espejo, Yautepec, 9/25/1857.

40. Ibid.

41. "Recollections of an American Journal."

Chapter Five

1. The novel *El Zarco the Bandit*, by Ignacio Manuel Altamirano, paints a vivid picture of the influence of banditry in Morelos centered in and around the town of Yuatepec. Altamirano lived during the period about which he writes, served in the Mexican resistance to the French occupation, knew and corresponded with many Liberal leaders, including Francisco Leyva, the first governor of Morelos, and Mariano Riva Palacio, governor of the state of Mexico. His novel offers a firsthand impression of life at the time.

2. The AJTS contains the case of the pueblo of Apatlaco versus the hacienda Cuahuixtla, which is replete with references to bandits and the support they received from the rural population and which is discussed more fully in the following chapter. The fact that they were seen by the owner and administrator of the hacienda as an insidious element corrupting other workers on the estate inadvertently reflected their appeal.

3. Popoca y Palacios, *Historia del bandalismo*.

4. This description of los plateados comes from ibid., 16; and Altamirano, *Zarco*.

5. This episode is cited in Popoca y Palacios, *Historia del bandalismo*, 36, and although the storytelling is embellished, it corresponds with others about administrators being kidnapped, killed, and bullied. See also López

González, *Plateados*; Illescas, "Agitación social."

6. For a discussion of the plateados with a more skeptical impression of the social content of their activities, which sees them in large part as indiscriminate marauders attacking villagers as often as hacendados, see Mallon, *Peasant and Nation*, esp. 148; also see Womack, *Zapata* and Brunk, *Emiliano Zapata*. For fundamental discussions of banditry, see Hobsbaum, *Primitive Rebels*; and Anton Blok, "Peasant and Brigand." For treatments of Latin American banditry, see Joseph, *On the Trail of Latin American Bandits*, and Paul Vanderwood, "Nineteenth-Century Mexico's Profiteering Bandits," in Richard Slatta, *Bandidos*, which offers a different interpretation than mine. For commentary on debt peonage in the 1850s, see MRP, BLAC, doc. 6965, 9/13/1857, which reports the practice and resistance to it around Tulancingo, State of Mexico. For more on Leyva's lengthy comments about the social origins of Zapatismo in historical perspective, see AGN, Secretaría de Gobernación, Asuntos Varios, Islas Marías, Estados 1911–1914, exp. 298.

7. See Popoca y Palacios, *Bandalismo*; Mallon, *Peasant and Nation*, 23; and Thomson, with LaFrance, *Patriotism, Politics*, for more on popular resistance, especially in Puebla. See also López González, *Plateados*.

8. Robelo, *Revistas descriptivas*.

9. AGN, no section, caja 499, exp. 10, 1863. The collection Justicia Imperio at the AGN has another of Sourquet's complaints filed under vol. 9, exp. 27, fojas 174–99.

10. Ibid.

11. Ibid.

12. AJTS, doc. 118, has data on the haciendas Zacatepec and Treinta, including acreage planted in sugarcane, the amount irrigated, the amount of sugar produced and its value per loaf, as well as information about wages and material improvements. The documents also record things like the 300 mules and 234 oxen at Treinta, as well as the inventory of the tienda de raya.

13. AJTS, doc. 114, is a rental agreement between Ignacio Cortina Chávez, owner of Tenextepango, and José Aguayo. It has Aguayo's explanation for why he could not fulfill the agreement.

14. AGN, no section, caja 499, exp. 11, 1863. For the jail break, see Justícia Imperio, vol. 10, exp. 50, 466–69.

15. AJTS, doc. 118.

16. Ibid.

17. AJTS, doc. 2, is an inventory for the hacienda Acamilpa with a record of production and costs, including salaries, from May 1862 to January 1864. For an important discussion of "Labor Conditions on Haciendas in Porfirian Mexico," see Katz's breakdown of tenants, sharecroppers, peones acasillados, and day laborers on Mexican haciendas. Katz states, "Among smaller tenants and sharecroppers arrangements generally were for a short time only and the hacendado felt free to revoke or change them at any time." That was true in Morelos. Villagers-turned-sharecroppers did not share the same laissez faire attitude to arrangements governing their livelihood as hacendados did, as evidenced by episodes like the one at Chiconcuac mentioned earlier.

18. Von Mentz, *Pueblos de indios*, 133.

19. Ibid., 134. For more on the issue of taxes and local-level political responses to them at this time in neighboring Guerrerro, see Guardino, *Peasants, Politics*.

20. AJTS, doc. 2. Katz discusses the ramifications of this so far as social movements are concerned and has mentioned that peones acasillados, cowboys, and the like were less likely to rebel against hacendados than were neighboring free Indian villagers fighting to defend lands, or tenants and

sharecroppers. During the nineteenth century, Morelos seems to fit the pattern explained by Katz, as estate workers did join village uprisings and engage in banditry and strikes, and peones acasillados became members of the hacienda armed guards and received forms of preferential treatment. It is important to note, however, that during the revolution many resident peónes on the estates joined the Zapatistas. (See also Silva Herzog, *Agrarismo mexicano*; González Navarro, *Raza y tierra*, 87.)

21. AJTS, doc. 2. Their average daily wage is not absolutely certain because the number of workers on the estate was not included in the company books, but the figure has been estimated in an earlier chapter. Based on other data, it appears that while worker wages varied depending on the tasks they performed, wages for similar work held fairly constant across the sugar estates in Morelos. Information from the AGN, AJTS, and the *compilación estadistica nacional* suggest as much. It is hard to say how the percentages of workers broke down, but hacienda resident populations grew during the late nineteenth and early twentieth centuries, while many independent pueblos shrunk, or even disappeared.

22. See the hacendado survey from 1912, AGN, Secretaría de Gobernación, Asuntos Varios, Islas Marías, Estados 1911–1914, exp. 298, in which seven of the main landowners in Morelos responded to the Madero government's inquiries about the social disorder in the state. In this context Manuel Araoz's response concerning widows and orphans and medical care is useful, even though it comes fifty years after this date, because it represents long-standing reciprocal relationships and expectations between hacendados and resident workers.

23. Eight reales equaled one peso.

24. This was true in Morelos and elsewhere in the nation as well. At the Hercules textile mill and hacienda in Querétaro, and the Rascón sugar hacienda of San Luis Potosí, the salary of the chief administrators typically exceeded their workers by more than fifteen times. See Hart, *Empire and Revolution*.

25. The documents of the Junta Protectora are at the AGN under that title.

26. JPCM, vol. 4, exp. 15, is the petition submitted by Atlacholaya and others. In this sense I think they mean native dweller, not necessarily "Indian" villager.

27. Ibid.

28. JPCM, vol. 4, exp. 15, is the petition from these towns submitted in joint complaint of the "vexations and bad treatment of which they are the victims at the hands of the neighboring hacendados."

29. Von Mentz, *Pueblos de indios*, 82. See also García Cubas, *Diccionario geográfico*.

30. For a good theoretical discussion of nationalism and its origins in a recognition of shared experiences and traits, see B. Anderson, *Imagined Communities*.

31. Von Mentz, *Pueblos en el siglo XIX*, contains the reprinted primary document of the report of the prefecture of Cuernavaca in 1850, which, among much other information, offers the numbers and equipment of the rural security forces at the time.

32. It seems clear from a variety of documents from various archives, including the Junta Protectora and the Tribunal Superior that this is what they actually felt; it did not represent something foisted on them by a group of lawyers or document producers.

33. JPCM, vol. 4, exp. 15, June 1866.

34. These sorts of takeovers occurred in Morelos and elsewhere in the 1850s and 1860s. The best source of information on peasant mobilizations is Reina, *Luchas populares*; and Reina, *Rebeliones campesinas*. For more particular episodes in Morelos, see Mallon's treatment of the 1840s and 1850s.

35. JPCM, vol. 4, exp. 15, June 1866.

36. Ibid.
37. For the best discussions of this process in a single town, see Sotelo Inclán, *Raíz y razón*; and Hernández Chávez, *Anenecuilco*.
38. JPCM, vol. 4, exp. 15, and for the quote from Corona, see AGN, Secretaría de Gobernación, Asuntos Varios, Islas Marías, Estados 1911–1914, exp. 298, tomo 82, May 28, 1912.
39. Ibid. Of course, the town may have sold these lands to hacendados in the intervening centuries since they were granted the colonial *mercedes*. It is impossible to tell from these documents; however, it is clear that they retained the original grants that had once been considered inviolable as communal property, before the ideal of communal property came under governmental assault.

Chapter Six

1. The Archivo Histórico del Tribunal Superior del Distrito Federal contains the case of the hacienda Cuahuixtla versus the town of San Pedro Apatlaco, docket 17.
2. See Edelman, *Proletarian Peasants*.
3. AJTS, doc. 17.
4. Ibid.; italics are mine.
5. AJTS, doc. 17. Also see the preceding chapter for salaries of laborers performing different jobs on sugar haciendas across Morelos at this time.
6. AJTS, doc. 17.
7. The decision was extremely prejudicial because the financial costs precluded most workers in Morelos from pursuing individual claims.
8. Ibid.
9. See Sotelo Inclán, *Raíz y razón*; and Salinas, *Historias y paisajes*. Also see the archive of San Miguel Anenecuilco at the special collections of the AGN, carpeta 6, which contains copies of the letter from Anenecuilco to the Alcalde Municipal of the Villa de Ayala, complaining of water usurpations by hacienda Cuahuixtla, and Mendoza Cortina, in March 1878. These mid-nineteenth century disputes formed part of the collective memory of pueblo citizens and hacienda residents through the revolution. When those groups mobilized, they attempted to correct contemporary problems and also rectify wrongs they felt they had suffered in the past.
10. The incident is described in great detail in AJTS, doc. 17.
11. The events at Apatlaco demonstrate how abstract economic processes and changing social structures are actually experienced, and how they become part of a larger collective history.
12. See Womack, *Zapata*, 41; and the letters of Luis García Pimintel to Joaquín García Pimentel, made available by the INAH. The author would like to thank Antonio Saborít, investigator and former director of Estudios Históricos at INAH, for providing the documents.
13. AGN, Secretaría de Gobernación, Seguridad Pública, no section, caja 689, exp. 8. Morelos had the third-highest mortality rate in the country in 1893, at 52.69 deaths per 1,000 inhabitants.
14. AJTS, doc. 17. The men González mentioned were well-known bandits in Morelos, heroes to some, despised by others.
15. Although they sometimes supported bandits, and bandits came from within their ranks, these same villagers and workers could occasionally fall prey to the bandits as well. Mallon, *Peasant and Nation*, points this out and offers a specific account to support her position.
16. AJTS, doc. 17.

17. In the year 1850, the prefect of the district of Cuernavaca, Alejandro Villaseñor, reported Cuahuixtla's contribution to the *fuerza rural* of the district. By the early twentieth century the fluid nature of rural society had blurred occupational categories and resident peóns suddenly began to join the revolution en masse. See Chiu, "Peónes y campesinos." See also the invaluable Zapatista interviews conducted for the Programa de Historía Oral, by members of INAH and cited extensively below in Chapters 7, 8, and 9.

18. For the significance of nonviolent, yet noncompliant everyday forms of behavior as resistance, see Scott, *Weapons of the Weak*. In this case, the persons against whom that behavior was directed judged it to be contaminating and took action to eradicate it. Those actions implicitly acknowledged its potential effectiveness or "influence."

19. The letters of Luis García Pimentel, who was seeking medical treatment in France, to his son, Joaquín, reveal the importance elites placed in the contested realms of education and religion. Both are discussed more fully in Chapter 7 below.

20. For examples of yearly account books and inventories and the lack of debt owed to, or due from, workers, see the AJTS, doc. 2, which contains records of the hacienda Acamilpa, and doc. 118, which holds records of the hacienda Treinta Pesos.

21. Apatlaco's case at the AJTS, makes reference to their "natural rights." Tutino, *Insurrection to Revolution*, discusses the security of hacienda life as a mollifying substitute for those who lost the independence enjoyed by free campesino villages. The general process he describes reflects the transition taking place in Morelos at the time and was reflected at Apatlaco. But the "security" gained as a hacienda dependent ended up being even more tenuous than a problematic peasant lifestyle, since the worker could be fired, evicted, or laid off at any time. The campesino was left to confront and bargain with the employer on a basis of individual versus individual, with the market playing a larger mediating role as time went on. Hacendados pursued that relationship because they enjoyed a privileged position. At the same time, they tried to retain some of the more archaic social relations that had prevailed between peón and patrón since the colonial era, but under changing conditions that further exposed the lower classes to the vicissitudes of the marketplace.

22. AJTS, doc. 17. Although the hacendado may have exaggerated his overhead, the point remains.

23. Ibid.

24. Ibid.

25. Ibid. See the interviews of the Oral History Project (INAH), including that of Colonel Carmen Aldana conducted by Laura Espejel López, Mar. 2 and 30, 1974 (Pho-Z/1/32). At this point it is important to consider the degree to which lawyers writing these documents like the one upon which this story of Apatlaco is based, interjected their perspectives, educations, and values into the written record, which is all that is left of this dispute. Those influences, no doubt, played some part, but the sentiments of the vecinos come through nonetheless, especially in their actions, in the information they gave the lawyer, and the things they chose to emphasize. The fact that a lawyer prepared this appeal does not take away its authenticity, but it does add another issue to ponder. For Zapata's experience and feelings about this, see Womack, *Zapata*, 7.

26. Popoca y Palacios, *Historia del bandalismo*, 40, describes the plateados blackmailing the administrator of San Vicente and Chiconcuac, with threats to burn the cane fields. The storytelling is probably embellished, but the

behavior described is corroborated.

27. AJTS, doc. 17.

28. The term *españoles*, when used by the populace at large, carried a cultural connotation that included, and went beyond, one's national citizenship. It usually implied a more urban, well-groomed background. Spaniards were usually hacendados, landholders, administrators, or skilled laborers and belonged to segregated guilds. The use of the term also implied a resentful commentary on the higher social standing and better treatment afforded "Spaniards" in general.

29. AJTS, doc. 17. Although I have argued that a level of class consciousness was developing, this statement shows that rural working people in Morelos, while able to overcome the ethnic barriers within the lower castes, were still alert to the social stratification and felt that "Spaniards" and their cultural descendants occupied privileged positions vis-à-vis the rural population made up of mestizos and others.

30. To resume a discussion from before; this was not just the case of an experienced lawyer foisting his impressions on his clients, manipulating public opinion or Maximilian's junta. It resonated too closely with other occurrences, litigation, and popular acts that took place outside official channels to be dismissed that flippantly. A variety of issues played a role in the way the lawyer for Apatlaco carried out the case, but the structural changes underway were what created the circumstances in the first place, while the wobbly nature of the larger political situation in the country allowed for some astute maneuvering as Maximilian attempted to use the junta to placate the rural masses.

31. AJTS, doc. 17.

32. Ibid. Today the pueblo and ejido of Apatlaco sit near the burned-out remains of Cuahuixtla.

Chapter Seven

1. See Sotelo Inclán, *Raíz y razón*, 311–12, on Morelos hacendados Jesús Goribar, the Icazbalceta's, Ignacio Cortina Chávez, Francisco Pimentel, Manuel Escandón, Isidoro de la Torre, and others, sending a petition to Mexico City to protest proposed land redistribution by the governor of Aguascalientes. They viewed it as an alarming precedent and something they did not want to happen in Morelos. For more on Leyva and his antagonistic relationship with the hacendados, see Pittman, "Planters, Peasants"; and Rueda Smithers, *Paraíso de la caña*.

2. Pittman offers the slate proposed by the planters for the elections of 1869 and shows their unified interests and efforts at political appointment. Their choices read as follows: Governor, Porfirio Díaz; Federal Deputy, Cuernavaca, José G. Partearroyo, and alternate, Juan de la Peña y Barragan (formerly of the Hospital estate); Federal Deputy, Yautepec, Feliciano Chavarría, and alternate, Jesús Goribar (Cocoyoc estate); Tetecala, Miguel Mosso (formerly of the San José Vistahermosa estate), and alternate, Francisco Celis (Santa Cruz estate); Morelos, Faustino Goribar (Casasano estate), and alternate, Lorenzo García Icazbalceta (Santa Clara, Santa Ana Tenango, and San Ignacio estates); Jonacatepec, Ignacio de la Peña y Barragan (formerly of Hospital estate). Francisco Celis of Santa Cruz hacienda, Agustín Róbalo of Santa Inés, and a few other individuals not associated with the estates were nominated by both the Juárez group and the landowners supporting Díaz. Pittman, "Planters, Peasants," 50.

3. See Vicente Riva Palacio Papers at University of Texas, doc. 789, 5/16/71, reporting Negrete and pueblos around Tenango disrupting the peace. See also Pittman, "Planters, Peasants," 47–48; and see Díaz Soto y Gama, *Revolución del sur*, ch. 2.

4. Pacheco, *Memórias* (ms. can be located at Bancroft Library, Berkeley, CA).

5. Rosecrans Papers, box 90, Special Collections, Graduate Research Library, UCLA. One arroba equaled eleven kilos, or almost twenty-five pounds. A barrel was about thirty-one pounds.

6. Landazuri Benitez and Vázquez Mantecón, *Azúcar y estado*, 152. For an original analysis of the revolution of Tuxtepec that ousted Lerdo and brought Díaz to power, and insight into the international implications, see Hart, *Empire and Revolution*.

7. Memória de Secretaría de Fomento, tomo II, 486, 1877–1882.

8. See García Pimentel letters for role of church and school as agents of socialization on the haciendas, also briefly discussed in Chapter 8 here.

9. Melville, *Crecimiento y rebelión*, 22.

10. Preciado, *Memória*.

11. See Crespo, "Pueblos de Morelos."

12. See Crespo and Vega Villanueva, *Tierra y propiedad*, derived from the Manifestaciones de haciendas, ranchos y bienes comunales in Morelos, in response to a "Revaluo general de Bienes Raices" ordered by Governor Pablo Escandón in 1909. It is an important source for information about the haciendas and the bienes comunales that indicates that communal property had been nearly liquidated. That development contributed to the Zapatista rebellion.

13. See Melville, *Crecimiento y rebelión*; Crespo, *Hacienda azucarera*.

14. AGN, Fomento, época del imperio, 1864, caja 9, exp. 9, contains statistical data from 1864 on the quantity and value of products and the extension of irrigated and total surface area of haciendas in Morelos. Similar data exists for 1903 gathered by the Comisión Mexicana para la Exposición de París in 1900. Those sources give an idea of changes in land tenure taking place during that time period, and the information presented in Crespo and Vega Villanueva, *Tierra y propiedad*, which contains the "manifestaciones de haciendas, ranchos y bienes comunales" for 1909, helps complete the picture.

15. See AGN, Secretaría de Gobernación, Asuntos Varios, Islas Marías, Estados 1911–1914, exp. 298, for the government questionnaire and the comments of García Pimentel, other Morelos hacendados, and Patricio Leyva.

16. See interview with Carmen Aldana (Pho-A/1/32), see n. 17. A carga was 181.6 liters. The term *ahijado* means godchild, or adopted child.

17. See the Instituto de Geografía y Estadística for the *Memória de la administración pública de Morelos*, which has the census of Morelos in 1900.

18. The information on these individuals comes from the collection of oral interviews conducted by the Instituto Nacional de Antropología y Historia for their Programa de Historia Oral (1974–75), generously made available to me by Antonio Saborit, Salvador Rueda Smithers, and Laura Espejel López. The coordinator of the program was Alicia Olivera de Bonfil, the investigators Laura Espejel López, Eugenia Meyer, Carlos Varreto Marc, and collaborators Citlai Marino Uribe and Salvador Rueda Smithers. Coronel Aldana was interviewed by Laura Espejel López in March 1974; the transcript can be found in (Pho-Z/1/32). For more on Lorenzo Vergara, see (Pho-Z/1/1). For the interview with Agapito Pariente, see (Pho-Z/1/12).

19. Hegemony is a mixture of coercion and consent, but the goal of achieving hegemony for the ruling class is to be seen to rule legitimately in order to carry out their agendas and channel dissent into predictable avenues. That

allows dissent to be voiced without fundamentally challenging the status quo. That dissent, in turn, by its very existence and failure to effect change, provides legitimacy for the rulers. See Herbert Marcuse, "Repressive Tolerance," in Wolff, *A Critique of Pure Tolerance.*

20. See Womack, *Zapata*, 45; Crespo and Vega Villanueva, *Tierra y propiedad*; and interview with Señora Leonor Alfaro, conducted by Ximena Sepulveda y María Isabel Souza, in Cuautla, Morelos, Aug. 31, 1973.

21. Memória de Secretaría de Fomento, tomo IV, 108, 1883–1885. For description of Zacatepec and other haciendas during the Porfiriato, see Robelo, *Revistas descriptiva.* See also *Boletín de la Sociedad Agrícola de México*, May 7, 1903. The bulletin is available at the Hemeroteca at the UNAM.

22. For good histories of sugar manufacturing in Cuba, see Fraginal, *Ingenio*; and Bergad, *Cuban Rural Society.*

23. See interview with Soldado Plácido Amacende Pérez (Pho-Z/1/30), and interview with Coronel Carmen Aldana (Pho-Z/1/32), and interview with Señor Lorenzo Vergara (Pho-Z/1/1). For a good general description of hacienda land use, see Melville, *Crecimiento y rebelión*, 23. For good primary data, see the Secretaría de Fomento, 1864, Época del Imperio, serie: Agricultura, caja 9, exp. 8, for data on sizes of land holdings of numerous haciendas in Morelos, as well as their values, amount of irrigated and unirrigated land, the value of products, operational expenses, and yearly profits. For similar data that demonstrates change over time, see Fomento-Exposiciones Extranjeras, Comisión Mexicana para la Exposición de Paris, 1900, caja 51, exp. 11.

24. AGN, Secretaría de Gobernación, Asuntos Varios, Islas Marías, Estados 1911–1914, exp. 298.

25. Condumex Archive, "ideas generales sobre el cultivo de la caña de azúcar en el estado de Morelos," anónimo, although it is thought that Tomás Ruíz, administrator of Zacatapec, was the author, Secretaría de Fomento, 1885."

26. Interview with José Lora Mirasol by Laura Espejel López, (Pho-A/1/14), INAH. See also *El Cronista de Morelos*, Aug. 2, 1886; and Salinas, *Historias y paisajes.*

27. Condumex, "el cultivo de la caña de azúcar." The interviews of former hacienda workers corroborate the wages mentioned here.

28. See interview with Señor Agapito Pariente conducted by Alicia Olivera de Bonfil, in Tepalcingo, Morelos, Mar. 2, 1974 (INAH).

29. See interview with Capitán de Caballeria, Miguel Dominguez Peña, by Laura Espejel López (Pho-Z/1/36).

30. See *El Cronista de Morelos*, Aug. 9, 1886, for information on wages in Morelos and the Mesa Central, and see the collection of Zapatista interviews for variations in salaries across Morelos.

31. AGN, Secretaría de Gobernación, Asuntos Varios, Islas Marías, Estados 1911–1914, exp. 298.

32. For excellent descriptions of the sugar-making process, see Crespo et al., *Historia del azúcar*, vol. 2. For a comparison with the process in Brazil, see Schwartz, *Sugar Plantations.*

33. Ibid. Some crushers were so effective at squeezing the juice out of the plants that the bagazo was dry enough to go straight into the furnace.

34. *Boletín de la Sociedad Agrícola de México*, Sept. 1883. This issue is based largely on the practices of the hacienda Miacatlan, according to the administrator.

35. Ibid.

36. Ibid.

37. See Robelo, *Revistas descriptivas.*

38. *El Cronista de Morelos*, 5, June 16, 1883.

39. See interview with Coronel Carmen Aldana (Pho-Z/132), and separate

interview with Brigadier General Manuel Sosa Pavon (Pho-Z/1/48).
40. Interview by Laura Espejel López with Capitán de Caballeria Miguel Dominguez Peña (Pho-Z/1/36).
41. Ruíz de Velasco, *Estudios sobre el cultivo de la caña*, 145.
42. Melville, *Crecimiento y rebelión*, 35.
43. Domenéch, *Guía general*.
44. Preciado, *Memórias*, Apr. 12, 1887. This report indicates that the haciendas were indeed providing large labor opportunities, and even if their growth was resented, the practical benefits they brought balanced out the negative ones, at least for the time being.
45. Melville, *Crecimiento y rebelión*, 36, and also his index.
46. Womack, *Zapata*, 49.
47. Melville, *Crecimiento y rebelión*, 37.
48. *Mexican Yearbook*.
49. Coatsworth, *Growth against Development*, 50.
50. Sotelo Inclán, *Raíz y razón*, 374.
51. *El Cronista de Morelos*, Aug. 1884, contains an article discussing the origins and contributions of the railway in the state.
52. Cosío Villegas, *Historia Moderna de México*, 2:568.
53. Diez, *Bibliografía*, ccxxii.
54. Womack, *Zapata*, 49.

Chapter Eight

1. *The Mexican Financier* 3, no. 17, Mexico City, Jan. 26, 1884.
2. See interview by Salvador Rueda Smithers and Laura Espejel López (Pho-Z/1/.77).
3. *El Hijo del Trabajo*, July 18, 1880.
4. Ibid., Apr. 19, 1886.
5. *El Cronista de Morelos*, June 7, 1884. See also Vanderwood, *Disorder and Progress*.
6. *El Progreso de Morelos*, 22, May 28, 1892. See MacLean y Esteños, *Revolución de 1910*.
7. APD, Universidad Iberoamericana, leg. 11, caja 17, doc. 008213. Also see Warman, *"We Come to Object,"* 42. The manner in which pueblo petitions changed after the revolution indicated the profound psychological transformation wrought by that upheaval.
8. Ibid.
9. APD, doc. 012988.
10. Ibid.
11. APD, L-10, C-19, D-009392.
12. Ibid.
13. APD, L-14, C-27, doc. 013209, Dec. 1889.
14. Ibid.
15. Letters from France from Luis García Pimentel to his son, Joaquín, 1904. Made available by INAH. For more on the basic reading and writing skills acquired, or, more accurately, not acquired, at these schools, see the collection of interviews from the INAH.
16. Luis García Pimentel, Mar. 1904, INAH. It would make an interesting study to analyze the similarities or disparities between sermons on the estates and in the independent pueblos.
17. Ibid.
18. APD, L-15, C-4, D-001770, Feb., 1890.
19. Ibid.
20. See interview with Señor Andrés Ávila (Pho-Z/1/53). See also the *Memória de*

Jesús Preciado, 1890–91, Instituto de Geografía y Estadística. See interview with Soldado Plácido Amacende Pérez, by Laura Espejel López, Mar. 2, 1974 (Pho-Z/1/30).

21. *Semanario Oficial del Estado de Morelos*, June 12, 1897.

22. *Semanario Oficial del Estado de Morelos*, 1900.

23. *Semanario Oficial del Estado de Morelos*, June 17, 1905.

24. *La Tierra de México*, 1902.

25. Ibid.

26. APD, L-29, C-6.

27. AGN, Suprema Corte de Justicia. Rafael Ramos Alarcón may have been related to Governor Manuel Alarcón and his brother Juan Alarcón, administrator of the hacienda Atlihuayán in Yautepec.

28. Ibid.; italics are mine.

29. For arguments that see change being orchestrated mainly from the top-down and that present the state as the primary agent or manipulator of social change instead of the populace, see Joseph, *Revolution from Without*. In a mainly postrevolutionary context dealing mainly with cultural rather than material change, see Knight, "Revolutionary State, Recalcitrant People."

30. It is obvious in this chapter that much of the social conflict being discussed is being caused by hacendado acquisition of other resources, not just land. The question of exactly when the hacendados succeeded in acquiring the bulk of pueblo lands and whether it was during the mid-nineteenth century as a result of the Ley Lerdo, or was more pronounced later with the rule of Díaz, is very hard to answer. What is clear is that it was an ongoing process from mid-century through the outbreak of the revolution, and that Díaz's rule allowed for the consolidation of those holdings and the maximizing of the areas sugar producing capabilities through greater hacendado control of water needed for irrigation.

31. Warman, *"We Come to Object,"* 83. Punishing entire pueblos was not new. During the agrarian unrest of the late 1860s the entire pueblo of Chicoloapan, in Mexico State near Chalco, was banished to Yucatán as punishment for its support of the Chavez López uprising there. For more on that episode, see Hart, *Anarchism*, ch. 3.

32. See Womack, *Zapata*, ch. 1; Brunk, *Emiliano Zapata!*, ch. 3. The anti-Escandón movement was significant and brought together a broader pueblo and hacienda worker opposition that then exploded beyond the parameters of the election, the control of middle-class allies, and the candidacy of Patricio Leyva.

33. Rosenzweig, "La Vida Económica," in Cosío Villegas, *Historia Moderna*, 1:81–82.

34. *El Cronista de Morelos*, 29, July 19, 1884.

35. *Boletín de la Sociedad Agrícola de México*, Aug. 3, 1903, p. 591.

36. Ibid., Oct. 13, 1903, p. 775.

37. Melville, *Crecimiento y rebelión*, 57.

38. APD, L-28, C-14, doc. 005521.

39. Ibid.

40. Melville, *Crecimiento y rebelión*.

41. For Mexican sugar prices, see the invaluable Crespo et al., *Historia del azúcar*, 1:734. See also Womack, *Zapata*, 48.

42. *Bureau of the American Republics*, serial 5804.

43. Luis García Pimentel to his son in 1904, INAH.

44. *Monthly Consular and Trade Reports* 344 (Washington, DC: Government Printing Office, 1909). For the economic malaise of the late Porfiriato, see Rosenzweig in Cosío Villegas, *Historia Moderna*; and see R. E. Ruíz, *Great*

Rebellion; Hart, *Revolutionary Mexico*; Katz, *Secret War*; Knight, *Mexican Revolution*.

45. *Daily Consular and Trade Reports*, 1911, no. 256, p. 562.
46. Crespo et al., *Historia del azúcar*.
47. *Daily Consular and Trade Reports*, 1911, no. 546.
48. *Boletín de la Sociedad Agrícola de México*, Jan. 1910. See also Crespo et al. *Historia del azúcar*, 1:734, for price data.
49. *Daily Consular and Trade Reports*, Sept. 19, 1909. The literature on Cuba is extensive. For two good histories of Cuba that treat U.S. Cuban relations, see Pérez, *Cuba*; and Pérez, *War of 1898*. Two good monographs are Ayala, *American Sugar Kingdom*; and Pérez-López, *Economics of Cuban Sugar*.
50. *Boletín de la Sociedad Agrícola de México*, Jan. 1910. See also Crespo, *Historia del azúcar*, 1:2.
51. For a good description of the election and its part in the revolution, see Womack, *Zapata*, 18. Another good discussion of the election can be found in Rueda Smithers, *Paraíso de la caña*, 182–201.
52. See interview with Pedro Placencia. These interviews were conducted about fifty years after the events they record. The flaws in human memory, and the possibility that these individuals' recollections of the revolution were clouded by events that transpired during the intervening years, or were colored by the ways in which the revolution has been interpreted over that time, should be kept in mind. After reading the interviews, I decided that when corroborated by other evidence I would rather rely on these accounts from people who were actually there, instead of accounts by people, including historians, who were not. For insight into how these interviews were conducted and a discussion of their value and "what was lost and what was found," see Olivera de Bonfil, "Lo que dijeron."
53. See interview with Señor Pedro Plasencia (Pho-Z/1/62) and interview with Capitán segundo de Caballeria Serafín Plasencia (Pho-Z/1/59). The two men were related.
54. See interview with Brigadier General Manuel Sosa Pavon, by Eugenia Meyer (Pho-Z/1/48).
55. APD, L-34, C-3, 1909.
56. APD, doc. 000646.
57. APD, L-34, C-6, Feb. 1, 1909.
58. APD, L-34, C-3, 1909. Also see the interview with General Prospero García Aguirre, by Laura Espejel López and Salvador Rueda Smithers (Pho-Z/1/117).
59. See the assorted INAH collection of Zapatista interviews, no. 298.
60. See Hacienda Publica de los Estados 1911, José Yves Limantour, on frosts of 1909, at the Hemeroteca Nacional, UNAM.
61. See interview with Soldado Plácido Amacende Pérez (Pho-Z/1/30).

Chapter Nine

1. See Womack, *Zapata*, 66.
2. Ibid., 87.
3. Ibid., 78.
4. For the death of Segovia, see interview with Señor Luis Hernandez García of Tenango (Pho-Z-1/76).
5. The Morelos revolutionaries have been portrayed as primarily pueblo or peasant villagers in many works. See, for example, Cumberland, *Mexican Revolution*; and Womack, *Zapata*. Some have argued that dependent peons in various parts of Mexico did not, generally, join the revolution and that,

instead, it was mainly peasant villagers in places like Morelos, or rancheros, miners, and other workers in place like Chihuahua and Durango that did. Every place had a different dynamic; see Joseph, *Revolution from Without*, where that argument is applied to Yucatán; or Buve, "Peasant Movements"; and Knight, *Mexican Revolution*, 1:86–87, where the idea of the docility of resident peons is discussed, although neither he nor Womack argue that is absolute. Also see Knight, *Mexican Revolution*, 1:157–59, where the important role of peasant communities is discussed, but the part of hacienda workers is overlooked. Womack emphasizes the role of the pueblos in his work, but recognizes in passing that workers were involved by 1912, when large numbers from the hacienda Cocoyoc joined the revolution. The testimony of the actual participants in Morelos, many who were "peónes de hacienda," indicates that, at least in that region, hacienda peons were not a reluctant mass that "preferred their bonded security."

6.   See interview with Señor Pedro Plasencia, by Laura Espejel López (Pho-/Z/1/62).

7.   Interview by Laura Espejel López with Serafín Placencia.

8.   The detailed story of the Zapatista revolution has been told well elsewhere, for the classic history of it, see Womack, *Zapata*; and for a valuable reinterpretation drawing on sources unavailable in earlier studies, see Brunk, *Emiliano Zapata!*

9.   For more on Zapata's orders to pueblos to reclaim their lands, see Womack, *Zapata*, 87, and his footnote 3 in that chapter.

10.   Womack, *Zapata*, 99, 102.

11.   The plan is reproduced in Womack, *Zapata*, Appendix B.

12.   See doc. 114 from the AGN, *Documentos Ineditos sobre Emiliano Zapata y el Curatel General*, Seleccionados del Archivo de Genovevo de la O, Comisión para la conmemorización de Emiliano Zapata, Mexico, 1979.

13.   See Womack, *Zapata*; Piñeda Gómez, *Irrupción zapatista*. See also interview with Carmen Aldana on the burning of Tepalcingo; interview with José Epitia Ruíz on the burning of the Tenango ranchería; and interview with Señor Pascual Aguirre on Tepalcingo.

14.   See AGN, Secretaría de Gobernación, Asuntos Varios, Islas Marías, Estados 1911–1915, exp. 298.

15.   AGN, Secretaría de Gobernación, Asuntos Varios, Islas Marías, Estados 1911–1915. The response represented a cross-section of the Morelos ruling class and was signed by Manuel Araoz, Juan Pagaza, the sons de Antonio Escandón, Luis García Pimentel, and the widow of Vicente Alonso.

16.   Ibid.

17.   See interview with José Lora Mirasol.

18.   See interview with Serafín Placencia on the reasons for Zapata ordering Felipe Neri's murder (Pho-2/1/59); and the interview with Carmen Aldana.

19.   See interview with Dr. Juan Olivera López; for more on Zapatista excesses, see Brunk, *Emiliano Zapata!*

20.   AGN, Secretaría de Gobernación, 298, La Comisión Agraria Ejecutiva, May 1, 1912. Emphasis appears in original.

21.   AGN, *Documentos Ineditos sobre Emiliano Zapata y el Cuartel General*, Seleccionados del Archivo de Genovevo de la O, Comisión para la conmemorización de Emiliano Zapata, Mexico, 1979.

22.   See interview with Coronel Carmen Aldana.

23.   See Katz, *Life and Times of Pancho Villa*. Katz says, "In many respect, the coup against Madero was the forerunner of the many similar twentieth-century coups in which reform-minded presidents, such as Romulo Gallegos in Venezuela, Jacobo Arbenz in Guatemala, and Salvador Allende in Chile,

would be toppled by the military with varying degrees of covert or even overt support form foreign, mainly U.S., sources. . . . The [U.S.] ambassador encouraged Huerta to overthrow Madero and told him that the United States would recognize a government arising out of such a coup" (194–95). The same author is working on a history of the larger U.S. role in the pro-Huerta, anti-Madero coup that should be illuminating.

24. Quoted in Womack, *Zapata*. For the important role of Carranza in the revolution, see Richmond, *Venustiano Carranza's Nationalist Struggle*.

25. See letter from General Calixto Contreras to Emiliano Zapata, from Cuencame, Durango, June 5, 1914, in which he expresses support for Zapata's agrarian goals. AGN, Archive of Genovevo de la O, caja 14, exp. 7.

26. For the goals of the enigmatic Villa and the Villistas, see Katz, *Life and Times of Pancho Villa*.

27. For a biography of Obregón and history of his role in the revolution, see Hall, *Álvaro Obregón*. For information of the U.S. role at Veracruz and its impact on the revolution, see Hart, *Revolutionary Mexico*.

28. See interview with Pedro Plasencia.

29. Womack, *Zapata*, 227, 231, and Chapter 8 offer a good discussion of the process. Gilly, *Mexican Revolution*.

30. Millon, *Zapata*.

31. Interview with Señora Leonora Alfaro.

32. See interviews with Señor Andrés Ávila for mention of Chavarria, and Serafín Plasencia for "Amalia." Señor Valentín López González, noted historian of Morelos, told me about the conditions in Cuernavaca and the coyotes in the streets.

33. Interview with Manuel Sosa Pavon.

34. See Millon, *Zapata*, 54.

35. That position is expressed in literature as well, see for example, Azuela, *Los de abajo*, translated as *The Underdogs*. For a good discussion of this and other matters of interpretation of the revolution, see Joseph and Nugent, *Everyday Forms*, esp. the first chapter by the editors.

36. AGN, *Documentos Ineditos sobre Emiliano Zapata y el Cuartel General*, Seleccionados del Archivo de Genovevo de la O, Comisión para la conmemorización de Emiliano Zapata, Mexico, 1979.

37. For a more detailed account of the intrigue and events surrounding Zapata's murder, see Womack, *Zapata*; Brunk, *Emiliano Zapata!*

38. For more on Obregón and his political acumen and cooptation of urban workers, see Hall, *Álvaro Obregón*; and Lear, *Workers, Neighbors*.

39. For a detailed presentation of the land reform in Morelos, see the Appendix. For more on Obregón, see Hall, *Álvaro Obregón*.

Conclusion

1. See Albro, *Always a Rebel*; Brunk, "Zapata and the City Boys"; Cockcroft, *Intellectual Precursors*; Hart, *Anarchism*, esp. ch. 5; Mallon, *Peasant and Nation*; and Thomson, with LaFrance, *Patriotism, Politics*. See also the AGN, Secretaría de Gobernación 298, La Comisión Agraria Ejecutiva, 1912, for hacendado complaints of "outside agitators" spurring the pueblos to rebellion with talk of their inherited rights.

2. B. Andersen's phrase, see *Imagined Communities*.

3. When the government has been seen as having failed in that regard, it has been challenged as not having lived up to its revolutionary responsibilities. That failure has been offered as justification for insurrections from that of Ruben Jaramillo in Morelos during the 1940s, to Lucio Cabañas in Guerrero

in the 1970s, to the Zapatistas in Chiapas today.

4.   On the Zapatista rebellion in Chiapas, see the historically informed anthropological work by Stephen, *Zapata Lives!* Harvey, *Chiapas Rebellion*, provides an excellent history of the origins of the movement. See also Womack,
Rebellion in Chiapas. Ponce de León, *Our Word Is Our Weapon*, offers
insights into the causes and goals of the Zapatistas through the writings of
their intellectual spokesman. Hayden, *Zapatista Reader*, is an interesting
compilation treating the origins and meaning of the Chiapas uprising. Since
the 2000 elections, the state government has exhibited a more compassion-
ate policy toward the Zapatistas, although that could change at any time.

Bibliography

Archival Collections
Archivo General de la Nación (AGN), Mexico City
    Archivo de Genovevo de la O
    Comisión Nacional Agaria, Resoluciones Presidenciales
    Jesús Sotelo Inclán Papers (JSI)
    Junta Protectora de las Clases Menesterosas (JPCM)
    Ramo de Bienes Nacionalizados
    Ramo de Fomento
    Ramo de Gobernación
    Ramo de Tierras
Archivo Histórico del Estado de Morelos, Cuernavaca
Archivo Histórico de Valentín López González, Cuernavaca
Archivo Histórico de Instituto Nacional de Historia e Antropología (INAH)
    García Pimentel Papers
Archivo Judicial del Tribunal Superior (AJTS)
Archivo Porfirio Díaz (APD), Universidad Iberoamericana
Archivo de la Programa de Historia Oral
Bancroft Manuscript Collection, University of California, Berkeley
Benson Latin American Collection (BLAC), University of Texas, Austin
    Mariano Riva Palacio Papers (MRP)
    Vicente Riva Palacio Papers (VRP)
Condumex Archive, Mexico City
Rosecrans Papers, Graduate Research Library, University of California, Los Angeles

Newspapers and Journals
Boletín de la Sociedad Agrícola de México
Bureau of the American Republics
Daily Consular and Trade Reports
El Cronista de Morelos

El Higo del Trabajo
El Monitor Republicano
El Progreso de Morelos
El Tiempo
La Tierra de México
Monthly Consular and Trade Reports
Semanario Oficial del Estado de Morelos
The Mexican Financier
The Mexican Yearbook
The Two Republics

Books and Articles

Aguirre Beltrán, Gonzalo. *La población negra de México, 1519–1810*. Mexico City: Editiones Fuente Cultural, 1946.

———. *Regiones de refugio: El desarollo de la comunida y el proceso dominical en mestizo América*. Mexico City: Instituto Indigenista Interamericano, 1967.

Alamán, Lucas. *Documentos diversos, ineditos y muy raros*. Vol. 4. Mexico City: Editorial Jus, 1945–47.

Albro, Ward S. *Always a Rebel: Ricardo Florés Magón and the Mexican Revolution*. Fort Worth: Texas Christian University Press, 1992.

Altamirano, Ignacio Manuel. *El Zarco the Bandit*. London: Folio Society, 1957.

Álvarez, General D. Juan. "Manifiesto del ciudadano Juan Álvarez, a los pueblos cultos de Europa y America." Ed. Valentín López González. Cuernavaca, Morelos: Cuadernos Histórico Morelenses, 2000.

Anderson, Benedict. *Imagined Communities: Reflections on the Origin and Spread of Nationalism*. London: Routledge, 1985.

Anderson, Rodney. *Outcasts in their Own Land: Mexican Industrial Workers, 1906–1911*. DeKalb: Northern Illinois University Press, 1976.

Ávila Espinosa, Felipe Arturo. *Los origenes del zapatismo*. Mexico City: El Colégio de México, 2001.

Ayala, César J. *American Sugar Kingdom: The Plantation Economy of the Spanish Caribbean, 1898–1934*. Chapel Hill and London: University of North Carolina Press, 2000.

Azuela, Mariano. *The Underdogs*. New York: Signet Classics, 1962.

Barrett, Ward. *The Sugar Hacienda of the Marqueses del Valle*. Minneapolis: University of Minnesota Press, 1970.

Bazant, Jan. *Los bienes de la iglesia en México (1856–1875): Aspectos economicos y sociales de la revolución liberal*. Mexico City: El Colégio de México, 1977.

Bazant, Milada. "La Desamortización." In *El estado de México durante la segunda república*. ed. Ma. del Pilar Iracheta Cenecorta. Zinacantepec: Estado de Mexico, El Colegio Mexiquense, 1999.

Beezley, William H. *Judas at the Jockey Club and Other Stories of Porfirian Mexico*. Lincoln: University of Nebraska Press, 1987.

Beezley, William H., Cheryl English Martin, and William French, eds. *Rituals of Rule, Rituals of Resistance*. New York: Scholarly Resources, 1994.

Bergad, Laird W. *Cuban Rural Society in the Nineteenth Century: The Social and Economic History of Monoculture in Matanzas*. Princeton, NJ: Princeton University Press, 1990.

Bergquist, Charles. *Labor in Latin America: Comparative Essays on Chile, Argentina, Venezuela, and Colombia*. Palo Alto, CA: Stanford University Press, 1986.

Birkbeck, Christopher. "Latin American Banditry as Peasant Resistance: A Dead-End Trail?" *Latin American Research Review* 26, no. 1.

Blok, Anton. "The Peasant and the Brigand: Social Banditry Reconsidered."

Comparative Studies in Society and History 14, no. 4.

Bocanegra, José María. *Memória para la historia de México independiente.* Vol. 1. Mexico City: n.p., 1892.

Borah, Woodrow W., and Sherburne F. Cook. *The Population of Central Mexico in 1548: An Analysis of the Suma de visitas de pueblos.* Berkeley: University of California Press, 1960.

Brading, David. *The Origins of Mexican Nationalism.* Cambridge: Cambridge University Press, 1985.

Brady, Robert LaDon. "The Emergence of a Negro Class in Mexico, 1524–1640." PhD diss. University of Iowa, 1965.

Brunk, Samuel. *Emiliano Zapata! Revolution and Betrayal in Mexico.* Albuquerque: University of New Mexico Press, 1995.

———. "Zapata and the City Boys: In Search of a Piece of the Revolution." *Hispanic American Historical Review* 73 (1993): 33–65.

Buve, Raymond Th. J. "Peasant Movements, Cuadillos and Land Reform during the Revolution (1910–1917) in Tlaxcala, Mexico." *BdEL* 18 (June 1975).

Carrasco, Pedro. "The People's of Central Mexico and Their Historical Traditions." In *Handbook of Middle American Indians*, vol. 11. Austin: University of Texas Press, Robert Wauchipe, general editor (1964–1976).

Carroll, Patrick J. *Blacks in Colonial Veracruz: Race, Ethnicity, and Regional Development.* Austin: University of Texas Press, 1991.

Chevalier, François. *La formación de los grandes latifundios en México.* Mexico City: Fondo de Cultura Ecuadora, 1975.

———. *Land and Society in Colonial Mexico: The Great Hacienda.* Berkeley: University of California Press, 1963.

Chiu, Aquiles. "Peónes y campesinos Zapatistas." In *Emiliano Zapata y el movimiento Zapatista: Cinco ensayos.* Mexico City: INAH, 1980.

Chowning, Margaret. *Wealth and Power in Provincial Mexico: Michoacán from the Late Colony to the Revolution.* Palo Alto, CA: Stanford University Press, 1999.

———. "The Contours of the Post-1810 Depression in Michoacán." Unpublished Paper.

Cline, S. L., ed. Libro de tributos*: Early 16th Century Nahuatl Censuses from Morelos.* Berkeley: University of California Press, 1993.

Coatsworth, John. *Growth against Development: The Economic Impact of Railroads in Porfirian Mexico.* DeKalb, IL: Northern Illinois University Press, 1981.

———. "Patterns of Rural Rebellion in Latin America: Mexico in Comparative Perspective." In *Riot, Rebellion, and Revolution.* Princeton, NJ: Princeton University Press, 1988.

Cockcroft, James D. *Intellectual Precursors of the Mexican Revolution.* Austin: University of Texas Press, 1968.

Cosío Villegas, Daniel, ed. *Historia moderna de México.* 9 vols. Mexico City: Editorial Hermes, 1955–73.

Crespo, Horacio. *La hacienda azucarera del estado de Morelos: Modernización y conflicto.* Mexico City: Facultad de Filosofia y Leteras, UNAM, 1996.

———. "Los pueblos de Morelos, la comunidad agraria, y la desamortización liberal en Morelos y una fuente para el estudio de la diferenciándión social campesina." In *Estudios sobre el zapatismo*, coord. Laura López Espejel. Mexico City: INAH, 2001.

Crespo, Horacio, et al., eds. *Historia del azúcar en México.* 2 vols. Mexico City: Fondo de Cultura Económica, 1988–90.

Crespo, Horacio, and Enrique Vega Villanueva. *Tierra y propiedad en el fin del porfiriato.* Mexico City: Centro de Estudios Históricos del Agarismo en Mexico, 1982.

"El Cristo Negro de San Gaspar." In *Crónica morelense.* Morelos, Mexico: Instituto de Cultura de Morelos, Tlaquiltenango, 1996.

Cumberland, Charles. *Mexican Revolution: Genesis under Madero.* Austin:

University of Texas Press, 1952.

De la Peña, Guillermo. *A Legacy of Promises: Agriculture, Politics and Ritual in the Morelos Highlands of Mexico*. Austin: University of Texas Press, 1981.

Díaz Soto y Gama, Antonio. *La revolución agraria del sur y Emiliano Zapata su caudillo*. Mexico City: Policromia, 1961.

Diez, Domingo. *Bibliografía del estado de Morelos*. Mexico City: Secretaria de Relaciones Exteriores, 1933.

Diplomatic Correspondence of the United States, Inter-American Affairs. Vol. 8. Documents 3128–3771. Washington, DC: Carnegie Endowment for International Peace, 1937.

Doménéch, J. Figuero. *Guía general descriptivo de la República Mexicana*. Vol. 2. Mexico City: n.p., 1899.

Edelman, Robert. *Proletarian Peasants: The Revolution of 1905 in Russia's Southwest*. Ithaca, NY: Cornell University Press, 1987.

Fraginal, Manuel Moreno. *El ingenio: Complejo económico social cubano del azúcar*. 3 vols. Havana: Editorial de Ciencias Sociales, 1978.

García Cantú, Gastón. *Utopías mexicanas*. Mexico City: Fondo de Cultura, 1978.

García Cubas, Antonio. *Diccionario geográfico, histórico y biográfico de los Estados Unidos Mexicanos*, 5 vols. Mexico City: n.p., 1896.

Garza y Villareal, Luis.

Geertz, Clifford. *The Interpretation of Cultures*. New York: Basic Books, 1973.

Gerhard, Peter. *A Guide to the Historical Geography of New Spain*. Cambridge: Cambridge University Press, 1972.

Gilly, Adolfo. *The Mexican Revolution*. London: NLB, 1983.

Gimenez, Catalina H, de. *Así cantaban la revolución*. Mexico City: Editorial Grijalbo, 1996.

González Navarro, Moisés. *Anatomía del poder en México*. Mexico City: Colegio de Mexico, 1977.

———. *Raza y tierra: La guerra de castas y el henequen*. Mexico City: Colegio de Mexico, 1979.

Gramsci, Antonio. *Selections from the Prison Notebooks*. Ed. Quintin Hoare and Geoffrey Nowel Smith. London: New York: International Publishers, 1971.

Gruzinski, Serge. *Man-gods in the Mexican Highlands: Indian Power and Colonial Society, 1520–1800*. Palo Alto, CA: Stanford University Press, 1989.

Guardino, Peter. "Barbarism or Republican Law? Guerrero's Peasants and National Politics, 1820–1846." *Hispanic American Historical Review* (1995).

———. *Peasants, Politics and the Formation of Mexico's National State, 1800–1857*. Palo Alto, CA: Stanford University Press, 1996.

Hale, Charles. *Mexican Liberalism in the Age of Mora, 1821–1853*. New Haven, CT: Yale University Press, 1968.

Hall, Linda. *Álvaro Obregón, Power and Revolution in Mexico 1911–1920*. College Station: Texas A&M Press, 1981.

Hamill, Hugh. *The Hidalgo Revolt*. Gainesville: University of Florida Press, 1966.

Hamnett, Brian. "The Economic and Social Dimension of the Revolution of Independence in Mexico, 1800–1824." PhD diss. Universitat Brelefeld, 1979.

———. *Roots of Insurgency*. Cambridge: Cambridge University Press, 1986.

Hart, John Mason. *Anarchism and the Mexican Working Class, 1860–1931*. Austin: University of Texas Press, 1978.

———. *Empire and Revolution: The Americans in Mexico Since the Civil War*. Berkeley: University of California Press, 2002.

———. "Miguel Negrete: La epopeya de un revolucionario." *Historia Mexicana* (July–Sept. 1974).

———. *Revolutionary Mexico: The Coming and Process of the Mexican Revolution*. Berkeley: University of California Press, 1987.

BIBLIOGRAPHY

Harvey, Neil. *The Chiapas Rebellion: The Struggle for Land and Democracy.* Durham, NC: Duke University Press, 1998.

Haskett, Robert. *Indigenous Rulers: An Ethnohistory of Town Government in Colonial Cuernavaca.* Albuquerque: University of New Mexico Press, 1993.

Hayden, Tom, ed. *The Zapatista Reader.* New York: Thunder's Mouth Press, Nation Books, 2002.

Heau, Catherine. "La tradición autonomista y legalista de los pueblos en territorio zapatista." In *Estudios sobre el zapatismo,* coord. Laura López Espejel. Mexico City: INAH, 2000.

Helguera, Laura R., Sinecio López M., and Rámon Ramirez M. *Los campesinos de la tierra de Zapata.* Mexico City: INAH, 1974.

Hernández Chávez, Alicia. *Anenecuilco, memória y vida de un pueblo.* Mexico City: El Colégio de México, 1991.

———. *Propiedad comunal y desarrollo capitalista en el estado de Morelos, 1535–1920.* Mexico City: El Colégio de México, 1973.

Hobsbawm, Eric. *Bandits.* New York: Dell, 1969.

Hobsbawm, Eric, and George Rude. *Captain Swing.* London: Orion Publishing, 2001.

Huerta, María Teresa. *Empresarios del azúcar en el siglo XIX.* Mexico City: INAH, 1993.

Illescas, María Dolores. "Agitación social y bandidaje en el estado de Morelos durante el siglo xix." *Estudios Mexicanos* (fall 1988): 79–84.

James, C. L. R. *The Black Jacobins: Toussaint L'Ouverture and the San Domingo Revolution.* New York: v, 1963.

Johnson, Richard. *The Mexican Revolution of Ayutla, 1854–1855: An Analysis of the Evolution and Destruction of a Latin American Dictatorship.* Westport, CT: Greenwood Press, 1974.

Joseph, Gilbert M. "On the Trail of Latin American Bandits: A Reexamination of Peasant Resistance." *Latin American Research Review* 25 (1990).

———. *Revolution from Without: Yucatán, Mexico and the United States, 1880–1924.* Cambridge: Cambridge University Press, 1982.

Joseph, Gilbert M., and Daniel Nugent, eds. *Everyday Forms of State Formation.* Durham, NC: Duke University Press, 1994.

Katz, Friedrich. "Labor Conditions on Haciendas in Porfiran Mexico: Some Trends and Tendencies." *Hispanic American Historical Review* 54 (1974).

———. "Rural Rebellions after 1810." In *Riot, Rebellion and Revolution: Rural Social Conflict in Mexico.* Princeton, NJ: Princeton University Press, 1988.

———. *The Secret War in Mexico: Europe, the United States and the Mexican Revolution.* Chicago: University of Chicago Press, 1981.

Katz, Friedrich, ed. "Rural Revolts in Mexico." In *Riot, Rebellion and Revolution: Rural Social Conflict in Mexico.* Princeton, NJ: Princeton University Press, 1988.

Knight, Alan. *The Mexican Revolution.* 2 vols. Cambridge: Cambridge University Press, 1986.

———. "Revolutionary State, Recalcitrant People: Mexico, 1910–1940." In *The Revolutionary Process in Mexico: Essays on Political and Social Change, 1880–1940,* ed. Jaime E. Rodríguez. Los Angeles: UCLA Latin American Center Publications, 1990.

———. "Weapons and Arches in the Mexican Revolutionary Landscape." In *Everyday Forms of State Formation,* ed Gilbert M. Joseph and Daniel Nugent. Durham, NC: Duke University Press, 1994.

Knowlton, Robert. *Los bienes del clero y la Reforma mexicana, 1856–1910.* Mexico City: Fondo de Cultura Económica, 1985.

Ladurie, Emanuel Leroy. *The Peasants of Languedoc.* Urbana, Chicago, and London: University of Illinois Press, 1976.

Landazuri Benitez, Gisela, and Veronica Vázquez Mantecón. *Azúcar y estado: 1750–1880.* Mexico City: Fondo de Cultura, 1988.

Lear, John. *Workers, Neighbors, and Citizens: The Revolution in Mexico City.* Lincoln and London: University of Nebraska Press, 2001.

Leonard, Irving. *Baroque Times in Old Mexico.* Ann Arbor: University of Michigan Press, 1959.

Lewis, Oscar. *Life in a Mexican Village: Tepozlán Restudies.* Urbana: University of Illinois Press, 1963.

Lira, Andrés. *Espejo de discordias: La sociedad mexicana vista por Lorenzo de Zavala, José María Luis Mora y Lucas Alamán.* Mexico City: Secretaría de Educación Pública, 1984.

López Espejel, Laura, coord. *Estudios sobre el zapatismo.* Mexico City: INAH, 2001.

López González, Valentín. *Los plateados en el estado de Morelos, 1861–1865.* Cuernavaca, Morelos: Cuadernos Histórico Morelenses, 1999.

MacLean y Esteños, Roberto. *La revolución de 1910 y el problema agraria en México.* Mexico City, 1959.

Mallon, Florencia E. *Defense of Community in the Peruvian Highlands: Peasant Struggle and Capitalist Transition, 1860–1940.* Princeton, NJ: Princeton University Press, 1983.

———. *Peasant and Nation: The Making of Post Colonial Mexico and Peru.* Berkeley: University of California Press, 1995.

———. "Peasants and State Formation in Nineteenth-Century Mexico: Morelos, 1848–1858." *Political Power and Social Theory* 7 (1988).

Martin, Cheryl English. *Rural Society in Colonial Morelos.* Albuquerque: University of New Mexico Press, 1985.

Márquez, Enrique, and María Isabel Abella. *Ponciano Arriaga, obras completas.* 5 vols. *La experiencia nacional,* vol. 2. Mexico City: UNAM, 1992.

Mazari, Manuel. *Bosquejo histórico del estado de Morelos.* 1930; reprint, Morelos: Universidad autonoma del estado de Morelos, 1986.

Mejia Fernandez, Miguel. *Politica agraria en México en el siglo XIX.* Mexico City: Siglo Veinteuno, 1979.

Melville, Roberto. *Crecimiento y rebelión: El desarrollo económico de las haciendas Azucareras en Morelos (1880–1910).* Mexico City: Nueva Imagen, 1979.

Mendieta y Nuñez, Lucio, Dr. *El problema agrario de México.* Mexico City: Porrua, 1971.

Meyers, William. *Forge of Progress, Crucible of Revolt: Origins of the Mexican Revolution in the Comarca Lagunera, 1880–1911.* Albuquerque: University of New Mexico Press, 1994.

Millon, Robert. *Zapata: The Ideology of an Agrarian Revolutionary.* New York: International Publishers, 1970.

Molina Enriquez, Andrés. *Los grandes problemas nacionales.* Mexico City: Ediciones Eia, 1978.

Moore, Barrington, Jr. *Social Origins of Dictatorship and Democracy: Lord and Peasant in the Making of the Modern World.* Boston: Beacon Press, 1966.

———. *Injustice: The Social Bases of Obedience and Revolt.* White Plains, NY: M. F. Sharpe, 1978.

Mora, José María Luis. *Obras sueltas de José María Luis Mora.* Mexico City: Editorial Porrua, 1963.

Muñoz y Perez, Daniel. "El General Don Juan Álvarez." In *Ensayo biográfico y selección de documentos.* Mexico City: Academia Literaria, 1959.

Nugent, Daniel. *Spent Cartridges of Revolution: An Anthropological History of Namaiquuipa, Chihuahua.* Chicago: University of Chicago Press, 1993.

Olivera de Bonfil, Alicia. "Lo que dijeron y lo que dicen que dijeron." In *Estudios sobre el zapatismo,* coord. Laura López Espejel. Mexico City: INAH, 2001.

Pacheco, Francisco. *Memórias de Francisco Pacheco.* Mexico City: n.p., 1877.

Palmer, Colin. *Negro Slavery in Mexico, 1570–1650.* Madison: University of Wisconsin Press, 1971.

———. *Slaves of the White God: Blacks in Mexico, 1570–1650*. Cambridge, MA: Harvard University Press, 1976.

Pérez, Louis A., Jr. *Cuba: Between Reform and Revolution*. New York and Oxford: Oxford University Press, 1988.

———. *The War of 1898: The United Sates and Cuba in History and Historiography*. Chapel Hill and London: University of North Carolina Press, 1998.

Pérez-López, Jorge F. *The Economics of Cuban Sugar*. Pittsburgh: University of Pittsburgh Press, 1991.

Perry, Laurens Ballard. "El modelo liberal y la politica practica en la republica restaurada, 1867–1876." *Historia Mexicana* (Apr.–June 1974).

Piñeda Gómez, Francisco. *La irrupción zapatista. 1911*. Mexico City: Ediciones Era, 1997.

Pittman, Dewitt Kenneth. "Planters, Peasants, and Politicians: Agrarian Classes and the Installation of the Oligarchic State in Mexico, 1869–1876." PhD diss. Yale University, 1983.

Ponce de León, Juana, ed. *Our Word Is Our Weapon: Selected Writings of Subcomandante Marcos*. New York: Seven Stories Press, 2001.

Popkin, Samuel. *The Rational Peasant. The Political Economy of Rural Society in Vietnam*. Berkeley: University of California Press, 1979.

Popoca y Palacios, Lamberto. *Historia del banalismo en el estado de Morelos. ¡Ayer como ahora! ¡1860 "Plateados"! ¡1911 "Zapatistas"!* Mexico City: n.p. 1912.

Potash, Robert. *El Banco de Avio de México: El fomento de la industria 1821–1846*. Mexico City, 1959.

Powell, T. G. "Los Liberales, el campesinado indígena y los problemas agrarios durante La Reforma." *Historia Mexicana* 21, no. 4, 1972.

———. "Priests and Peasants in Central Mexico: Social Conflict during 'La Reforma.'" *Hispanic American Historical Review* 57 (1977).

Preciado, Jesús. *Memória sobre el estado de la administración pública de Morelos*. Cuernavaca, Morelos: n.p., 1887.

Purnell, Jennie. *Popular Movements and State Formation in Revolutionary Mexico: The Agraristas and Cristeros of Michoacan*. Durham, NC: Duke University Press, 1999.

———. "With All Due Respect: Popular Resistance to the Privatization of Communal Land in 19th Century Michoacan." *Latin American Research Review* 34, no. 1, 1999.

Ramírez, Ignacio. *Obras completas*. 3 vols. Ed. David Maciel and Boris Rosen. Mexico City: Centro de Investigación Científica "Jorge L. Tamayo," 1984.

Redfield, Robert. *Tepoztlán: A Mexican Village*. Chicago: University of Chicago Press, 1930.

Reed, Nelson. *The Caste War of Yucatán*. Palo Alto, CA: Stanford University Press, 2001.

Reina, Leticia. *Las luchas populares en México en el siglo XIX*. Mexico City: SEP, CIESAS, 1983.

———. *Las rebeliones campesinas en México (1819–1906)*. Mexico City: Siglo vienteuno, 1980.

"Respuesta de los propietarios de los distritos de Cuernavaca y Morelos, a la parte que les concierne en el manifiesto del señor General D. Juan Álvarez, 1857." Ed. Valentín López González. Cuernavaca, Morelos: Cuadernos Histórico Morelenses, 2000.

Reyes Heroles, Jesús. *El liberalismo mexicano*. 3 vols. Mexico City: Fondo de Cultura Económica, 1974.

Richmond, Douglas. *Venustiano Carranza's Nationalist Struggle, 1893–1920*. Lincoln: University of Nebraska Press, 1983.

Riley, G. Michael. *Fernando Cortés and the Marquesado in Morelos, 1522–1547*. Albuquerque: University of New Mexico Press, 1973.

Robelo, Cecilio. *Revistas descriptivas del estado de Morelos*. Cuernavaca, Morelos: Sociedad Geografica y Estadística, 1885.

Rodríguez, Jaime E., ed., *The Origins of Mexican National Politics*. Wilmington, DE: Scholarly Resources, 1997.

Rueda Smithers, Salvador. "Oposición y subversión: Testimonios zapatistas." *Historias* no. 3 (Jan.–Mar. 1983).

———. *El paraíso de la caña: Historia de una construcción imaginaria*. Mexico City: INAH, 1998.

Rugeley, Terry. *Yucatán's Maya Peasantry and the Origins of the Caste War*. Austin: University of Texas Press, 1996.

Ruíz, Ramón Eduardo. *The Great Rebellion: Mexico, 1905–1924*. New York and London: Norton, 1980.

———. *The People of Sonora and Yankee Capitalists*. Tucson: University of Arizona Press, 1988.

Ruíz de Velasco, Felipe. *Historia y evoluciones del cultivo de la caña y de la industria azucarera en el estado de Morelos*. Mexico City: Editorial Cultura, 1937.

Saka, Mark. "We are Citizens! Agrarian Rebellion in the Huasteca, 1878–1883." PhD diss. University of Houston, 1995.

Salinas, Miguel. *Historias y paisajes morelenses*. Mexico City: E. Salinas, 1981.

Sandoval, Fernando. *Bibliografía general del azúcar*. Mexico City: Union Nacional de Productures de Azucar, 1954.

Sandstrom, Alan. *Corn Is our Blood*. Norman: University of Oklahoma Press, 1991.

Santa Anna y Juan Álvarez, frente a frente. Ed. Fernando Díaz Díaz. Mexico City: Sepsetentas, 1972.

Schwartz, Stuart. *Sugar Plantations in the Formation of Brazilian Society: Bahia, 1550–1835*. Cambridge: Cambridge University Press, 1985.

Scott, James. *Domination and the Arts of Resistance*. New Haven, CT: Yale University Press, 1990.

———. *The Moral Economy of the Peasant. Rebellion and Subsistence in Southeast Asia*. New Haven, CT: Yale University Press, 1976.

———. *Weapons of the Weak, Everyday Forms of Peasant Resistance*. New Haven, CT, and London: Yale University Press, 1985.

Sharrer Tamm, Beatriz. *Azúcar y trabajo*. Mexico City: CIESAS, 1997.

Silva Herzog, Jesús. *El agrarismo mexicano y la reforma agrarian: Exposición y crítica*. Mexico City: Fondo de Cultura Económica, 1974.

Sims, Harold. *The Expulsion of Mexico's Spaniards, 1821–1836*. Pittsburgh, PA: Temple University Press, 1990.

Síndico, Dominico. "Modernization in XIX Century Sugar Haciendas: The Case of Morelos." Unpublished paper, 1980.

———. "Azúcar y burguesía en Morelos en el siglo XIX."

Skocpol, Theda. *States and Social Revolutions*. Cambridge: Cambridge University Press, 1979.

Slatta, Richard. "Bandidos: The Varieties of Latin American Banditry." In *On the Trail of Latin American Bandits*. Ed. Gilbert Joseph. New York: Greenwood Press, 1990.

Sotelo Inclán, Jesús. *Raíz y razón de Zapata*. Mexico: Editorial Etros, 1943.

Stephen, Lynn. *Zapata Lives! Histories and Cultural Politics in Southern Mexico*. Berkeley: University of California Press, 2002.

Taylor, William B. *Drinking, Homicide, and Rebellion in Colonial Mexican Villages*. Palo Alto, CA: Stanford University Press, 1979.

———. *Magistrates of the Sacred: Priests and Parishioners in 18th Century Mexico*. Palo Alto, CA: Stanford University Press, 1996.

Tenorio-Trillo, Mauricio. *Mexico at the World's Fairs*. Berkeley: University of California Press, 1996.

Thomson, Guy P. C. "Bulwarks of Patriotic Liberalism: The National Guard, Philharmonic Corps, and Patriotic Juntas in Mexico, 1847–1888." *Journal of*

Latin American Studies 22 (Feb. 1990).

Thomson, Guy P. C., with David LaFrance. *Patriotism, Politics, and Popular Liberalism in Nineteenth-Century Mexico: Juan Francisco Lucas and the Puebla Sierra.* New York: Scholarly Resources, 1999.

Tinker-Salas, Miguel. *Under the Shadow of the Eagles: The Border and the Transformation of Sonora during the Porfiriato.* Berkeley: University of California Press, 1997.

Turner, Victor. *The Ritual Process.* Chicago: University of Chicago Press, 1969.

Tutino, John. *From Insurrection to Revolution in Mexico: Social Bases of Agrarian Violence, 1750–1940.* Princeton, NJ: Princeton University Press, 1986.

Vanderwood, Paul. *Disorder and Progress: Bandits, Police, and Mexican Development.* Wilmington, DE: Scholarly Resources, 1992.

Van Young, Eric. "Agrarian Rebellion and Defense of Community: Meaning and Collective Violence in Late Colonial and Independence-Era Mexico." *Journal of Social History* 2, no. 27 (1993).

———. *The Other Rebellion: Popular Violence, Ideology, and the Mexican Struggle for Independence, 1810–1821.* Palo Alto, CA: Stanford University Press, 2000.

———. "Paisaje de ensueño con figuras y vallados: Disputa y discurso cultural en el campo mexicano de fines de la colonia." In *Paisajes rebeldes: Una larga noche de rebelión indígena,* ed. Jane-Dale Lloyd et al. Mexico City: Universidad Iberoamericana, 1996.

Von Mentz, Brigida. *Pueblos de indios, mulatos y mestizos 1770–1870: Los campesinos y las transformaciones protoindustriales en el poniente de Morelos.* Mexico City: CIESAS, 1988.

———. *Pueblos en el siglo XIX através de sus documentos.* Mexico City: SEP, CIESAS, 1988.

Von Wobeser, Gisela. *San Carlos Borromeo: Endudiamiento de una hacienda colonial 1608–1729.* UNAM, 1980.

———. *La formación de la hacienda en la epoca colonial: El uso de la tierra y el agua.* Mexico City: UNAM, 1983.

Walker, David. "Homegrown Revolution: The Hacienda Santa Catalina del Alamo y Anexas and Agrarian Protest in Eastern Durango, Mexico, 1897–1913." *Hispanic American Historical Review* 72, no. 2 (1992): 239–73.

———. "The Villista Legacy and Agrarian Radicalism in Eastern Durango, Mexico, 1913–1930." Paper presented at the First Joint Conference of the Rocky Mountain Council for Latin American Studies and the Pacific Coast Council for Latin American Studies, Las Vegas, Nev., 1995.

Warman, Arturo. *"We Come to Object": The Peasants of Morelos and the National State.* Baltimore, MD, and London: Johns Hopkins University Press, 1980.

Wasserman, Mark. *Capitalists, Caciques, and Revolution: The Native Elite and Foreign Enterprise in Chihuahua, Mexico, 1854–1911.* Chapel Hill: University of North Carolina Press, 1984.

Whitmore, Thomas M. *Disease and Death in Early Colonial Mexico.* Boulder, CO: Westview Press, 1992.

Wolf, Eric. *Peasant Wars of the Twentieth Century.* New York: Harper and Row, 1969.

Wolff, Robert Paul, Barrington Moore, Jr., and Herbert Marcuse. *A Critique of Pure Tolerance.* Boston: Beacon Press, 1969.

Womack, John Jr. *Rebellion in Chiapas: An Historical Reader.* New York: New Press, 1999.

———. *Zapata and the Mexican Revolution.* New York: Alfred A. Knopf, 1969.

Zavala, Lorenzo de. *Viaje a los estados unidos de américa.* Merida, Yucatán: n.p., 1846.

Index

police: under Alarcón, Manuel, 151;
    failure of, to combat bandits,
    105; Mexican police, 104; pow-
    ers of, used to support hacen-
    dados, 187; private force of, 113;
    rural, 105
police protection, 104–5
police state, 151
political changes, 226
political clubs, 186
political rallies, 173
political riots, 190
Popoca y Palacios, Lamberto, 101
popular events, 253n7
popular hostility towards Spaniards,
    247–48n24
popular liberalism vs. urban liberal-
    ism, 66
Porfirian policies: on export-oriented
    economic growth, 171; as export
    supporters, 168
Porfiriato (Díaz's rule). *See also* Díaz
    regime: and *denuncios*, 84;
    overthrow of, 148
Preciado, Jesús, 166, 174–75, 176–77
primary sources, 266n52
private police force, 113
private property: and conservative leg-
    islation, 60; distribution of, 198;
    and economic plans, 84; inabil-
    ity of government to protect,
    56; and Liberal government, 83;
    rights of, 217
privatization. *See also* land privatiza-
    tion: and Morelos, 87; of state
    owned businesses, 227
privatization laws, 92
producer cooperatives, 213
El Progresso de Morelos, 173
property rights of hacendados, 135
propios (common lands), 245n9
protectionism, 184
protoindustrialism, 37
public parades, 253n7
Puebla, Mexico: battle at, 102; dispute
    between Zapatistas and federal
    troops, 199–200
Puebla Sierra, 42
pueblo land claims, 120
pueblos: allowed as squatters camps,
    122; bandits relationship with,
    130; as closed corporate commu-
    nities, 246–27n15; destroyed by
    government troops, 214; ethnic

composition of, 112–13; land dis-
    putes in Morelos, 86; land
    reform under Zapata, 213; Ley
    Lerdo, 86–87; litigation, 86;
    reduction in number of, 151; self
    government of, 213; unified as
    joint litigants in land claims,
    111–13
pueblo villagers, 266–67n5
Puente de Ixtla, 85
purgador (sugar cane processor), 160

Quaglia, Carlos, 173
Quijano, Benito, 60
Quintero, Carmen, 124, 127, 188, 225–26
Quintero, Vincente, 127
quinto, 16
Quiroga, Vasco de, 49

racial bias, 46
railroads: British investment in, 169;
    early, 166; effect of, on econo-
    my, 147; expansion of, 167–69
Ramírez, Ignacio, 55
rancherías, 20
el real (tenant houses), 124
real de esclavos, 17
rebellion: of indígenias, 174; indoctri-
    nation in, 175
recession, 184
reelection of president, 140, 146, 173
religious imagery, 163
repartamiento, 250n20
repression: fear of, 164–65; and pater-
    nalism, 176; punishment used to
    enforce, 188; suspension of indi-
    vidual rights to maintain, 172
reprisals: on campesinos, impact of,
    134; from hacendados, 127; pro-
    tection from, 129
revolution: considerations of by elite,
    57; discussions of, 175; and land
    claims, 198
rights: of community property owner-
    ship, 110; community property
    rights, 49; community rights,
    217; denial of, 39; equal rights,
    180; individual rights, 217; land
    rights, 16–17, 29, 62; natural
    rights, 113–14, 137; private prop-
    erty, 217; property, of hacenda-
    dos, 135; property rights, 60, 61,
    133, 135; rights strategy, 139–40;
    of rural Mexicans, 220; sacred

INDEX

strikes, 67
subsistence farming and economic
plans, 84
sugar industry: agriculture, 12; in
Anenecuilco, 30; cartels in, 183;
and colonial trade restrictions,
23–24; crisis in, 226; decline in
prices, 36; effects of, in
Morelos, 38, 223; effects of
growth of demand on, 20–21;
exports of, 182–84; growth of
demand for, 36–37, 107; harvesting, 38; industry, 12; investments in land and machinery,
167; and land tenure, 35; mechanization of, 166; significance of
exports, 35; and slavery, 17;
taxes levies on, 146; technology
and manufacturing changes in,
148; and wage-earning laborers,
38; world market sales, 167
sugar master, 161–62
sugar plantations. See also haciendas;
zafra (sugar cane harvest): cane
processing description, 159–61;
employment from, 146–47;
expansion of, 107, 150; fields set
ablaze, 67; growth of demand
for, 150; in Morelos, 33; taxation
of, 148; tax reductions on, 178
sugar production: averages of, 248n34;
changes in, 165–66; expansion
of, 171; growth in, 106; levels of,
147; reductions in, 192; urban
population growth, 35
survey companies, 177

tariff protections, 46
taxes and taxation: changing patterns
of, 42; levied on sugar industry,
146; reduction of, on sugar plantations, 178; of sugar plantations, 148; universal head tax, 187
temporal irrigation, 246n12
Tepalcingo, Mexico, 182, 202
Terranova, Duque de, 32
Terranova y Monteleóne, Duke of, 47
Ticumán, Mexico, 103
tiendas de raya, 94
tierras de comun repartamiento, 245n9
tierras de labor, 90
tierras de temporal (unirrigated land), 155
timber interests, 95
Tlaltizapan, Mexico, 93

Tlayacaque, Mexico, 51
Torres Burgos, Pablo, 188, 193, 194
trapicheros (mill workers), 109
Treaty of Ciudad, 198
Treaty of Guadalupe Hidalgo, 41
trickle-down theory, 178
Trist, Nicholas, 42
trusts, 183

unemployment, 177, 191–92
Unión Azucarera Mexico, 183
universal head tax, 187
unrest: agrarian, 34–35, 115; causes of,
202; in Cuautla, Mexico, 67; in
Cuernavaca, Mexico, 54; hacendados concerned over, 67–68;
in Morelos, 42, 49, 50, 51–52;
pattern of, 115; in rural population, 65; in Yucatán, 42, 52
urban discontent, 173
urban liberalism, 66
urban population growth, 35
U.S. Army: liberates Chiconcuac, 43;
occupies Mexico City, 42–43
U.S. government: drops support of
Huerta, 212; facilitates military
coup of Madero government,
211; imposition of Platt
Amendment of 1901, 185;
involvement in coups by,
267–68n20; weapons for
Carranza regime, 212

Valley of Cuautla Amilpas, 19
Vásquez Jiménez, Felix, 206–7, 208
vecinos indigenas, 110
Veracruz, Mexico, 13, 19, 102, 106
Vergara, Lorenzo, 152
Villa, Francisco (Pancho Villa):
Conventionalist faction, 212;
defeats Diaz, 197; Zapata sides
with, 212
Villa de Ayala, 20
Villa de Toluca, 14
Villaseñor, Alejandro: and agrarian law
reform, 48–49, 57–59, 67, 79, 80
Villistas vs. Carrancistas, 212–13
violence, justification of, 133
volteadores (sugar loaf makers), 109
von Humboldt, Alexander, 78

wage labor, 24
wages: average daily, 257n21; pay
scales during zafra (sugar cane